Ensemble:
Grammaire

Ensemble: Grammaire

An Integrated Approach to French

Raymond F. Comeau /*Boston University*
Francine L. Bustin /*Milton Academy*
Normand J. Lamoureux /*College of the Holy Cross*

HOLT, RINEHART AND WINSTON
New York • San Francisco • Toronto • London

Library of Congress Cataloging in Publication Data

Comeau, Raymond F.
  Ensemble grammaire.

  Includes index.
  1. French language—Grammar—1950–   I. Bustin,
Francine L., joint author. II. Lamoureux, Normand J.,
joint author. III. Title.
PC2112.C662   448'.2'421   76-49636
ISBN 0-03-018256-5

Illustration Credits

Marion Benntein from Editorial Photocolor Archives: 1 Skip Clarke (HRW): 15 Courtesy of French Embassy Press and Information Division: 40 HRW: 66, 175, 196 Helena Kolda: 66. 135, 151 (HRW), 196 (HRW), Courtesy of Photo Renault: 88 Metropolitan Museum of Art, Rogers Fund, 1920: 110

We wish to express our thanks to Harcourt Brace Jovanovich, Inc. for the permission to reproduce an excerpt from *Le Petit Prince* by Antoine de Saint-Exupéry.

Contents

Preface

ENSEMBLE is an integrated approach to the study of French language, literature and culture. It has been designed as a complete Intermediate French course, although it may profitably be used in more advanced courses as well. In concrete terms, *Ensemble* consists of three texts — a review grammar (with accompanying language laboratory program), a literary reader, and a cultural reader — which have been thematically and linguistically coordinated with one another, although each text may be used independently of the other two.

ENSEMBLE: GRAMMAIRE is comprised of eleven chapters. Chapter 1 has been devoted primarily to review, since intermediate students need a rapid yet comprehensive review of basic points of grammar at the very beginning of the course. This "mini-review" consists of two graded groups of exercises that stress key grammatical structures. It should be noted that no answers are given to these exercises. Instead, students are given specific page references indicating where particular points are treated in the text. In this way the mini-review provides a preliminary lesson in the use of the grammar text as a reference tool. The first chapter also contains a review of the literary past tense, the *passé simple,* and guidelines for writing compositions in French.

The remaining chapters (2 to 11) have the following format:

Chapter at a Glance is a capsule preview composed of model exercises treating all of the grammar points in the chapter. Answers are included at the end of the book. A preliminary self-diagnostic test for students, *Chapter at a Glance* will indicate to both student and instructor the amount of time and effort necessary to spend on a given chapter. This section can also be used as a study guide for quizzes and examinations.

The *Vocabulaire du thème* lists the thematic vocabulary used in the grammar examples and exercises. Students should familiarize themselves with this vocabulary before proceeding to the grammar explanations so that they will be able to manipulate the exercises. This section will also be useful in preparing written and oral reports based on the theme of each chapter.

The grammar presentations, in English, have been deliberately made as concise as possible. Special attention has been given to grammar points that normally present the most difficulty to English-speaking students. Exercises follow each grammar explanation.

The Exercices d'ensemble are a series of varied exercises that constitute a final review and synthesis of all of the grammar points in the chapter.

The *Sujets de discussion ou de composition* contain stimulating discussion and composition topics relating to the theme of the chapter. They are intended to encourage students to use the thematic vocabulary in meaningful contexts.

The *language laboratory manual* is designed to accompany the grammar text. The first chapter contains a review of pronunciation; the other ten chapters are composed of pattern practice drills and *dictées* intended to reinforce important points of grammar, develop oral expression and improve pronunciation.

R.F.C.

A word about ENSEMBLE: AN INTEGRATED APPROACH TO FRENCH

The three books — the review grammar, the cultural reader and the literary reader — which comprise the *Ensemble* series are each designed to stand alone, but more importantly they fit together to form an "ensemble." The review grammar and the laboratory manual which accompanies it integrate grammar and theme by incorporating thematic vocabulary in examples and exercises. The two readers, in turn, contain grammar exercises drawn directly from the literary and cultural readings.

A single program composed of three separate yet integrated texts offers distinct advantages. First of all, it provides greater opportunity for reading and exercises, thereby allowing for a more comprehensive, mature and articulate treatment of the subject. In addition, the recurrence of the same thematic vocabulary and grammar points in all three different texts provides continuous vocabulary and grammar reinforcement. The unique comprehensive and integrated nature of *Ensemble* will encourage, we believe, more lively and meaningful student participation.

For most intermediate classes it is recommended that instruction begin with a chapter in the grammar and proceed to the same chapter in either of the readers. Instructors may wish to vary the reading selections within a given chapter by alternating between the literary and the cultural reader. An instructor teaching an advanced course may wish to assign the grammar as outside work and spend class time with readings and oral reports. Since the three texts are thematically and grammatically coordinated, a lesson may even begin with the readings and end with a rapid grammar review.

Acknowledgments   We wish to express our appreciation to the staff of Holt, Rinehart and Winston and, in particular, to our development editor, Marilyn Hofer, for her ready availability and professional assistance. We want to acknowledge, too, the important contributions of our copy editor, Clifford Browder, whose stimulating suggestions helped enliven and tighten the final draft. Finally, we owe a very special debt of gratitude to our spouses — Jean Comeau, Edouard Bustin, and Priscilla Lamoureux — without whose unfailing support the three texts comprising this program could not have come to fruition.

R.F.C. / F.L.B. / N.J.L.

Ensemble:
Grammaire

1

Mini-review, passé simple, composition

Vocabulaire du thème: Les Jeunes

LES DISTRACTIONS DES JEUNES

l' **ami** (m), l'**amie** (f)   *friend, boyfriend, girlfriend*

le **copain,** la **copine** (fam.)   *chum, buddy*

le **petit ami,** la **petite amie**   *boyfriend, girlfriend*

lier amitié avec   *to make friends with*

avoir rendez-vous avec   *to have a date with*

sortir (seul, à deux, en groupe)   *to go out (alone, as a couple, in a group)*

aller au cinéma, au théâtre   *to go to the movies, to the theater*

aller à une soirée, à une partie   *to go to a party*

se **promener en voiture**   *to ride around in a car*

faire un voyage   *to take a trip*

regarder la télévision   *to watch television*

écouter la radio, des disques   *to listen to the radio, to records*

causer   *to talk, to chat*

faire la grasse matinée   *to sleep late*

faire des sports   *to play sports*

faire du ski   *to go skiing*

jouer au tennis, au golf, aux cartes   *to play tennis, golf, cards*

s' **amuser bien à lire, à faire du ski,** etc.   *to have a good time reading, skiing, etc.*

s' **intéresser aux sports, à danser,** etc.   *to be interested in sports, dancing, etc.*

gaspiller son temps   *to waste one's time*

LES JEUNES À L'UNIVERSITÉ

se **spécialiser en**   *to major in*

suivre un cours   *to take a course*

assister à un cours, à une conférence   *to attend a class, a lecture*

manquer un cours   *to miss a class*

le **cours facultatif**   *elective course*

le **cours obligatoire**   *required course*

les **devoirs** (m)   *homework*

le **cancre**   *bad student, dunce*

un **cerveau**   *brain*

passer un examen   *to take an exam*

bûcher (fam.)   *to cram*

réussir à un examen   *to pass an exam*

échouer à un examen   *to fail an exam*

rater un examen   *to flunk an exam*

la **note**   *grade*

le, la **camarade de chambre**   *roommate*

l' **interne** (m, f)   *on-campus student*

l' **externe** (m, f)   *off-campus student*

se **joindre à** (une **organisation**)   *to join (an organization)*

la **maison d'étudiants**   *dormitory*

le **réfectoire**   *dining hall*

Mini-review

EXERCICES DE GRAMMAIRE

The following two groups of exercises are intended as a rapid review of some important grammar points. The exercises in Group I are more basic than the ones in Group II. References in parentheses indicate where the grammar points are treated in the text. No answers are given.

I

1. *Complétez au* **temps présent.** (pp. 18–22, 69–70.)

   1. **parler:** je parle, tu _____, il (elle, on) _____, nous _____, vous _____, ils (elles) _____.
   2. **finir:** je finis, tu _____, il (elle, on) _____, nous _____, vous _____, ils (elles) _____.
   3. **perdre:** je perds, tu _____, il (elle, on) _____, nous _____, vous _____, ils (elles) _____.
   4. **avoir:** j'ai, tu _____, il (elle, on) _____, nous _____, vous _____, ils (elles) _____.
   5. **être:** je suis, tu _____, il (elle, on) _____, nous _____, vous _____, ils (elles) _____.
   6. **aller:** je vais, tu _____, il (elle, on) _____, nous _____, vous _____, ils (elles) _____.
   7. **faire:** je fais, tu _____, il (elle, on) _____, nous _____, vous _____, ils (elles) _____.
   8. **savoir:** je sais, tu _____, il (elle, on) _____, nous _____, vous _____, ils (elles) _____.
   9. **vouloir:** je veux, tu _____, il (elle, on) _____, nous _____, vous _____, ils (elles) _____.
   10. **se laver:** je me lave, tu _____, il (elle, on) _____, nous _____, vous _____, ils (elles) _____.

2. *Répondez par une phrase complète.* (pp. 18–22, 69–70.)

   1. Allez-vous souvent au cinéma?
   2. Réussissez-vous généralement aux examens?
   3. Liez-vous facilement amitié avec les gens?
   4. Voulez-vous sortir avec une personne intelligente, intéressante et séduisante ce week-end?
   5. Assistez-vous à tous vos cours?
   6. Le français est-il un cours obligatoire ou un cours facultatif à votre université?
   7. Avez-vous généralement envie d'étudier?
   8. Faites-vous des sports? Lesquels?
   9. Vous intéressez-vous aux affaires de l'université?
   10. Faites-vous quelquefois la grasse matinée?

3. *Complétez en traduisant les verbes et en les mettant à* **l'impératif.** (pp. 26, 71.)

   1. _____ (Finish) vos devoirs avant de sortir.
   2. _____ (Come) au cinéma avec nous si tu veux.
   3. _____ (Let's listen to) des disques chez vous ce soir!
   4. _____ (Have a good time) à la soirée chez Jean-Pierre.
   5. _____ (Speak) de vos propres affaires, s'il vous plaît!

4. *Replacez les mots en italiques par les pronoms personnels* **le, la, les, lui, leur.** (pp. 28–30.)

modèle: Je vois *Marie.*   **Je la vois.**

1. Les étudiants passent *les examens* cette semaine.
2. Jean fréquente *le bar du Dôme.*
3. Je téléphone *à mes parents* une fois par mois.
4. Je n'aime pas *le campus de mon université.*
5. Tiens! Le professeur a donné une bonne note *au cancre!*

5. *Replacez les tirets* (dashes) *par* **les** *ou* **des.** (p. 58.)

1. _____ externes n'habitent pas à l'université.
2. Avez-vous _____ frères?
3. On a trouvé _____ insectes dans la cuisine du réfectoire!
4. Notre professeur est bizarre. Il aime _____ cancres et déteste _____ cerveaux.
5. Où est Brigitte? —Elle est sortie avec _____ copines.

6. *Formulez une question en employant l'inversion.* (pp. 91–92.)

modèle: Oui, je suis un cours.   **Suivez-vous un cours?**

Oui, Marie est venue me voir.   **Marie est-elle venue vous voir?**

1. Oui, Jean a étudié jusqu'à minuit.
2. Oui, j'ai envie de parler français.
3. Oui, cet exercice est facile.
4. Oui, il faut étudier pour réussir.
5. Oui, Jeannine a assisté à la conférence.

7. *Répondez en employant l'adverbe négatif* **ne . . . pas.** (pp. 99–100.)

modèle: Avez-vous sommeil maintenant?   **Non, je n'ai pas sommeil maintenant.**

1. Aimez-vous la cuisine au réfectoire?
2. Acceptez-vous toutes les valeurs de la société?
3. Avez-vous manqué votre dernière classe?
4. Vous spécialisez-vous en japonais?
5. Aimez-vous rêver en classe?

8.

A. *Mettez les* **adjectifs** *au féminin.* (p. 114.)

1. paresseux	2. naïf
3. formidable	4. travailleur
5. blasé	

B. *Mettez les adjectifs à la position convenable* (appropriate) *en faisant l'accord* (agreement) *s'il y a lieu* (if necessary). (pp. 116–117.)

modèle: Quelle jeune fille! (vaniteux)   **Quelle jeune fille vaniteuse!**

1. Est-ce une auto? (français)
2. Marie habite dans une maison. (blanc)

3. Georges vient d'acheter une voiture! (sensationnel)
4. Marguerite est une étudiante. (bon)
5. Il était content parce qu'il avait des étudiants. (enthousiaste)

9. *Composez une phrase comparative en employant* **plus . . . que, moins . . . que** *ou* **aussi . . . que.** *Faites l'accord de l'adjectif s'il y a lieu.* (p. 128.)
modèle: l'Amérique; la France; grand
      L'Amérique est plus grande que la France.

1. un cancre; un cerveau; travailleur
2. un examen; une soirée; amusant
3. un melon; une orange; gros
4. le russe; l'espagnol; facile
5. les femmes; les hommes; raisonnable

10. *Changez les adjectifs en adverbes en employant* **-ment** *s'il y a lieu.* (p. 122.)
modèle: généreux   **généreusement**

1. curieux
2. général
3. probable
4. naïf
5. bon

11. *Formulez une phrase en employant les pronoms relatifs* **qui** *ou* **que.** (pp. 155–156.)
modèle: Voici un cours. Il a l'air ennuyeux!   **Voici un cours qui a l'air ennuyeux!**
       C'est un copain. Je l'admire.   **C'est un copain que j'admire.**

1. C'est un examen. Je le trouve facile.
2. Voici un étudiant. Il aime se promener en voiture.
3. Parlez-moi de votre ami. Il se moque de tout le monde!
4. Voici mon amie Geneviève. Elle aime manquer ses cours.
5. J'aime les cours difficiles. Nous les suivons.

12. *Remplacez* **un, une** *ou* **des** *par l'adjectif démonstratif* **ce, cet, cette** *ou* **ces.** (p. 164.)

1. des soirées
2. des jeunes
3. une note
4. un examen
5. un voyage

13. *Complétez au* **futur** *et au* **conditionnel.** (pp. 138–139.)

1. parler:
futur: je parlerai, tu _____, il (elle, on) _____, nous _____, vous _____, ils (elles) _____.
conditionnel: je parlerais, tu _____, il (elle, on) _____, nous _____, vous _____, ils (elles) _____.

2. **finir:**

futur: je finirai, tu _____, il (elle, on) _____, nous _____, vous _____, ils (elles) _____.

conditionnel: je finirais, tu _____, il (elle, on) _____, nous _____, vous _____, ils (elles) _____.

3. **perdre:**

futur: je perdrai, tu _____, il (elle, on) _____, nous _____, vous _____, ils (elles) _____.

conditionnel: je perdrais, tu _____, il (elle, on) _____, nous _____, vous _____, ils (elles) _____.

4. **avoir:**

futur: j'aurai, tu _____, il (elle, on) _____, nous _____, vous _____, ils (elles) _____.

conditionnel: j'aurais, tu _____, il (elle, on) _____, nous _____, vous _____, ils (elles) _____.

5. **être:**

futur: je serai, tu _____, il (elle, on) _____, nous _____, vous _____, ils (elles) _____.

conditionnel: je serais, tu _____, il (elle, on) _____, nous _____, vous _____, ils (elles) _____.

6. **aller:**

futur: j'irai, tu _____, il (elle, on) _____, nous _____, vous _____, ils (elles) _____.

conditionnel: j'irais, tu _____, il (elle, on) _____, nous _____, vous _____, ils (elles) _____.

7. **faire:**

futur: je ferai, tu _____, il (elle, on) _____, nous _____, vous _____, ils (elles) _____.

conditionnel: je ferais, tu _____, il (elle, on) _____, nous _____, vous _____, ils (elles) _____.

14. *Traduisez en français les verbes entre parenthèses.* (pp. 140–141, 142–143.)

1. Nous _____ (will go) à la soirée chez Robert.
2. Je _____ (would like) devenir médecin après avoir terminé mes études.
3. Après les examens semestriels je _____ (will sleep late) pendant toute une semaine!
4. Si j'étais à votre place, je _____ (would major) en psychologie.
5. Nous _____ (will live) dans un appartement au lieu d'une maison d'étudiants.

15. *Remplacez* **un, une** *ou* **des** *par l'adjectif possessif* **mon, ma** *ou* **mes.** (p. 200.)

1. une composition
2. un disque
3. un avenir
4. une université
5. des copains

16. **Les nombres:** (Appendix—Useful Expressions)

    1. Comptez de 1 à 20.
    2. Complétez: 10, 20, . . . 100.
    3. Exprimez en français: 21, 35, 61, 80, 81, 99, 100, 120, 1,000,000.
  -4. Traduisez en français: first, fifth, twentieth, forty-fifth, one hundredth.
    5. Traduisez en français en employant le suffixe *-aine:* about twenty, about thirty, about fifty, about one hundred.

17. **Les dates et le temps** (Appendix—Useful Expressions)

    1. Quels sont les jours de la semaine?
    2. Quels sont les mois de l'année?
    3. Traduisez en français: January 1, 1952; March 8, 1943; December 25, 1971.
    4. Quand êtes-vous né (mois, année)?
    5. Quel temps fait-il en hiver? au printemps?
    6. Quel temps fait-il en Floride?

18. **Quelle heure est-il?** (Appendix—Useful Expressions)

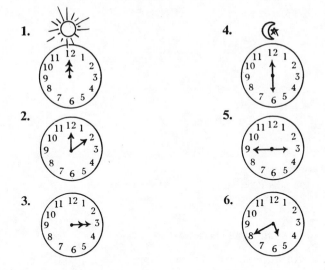

II.

    1. *Indiquez le genre* (**masculin** *ou* **féminin**) *sans consulter le dictionnaire.* (pp. 43–44.)

1. télévision	**4.** gentillesse	**7.** Californie
2. tableau	**5.** librairie	**8.** papier
3. classicisme	**6.** gouvernement	**9.** cigarette

2. *Remplacez les mots en italiques par* **y** *ou* **en.** (pp. 30–32).
   modèle: Je n'aime pas assister *aux cours obligatoires.*

   Je n'aime pas y assister.

   1. Nous allons *au cinéma* tous les jours.
   2. Malheureusement, j'ai échoué *à mon examen final.*
   3. Papa, j'ai besoin d'argent pour acheter *des livres.*
   4. Ma petite amie et moi, nous aimons étudier ensemble *à la bibliothèque.*
   5. J'ai suivi six *cours* le semestre passé.

3. *Remplacez les tirets par le partitif* **(du, de la, de l', des)** *ou par* **de (d')** *tout seul.* (pp. 56–57, 59–60.)

   1. Ce cancre fait beaucoup _____ fautes de grammaire!
   2. J'ai l'intention de faire _____ longs voyages.
   3. Cet étudiant solitaire n'a pas _____ copains.
   4. Ma copine a besoin _____ confiance.
   5. Cette étudiante va réussir parce qu'elle a _____ idées originales.

4. *Complétez au* **passé composé.** (pp. 74–76.)

   1. **parler:** j'ai parlé, tu _____, il (elle, on) _____, nous _____, vous _____, ils (elles) _____.
   2. **finir:** j'ai fini, tu _____, il (elle, on) _____, nous _____, vous _____, ils (elles) _____.
   3. **perdre:** j'ai perdu, tu _____, il (elle, on) _____, nous _____, vous _____, ils (elles) _____.
   4. **avoir:** j'ai eu, tu _____, il (elle, on) _____, nous _____, vous _____, ils (elles) _____.
   5. **être:** j'ai été, tu _____, il (elle, on) _____, nous _____, vous _____, ils (elles) _____.
   6. **aller:** je suis allé, tu _____, il (elle, on) _____, nous _____, vous _____, ils (elles) _____.
   7. **se lever:** je me suis levé, tu _____, il (elle, on) _____, nous _____, vous _____, ils (elles) _____.

5. *Mettez tous les verbes au* **passé composé.** (pp. 74–76.)

   1. Malheureusement, nous perdons nos cahiers.
   2. Les étudiants crient des slogans pendant la manifestation.
   3. Je fais du ski à la montagne.
   4. Je me réveille à cinq heures ce matin.
   5. Les jeunes se révoltent contre les préjugés de la société.
   6. Ils réussissent à l'examen parce qu'ils bûchent!
   7. Mes copains gaspillent leur temps!
   8. Nous nous promenons en voiture pendant le week-end.
   9. Marie sort en groupe quand elle va au théâtre.
   10. Mon camarade de chambre se spécialise en français.

6. *Complétez* à **l'imparfait.** (p. 79.)

   1. **parler:** je parlais, tu _____, il (elle, on) _____, nous _____, vous _____, ils (elles) _____.
   2. **finir:** je finissais, tu _____, il (elle, on) _____, nous _____, vous _____, ils (elles) _____.
   3. **perdre:** je perdais, tu _____, il (elle, on) _____, nous _____, vous _____, ils (elles)_____.
   4. **avoir:** j'avais, tu _____, il (elle, on) _____, nous _____, vous _____, ils (elles) _____.
   5. **être:** j'étais, tu _____, il (elle, on) _____, nous _____, vous _____, ils (elles) _____.

7. *Mettez les verbes entre parenthèses à* **l'imparfait** *et traduisez les phrases en anglais.* (pp. 80–81.)

   1. Comment! Il a manqué ce cours parce qu'il _____ (avoir) peur du professeur?
   2. Hier il _____ (faire) beau et les oiseaux _____ (chanter) dans les arbres.
   3. Je ne lui ai pas répondu parce que je _____ (être) timide.
   4. Quand je _____ (être) jeune, mon père et moi, nous _____ (faire) des promenades dans la neige.
   5. Quand le professeur m'a appelé, je _____ (dormir)!

8. *Formulez une question en employant les adverbes* **comment, où, pourquoi** *ou* **quand.** (pp. 93–94.)
   modèle: Je vais à Boston. **Où allez-vous?**

   1. Je vais à New York.
   2. François est travailleur et enthousiaste.
   3. Je travaille à mi-temps parce que je suis fauché (*broke*).
   4. Francine est blasée et paresseuse.
   5. Je commence à bûcher demain!
   6. Je viens à l'université en auto.

9. *Traduisez en français les verbes entre parenthèses en employant le verbe* **devoir.** (pp. 145–146.)

   1. Je _____ (have to) bûcher pour cet examen difficile!
   2. Vous _____ (should not) gaspiller votre temps.
   3. Nous _____ (must) assister à tous les cours qui nous restent.
   4. Michèle _____ (had to) trouver une autre camarade de chambre quand elle a changé d'appartement.
   5. Vous _____ (should have) passer votre temps libre à étudier, non pas à vous amuser!

10. *Remplacez les tirets par* **c'est** *ou* **il est.** (pp. 168–169.)

    1. J'aime beaucoup ce professeur parce que _____ sensationnel!

    2. Un «D»? _____ une mauvaise note!

    3. Quelle est la profession de votre père? —_____ avocat.

    4. Où est ton camarade de chambre sympathique? —_____ est avec mon camarade de chambre désagréable!

    5. _____ lui qui est sorti avec ta petite amie!

11. *Complétez au* **présent du subjonctif.** *Mettez* **il faut que** *devant chaque forme du verbe:* **il faut que je parle,** *etc.* (pp. 179–181.)

    1. **parler:** il faut que je parle, tu _____, il (elle, on) _____, nous _____, vous _____, ils (elles) _____.

    2. **finir:** il faut que je finisse, tu _____, il (elle, on) _____, nous _____, vous _____, ils (elles) _____.

    3. **perdre:** il faut que je perde, tu _____, il (elle, on) _____, nous _____, vous _____, ils (elles) _____.

    4. **avoir:** il faut que j'aie, tu _____, il (elle, on) _____, nous _____, vous _____, ils (elles) _____.

    5. **être:** il faut que je sois, tu _____, il (elle, on) _____, nous _____, vous _____, ils (elles) _____.

    6. **aller:** il faut que j'aille, tu _____, il (elle, on) _____, nous _____, vous _____, ils (elles) _____.

    7. **faire:** il faut que je fasse, tu _____, il (elle, on) _____, nous _____, vous _____, ils (elles) _____.

    8. **savoir:** il faut que je sache, tu _____, il (elle, on) _____, nous _____, vous _____, ils (elles) _____.

12. *Mettez les verbes au* **présent du subjonctif** *ou gardez* **l'infinitif,** *selon le cas* (as the case requires). (pp. 184–187)

    1. Je suis heureuse que mon copain _____ (pouvoir) m'accompagner au théâtre.

    2. Il fait si beau que je voudrais _____ (jouer) au golf aujourd'hui.

    3. Il faut que nous _____ (étudier) toute la nuit.

    4. Il est important que nous _____ (réussir) à cet examen.

    5. Notre professeur veut que nous _____ (lire) quatre livres en une semaine!

    6. Mon camarade de chambre veut _____ (regarder) la télévision au lieu d'étudier.

    7. Je suis étonné qu'une jeune fille si intelligente n' _____ (avoir) pas confiance en elle-même!

    8. Est-il important de _____ (passer) son temps à étudier si on veut réussir?

    9. Mes parents veulent que je _____ (se spécialiser) en médecine.

    10. Je ne veux pas que nous _____ (dîner) dans le réfectoire de l'université!

13. *Remplacez les tirets par la préposition* **à** *ou* **de**, *si nécessaire.* (pp. 210–212.)

1. J'ai enfin réussi _____ terminer l'examen!
2. Je n'ai jamais essayé _____ faire du ski.
3. Il faut _____ faire attention en classe.
4. Je vais commencer _____ parler très bien français cette année!
5. Marie veut _____ assister à la conférence de M. Barthes!

The passé simple

The **passé simple** or *past definite* is a literary past tense that is almost never used in conversation. To avoid confusion, students should be able to recognize it in the texts they read. The **passé simple** is generally translated in English in the same way as the **passé composé** or *compound past:* **j'ai parlé,** *I spoke;* **je parlai,** *I spoke.* The **passé simple** is formed by dropping the ending of the infinitive and adding the following endings:

-er verbs	-ir and -re verbs		avoir and être	
parler	**finir**	**perdre**	**avoir**	**être**
je parlai	je finis	je perdis	j' eus	je fus
tu parlas	tu finis	tu perdis	tu eus	tu fus
il	il	il	il	il
elle }parla	elle }finit	elle }perdit	elle }eut	elle }fut
on	on	on	on	on
nous parlâmes	nous finîmes	nous perdîmes	nous eûmes	nous fûmes
vous parlâtes	vous finîtes	vous perdîtes	vous eûtes	vous fûtes
ils }parlèrent	ils }finirent	ils }perdirent	ils }eurent	ils }furent
elles	elles	elles	elles	elles

The **passé simple** of common irregular verbs may be found in the verb charts in the Appendix. Other literary tenses are also explained there.

EXERCICE

Voici un extrait (*selection*) du *Petit Prince*, le roman célèbre d'Antoine de Saint-Exupéry. Venu d'un autre monde, le protagoniste explore l'univers en visitant une série de planètes.

Identifiez les verbes au **passé simple** *et traduisez ces verbes en anglais.*

La planète suivante était habitée par un *buveur.* Cette visite fut très courte mais elle plongea le petit prince dans une grande mélancolie:
—Que fais-tu là? dit-il au buveur, qu'il trouva installé en silence devant une collection de *bouteilles* vides et une collection de bouteilles pleines.
—Je bois, répondit le buveur, *d'un air lugubre.*
—Pourquoi bois-tu? lui demanda le petit prince.

—Pour oublier, répondit le buveur.

—Pour oublier quoi? *s'enquit* le petit prince qui déjà le *plaignait*.

—Pour oublier que *j'ai honte,* avoua le buveur en *baissant* la tête.

—Honte de quoi? s'*informa* le petit prince qui désirait le *secourir*.

—Honte de boire! *acheva* le buveur qui *s'enferma* définitivement dans le silence.

VOCABULAIRE

le buveur *drinker*
la bouteille *bottle*
d'un air lugubre *sadly, morosely*
s' **enquit** = demanda
plaindre *to pity*
avoir honte *to be ashamed*

avouer *to confess*
baisser *to lower*
s' **informa** = demanda
secourir = aider
acheva = conclut
s' **enfermer** *to shut oneself up*

Composition_____

A well-organized composition has an *introduction, transitions* and a *conclusion.* Study the following examples, which will be helpful in preparing compositions and oral reports.

1. Introductions

    Je vais discuter (décrire, examiner, traiter) . . .
    I am going to discuss (describe, examine, treat) . . .

    On dit souvent que . . .
    It is often said that . . .

    Je vais diviser mes remarques en deux parties: d'abord . . . et ensuite . . .
    I am going to divide my remarks into two parts: first . . . and then . . .

2. Transitions

    d'une part . . . d'autre part *on one hand . . . on the other hand*

    d'ailleurs *besides*
    de plus *furthermore, in addition, moreover*
    en plus de *in addition to*

    en ce qui concerne *concerning*
    quant à *as for*

    au contraire *on the contrary*
    cependant, pourtant *however*
    mais *but*
    tandis que *whereas*

    par exemple *for example*

3. Conclusions

en conclusion *in conclusion*
donc *therefore*
par conséquent *consequently*
à mon avis *in my opinion*
bref, en résumé *in short*

EXERCICE

Remplacez les tirets dans cette composition par **tandis que, par exemple, mais, cependant, donc, je vais discuter, au contraire** *ou* **en conclusion.**

_____ le fossé (*gap*) entre les générations. Je pense que les jeunes et les adultes doivent avoir des idées différentes parce qu'ils mènent des vies différentes.

Les jeunes passent beaucoup de temps à l'université où ils pensent à leurs études et aux rapports avec leurs copains. L'université, _____, est un monde fermé et protégé où les responsabilités sont réduites (_____, les étudiants ne sont pas toujours obligés de faire la cuisine!). Je ne dis pas que les étudiants n'ont pas de responsabilités, _____ leurs responsabilités sont limitées. Puisqu'ils manquent d'expérience dans le monde réel, ils ont tendance à être idéalistes et impatients. Ils veulent réformer la société en un jour!

Les adultes, _____, ont beaucoup d'expérience. Ils sont obligés de faire face aux réalités de la vie. C'est eux, _____, qui doivent payer les frais d'admission (*tuition*) de leurs enfants! Quand ils étaient jeunes, eux aussi ont essayé de réformer la société, _____ ils n'ont pas toujours réussi. Ils sont _____ devenus réalistes.

_____, on peut dire que les adultes acceptent de vivre dans un monde qui n'est pas parfait, _____ les jeunes rêvent d'une meilleure vie qu'ils veulent réaliser.

Sujets de discussion ou de composition

Employez au besoin (when useful) *les termes d'introduction, de transition et de conclusion qu'on vous a donnés ci-dessus* (above).

1. Décrivez un rendez-vous extraordinaire que vous avez eu. (Était-il bizarre, désastreux, formidable, amusant? Avec qui êtes-vous sorti? Où êtes-vous allé? etc.)

2. Quelles distractions préférez-vous le plus et lesquelles préférez-vous le moins? Pourquoi?

3. Vous avez l'air d'un cancre mais ce n'est pas parce que vous êtes stupide. C'est plutôt parce que vous vous révoltez secrètement contre le système d'enseignement supérieur que vous trouvez injuste et inefficace (*inefficient*). Expliquez précisément pourquoi.

4. Au début d'une année scolaire les étudiants doivent prendre beaucoup de décisions. Par exemple, il faut choisir des cours, des profs, une maison d'étudiants ou un appartement, des clubs ou des organisations, etc. Racontez les décisions que vous avez prises en indiquant les raisons de vos choix.

2

Present tense, imperative, personal pronouns

Chapter 2 at a glance

THE PRESENT TENSE

I. *Complétez* **au présent.**

1.	vous (flirter)	**5.**	je (boire)	**9.**	vous (apprendre)
2.	nous (finir)	**6.**	ils (aller)	**10.**	nous (divorcer)
3.	vous (mentir)	**7.**	ils (craindre)	**11.**	tu (acheter)
4.	ils (répondre)	**8.**	nous (mettre)	**12.**	elles (employer)

II. *Quelle traduction n'est pas correcte?*

1. Elle cherche une situation.
  a. She is looking for a job.
  b. She has been looking for a job.
  c. She does look for a job.
  d. She looks for a job.

2. Il est en train de terminer son travail.
  a. He is finishing his work on the train.
  b. He is busy finishing his work.
  c. He is in the act of finishing his work.

3. Elle est mariée depuis seize ans.
  a. She has been married for sixteen years.
  b. She got married at sixteen.

III. *Remplacez les mots entre parenthèses par* **depuis quand** *ou* **depuis combien de temps.**

1. (Since when) Jeannine flirte-t-elle avec mon petit ami?
2. (For how long) sortez-vous avec Robert?

IV. *Traduisez en français en employant l'expression* **venir de.**

1. Brigitte has just found a house.
2. They have just gone to Paris.

THE IMPERATIVE

V. *Mettez les verbes aux trois formes de* **l'impératif.**

1. (choisir) un mari!
2. (répondre) tout de suite!
3. (faire) la cuisine!
4. (être) indépendante(s)!

VI. *Mettez au négatif en employant* **ne . . . pas.**

1. Allons au cinéma!
2. Faites le lit!

VII. *Remplacez les tirets par* **tiens** *ou* **voyons.**

    1. _____! J'ai une bonne idée!
    2. _____! Vous n'êtes pas vraiment sérieuse!

PERSONAL PRONOUNS

VIII. *Remplacez les mots en italiques par un* **pronom** *et mettez le pronom à la place convenable.*

    1. Jeannine déteste *le chauvinisme du mâle!*
    2. Elle ne parle jamais *de son mariage.*
    3. Elles veulent habiter *à Paris.*
    4. Ne parlez pas *à mon petit ami!*

IX. *Remplacez les mots en italiques par deux* **pronoms** *et mettez les pronoms à la place convenable.*

    1. Robert donne *des cadeaux à Babette.*
    2. Laure a annoncé *son mariage à ses amies.*

X. *Traduisez en français en employant un* **pronom disjoint** (disjunctive).

    1. Je suis sûr que Madeleine est amoureuse de _____ (him)!
    2. _____ (You and I), nous sommes toujours en retard.

XI. *Complétez en employant le pronom* **le (l').**

    1. Votre sœur est-elle libérée? —Oui, _____ (she is).
    2. Hélène et Barbara sont-elles traditionalistes? —Non, _____ (they aren't).

Vocabulaire du thème: Les Femmes

LE MARIAGE

le **mari** *husband*	**avoir, élever des enfants** *to have, to bring up children*
la **femme** *wife*	
se **marier avec, épouser** *to marry (someone)*	**partager** *to share*
	fidèle *faithful*
se **marier** *to get married*	
marié *married*	**tromper** *to cheat on, to deceive*
être enceinte *to be pregnant*	**jaloux** *jealous*

L'AMOUR

flirter *to flirt*
être (tomber) amoureux de *to be (to fall) in love with*
embrasser *to kiss*
séduisant *attractive, sexy*
doux *sweet*
choyer *to pamper*

la liberté sexuelle *sexual freedom*
l' union libre (f) *living together out of wedlock, common-law marriage*
la limitation des naissances *birth control*
l' avortement (m) *abortion*
la pilule *pill*

LES TRAVAUX MÉNAGERS

les travaux ménagers *household chores*
faire la cuisine *to do the cooking, to cook*

faire la vaisselle *to do the dishes*
faire les courses *to do the shopping*
faire le ménage *to do the housework*

LA LIBÉRATION DES FEMMES

le, la féministe *feminist*
refuser les rôles féminins traditionnels *to refuse the traditional feminine roles*
l' égalité (f) *equality*
égal *equal*
indépendant *independent*
libéré *liberated*
la crèche *day-care center*

confus *confused*
frustré *frustrated*

chercher, trouver un poste *to look for, to find a job*
poursuivre une carrière *to pursue a career*

le chauvinisme du mâle *male chauvinism*
la discrimination *discrimination*
le stéréotype féminin *feminine stereotype*

L'APPARENCE

grossir *to get fat*
maigrir *to lose weight, to slim down*

suivre un régime *to be on a diet*
faire des manières *to put on airs*

The present tense

Formation of the present

Regular formations

Regular verbs can be classified in three major groups according to the ending of the infinitive.

1. Group 1: infinitive ending in **-er**

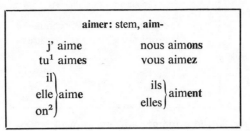

aimer: stem, **aim-**

j' aime	nous aim**ons**
tu¹ aimes	vous aim**ez**
il elle aime on²	ils elles aim**ent**

2. Group 2: infinitive ending in **-ir**
   a. Verbs like **finir.**

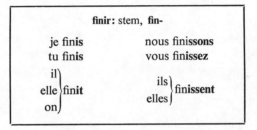

finir: stem, **fin-**

je finis	nous fin**issons**
tu finis	vous fin**issez**
il elle finit on	ils elles fin**issent**

   b. Verbs like **mentir.**

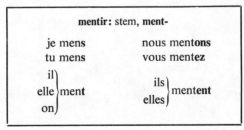

mentir: stem, **ment-**

je mens	nous ment**ons**
tu mens	vous ment**ez**
il elle ment on	ils elles ment**ent**

Common verbs like **mentir** are **dormir, partir, sentir, servir,** and **sortir.** Note that there is no **-iss-** in the plural, and that the consonant before the **-ir** ending is dropped in the singular but retained in the plural: **je dors,** but **nous dormons.**

---

¹ Remember that **tu,** the familiar form, is used in addressing members of one's family, close friends, children, and animals; otherwise, the more formal **vous** is used. Young people today use **tu** freely among themselves.

² **On** is an indefinite pronoun, meaning "one" or, in the indefinite sense, "you" or "they" or "people." It always takes a singular verb.

3. Group 3: infinitive ending in **-re**

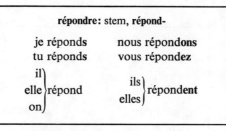

répondre: stem, répond-	
je réponds	nous répond**ons**
tu réponds	vous répond**ez**
il elle on ⎫répond	ils elles ⎫répond**ent**

The verbs **rompre** and **interrompre** add an unpronounced **t** in the third person singular: **il rompt, elle interrompt.**

EXERCICES

1. *Répondez affirmativement, puis négativement.*

   1. Réussissez-vous?
   2. Regardez-vous?
   3. Partez-vous?
   4. Interrompez-vous?
   5. Réfléchissez-vous?
   6. Vendez-vous?
   7. Grossissez-vous?
   8. Dormez-vous?
   9. Grandissez-vous?
   10. Travaillez-vous?

2. *Complétez au présent.*

   1. nous (attendre)
   2. vous (aimer)
   3. elles (punir)
   4. ils (entendre)
   5. nous (bâtir)
   6. tu (servir)
   7. vous (grandir)
   8. elle (embrasser)
   9. ils (gagner)
   10. nous (sortir)

Irregular formations

1. Verbs with irregular present tenses must be learned individually (see Appendix). Verbs with similar formations may be organized into groups.

   a. Common verbs

aller	dire	plaire
s'asseoir	être	prendre
avoir	faire	recevoir
boire	falloir[4]	rire
courir	lire	savoir
devoir[3]	mourir	valoir

   ---

   [3] See Chapter 7, pp. 145–148, for the use of **devoir**.
   [4] This verb is used only in the third person singular.

b. Common verb groups

> battre, mettre
> connaître, paraître
> croire, voir
> écrire, vivre, suivre
> offrir, ouvrir, souffrir
> pouvoir, vouloir, pleuvoir
> tenir, venir
> verbs ending in **-indre**: craindre, joindre, peindre, etc.
> verbs ending in **-uire**: construire, détruire, séduire, etc.

Note that compounds derived from these verbs are conjugated in the same way: **apprendre, comprendre,** and **surprendre** like **prendre; devenir, revenir,** and **se souvenir** like **venir;** etc.

2. Some common **-er** verbs undergo spelling changes.
   a. Verbs in **-cer** and **-ger: c** changes to **ç (c cédille)** and **g** to **ge** before the ending **-ons.**

> **commencer: je commence** but **nous commençons**
> **nager: je nage** but **nous nageons**

Other such verbs:

avancer	lancer	divorcer
changer	manger	partager

b. Verbs in **-yer: y** changes to **i** before endings in mute **-e: -e, -es, -ent.**

> **nettoyer: vous nettoyez** but **je nettoie, ils nettoient**

Other such verbs:

choyer	employer	essayer
essuyer	payer	envoyer

Note that verbs ending in **-ayer** may retain the **y: ils paient, ils payent.**

c. Verbs in **e** + *consonant* + **er: e** changes to **è (e accent grave)** before endings in mute **e.**

> **lever: nous levons** but **tu lèves, ils lèvent**

Other such verbs:

mener   promener
élever   peser

Verbs in **-eler** or **-eter** are exceptions. They double the **l** and **t** before endings in mute **e.**

> **appeler: nous appelons but elle appelle, ils appellent**

The verbs **acheter** and **geler,** however, change e to è: **j'achète, il gèle.**

d. Verbs in é + *consonant* + **er: é (e accent aigu)** changes to **è (e accent grave)** before endings in mute **-e.**

> **suggérer: nous suggérons but je suggère, ils suggèrent**

Other such verbs:

considérer   espérer   posséder
préférer   répéter

EXERCICES

1. *Complétez au présent.*

1. je, nous (craindre)
2. il, vous (savoir)
3. tu, elles (aller)
4. je, nous (découvrir)
5. il (pleuvoir)
6. tu, vous (faire)
7. je, vous (voir)
8. il, ils (venir)
9. tu, vous (commettre)
10. je, nous (devoir)
11. elle, nous (séduire)
12. je, nous (pouvoir)
13. tu, ils (écrire)
14. je, ils (être)
15. je, nous (boire)
16. tu, ils (avoir)
17. il (falloir)
18. je, vous (croire)
19. elle, elles (recevoir)
20. je, nous (vouloir)
21. tu, nous (rire)
22. elle, elles (plaire)
23. je, vous (valoir)

2. *Complétez au présent.*

1. nous (divorcer)
2. ils (changer)
3. nous (manger)
4. elle (payer)
5. tu (élever)
6. vous (acheter)
7. nous (appeler)
8. je (préférer)
9. vous (posséder)
10. nous (essayer)
11. ils (envoyer)
12. tu (espérer)
13. nous (mener)
14. elles (partager)
15. je (considérer)

Use of the present

The single form of the French present tense corresponds to several possible variations in English.

$$\textbf{j'aime} \begin{cases} \text{I love} \\ \text{I do love} \\ \text{I am loving} \\ \text{I have been loving} \end{cases}$$

The precise English equivalent of the French present tense depends on the use of the verb in the sentence.

Uses that correspond to the English present

Like the English present tense, the French present is used to indicate present or customary actions, and general truths.

Comment! Brigitte flirte-t-elle avec mon petit ami?
What! Is Brigitte flirting with my boy friend?

Hortense bavarde au téléphone tous les après-midi.
Hortense gossips on the phone every afternoon.

L'amour idéal n'existe pas.
Ideal love doesn't exist.

The English progressive present

The French present tense is used to express the English progressive present: *I am walking.*

Que fait Jeannine? —Elle cherche du travail.
What is Jeannine doing? —She's looking for work.

The expression **être en train de** + *infinitive* (*to be busy, or in the act or process of, doing something*) is used to stress the progressive nature of the present.

Silence! Je suis en train de travailler!
Quiet! I'm busy working!

La femme moderne est en train de se créer une nouvelle image.
Modern woman is in the process of creating a new image for herself.

With depuis, il y a . . . que, voici . . . que, voilà . . . que

The French present is used with **depuis, il y a . . . que, voici . . . que,** and **voilà . . . que** to express an action that began in the past and is still going on in the present (the English present perfect tense).

Charles et Emma sortent ensemble depuis longtemps.
Il y a longtemps que Charles et Emma sortent ensemble.

Voici (Voilà) longtemps que Charles et Emma sortent ensemble.
Charles and Emma have been going out together for a long time.

Note that the verb precedes **depuis,** but follows the other three expressions.
Il y a meaning *there is* (*are*) or *ago* should not be confused with **il y a . . . que.**

Il y a deux crèches en ville.
There are two day-care centers in the city.

Ils se sont mariés il y a deux ans.
They got married two years ago.

Il y a deux ans qu'elle suit un régime.
She has been on a diet for two years.

The immediate future

The French present can also be used with a future temporal expression to indicate an action in the immediate future.

Elle vient dans une heure.
She's coming in an hour.

Je vous téléphone demain.
I'll telephone you tomorrow.

EXERCICES

1. *Récrivez les phrases en employant le temps présent avec* **depuis.**

   1. Voilà six mois que ma femme est enceinte.
   2. Il y a deux ans que Jeannine se joint à toutes les organisations féministes.
   3. Voici quatre heures que Marguerite fait la cuisine!
   4. Il y a des siècles que l'homme domine la femme.
   5. Voilà des années que ma sœur grossit!

2. *Traduisez en français.*

   1. Jeannine is sweet, attractive, and very liberated.
   2. She has been married for four years.
   3. A true feminist, she refuses the traditional feminine roles.
   4. She and her husband Louis share the household chores.
   5. Louis, for example, is busy raising their two children.
   6. He also does the shopping, the cooking and the housework.
   7. He is so tired and frustrated that he is losing weight!
   8. And Jeannine? She is busy pursuing a career in business (*dans les affaires*).
   9. She does the dishes.
   10. They have been truly equal since the beginning of their marriage!

Related expressions

Depuis quand . . .? *and* Depuis combien de temps . . .? + *present tense*

1. **Depuis quand . . .?** (*how long, since when*) is used to ask a question concerning the origin of an action. The answer will usually indicate a specific point in time: a year, day of the month or week, hour of the day, etc.

   > **Depuis quand êtes-vous marié? —Je suis marié depuis 1970.**
   > How long (since when) have you been married? —I've been married since 1970.

2. **Depuis combien de temps . . .?** (*how long*) is used to ask a question concerning the duration of an action. The answer will usually indicate an amount of time.

   > **Depuis combien de temps êtes-vous divorcé? —Je suis divorcé depuis sept ans.**
   > How long have you been divorced? —I have been divorced for seven years.

Venir de + *infinitive*

The present tense of **venir de** + *infinitive* indicates that an action has just been completed.

> **Elle vient d'avoir un enfant.**
> She has just had a baby.

> **Elle vient de trouver un bon poste.**
> She just found a good job.

Note that the English equivalents do not use the present tense.

EXERCICES

1. *Répondez en français.*

   1. Depuis quand êtes-vous dans cette classe?
   2. Depuis combien de temps conduisez-vous une voiture?
   3. Depuis quand êtes-vous à l'université?
   4. Depuis combien de temps étudiez-vous le français?
   5. Depuis quand les États-Unis existent-ils?

2. *Traduisez en français.*

   1. Anne just found a boyfriend.
   2. They have just gone shopping.
   3, Jeannine has just gone out with Robert.
   4. Fifi just found a job!
   5. Marguerite and Guy have just had a baby.

The imperative_____

The imperative mood expresses a command or request. In French, it possesses three forms: the second person singular, and the first and second person plural.

Regular imperatives[5]

The imperatives of most verbs have the same form as the present indicative without the subject pronouns.

PRESENT INDICATIVE | IMPERATIVE

Tu attends.
You are waiting.

Attends!
Wait!

Vous suivez un régime.
You are on a diet.

Suivez un régime!
Go on a diet!

Nous faisons le ménage.
We're doing the housework.

Faisons le ménage!
Let's do the housework!

The negative imperative

The negative imperative is formed by placing **ne** before the verb and **pas** after it.

Ne trompez pas Robert!
Don't cheat on Robert!

Ne faisons pas cela.
Let's not do that.

The second person singular of -er verbs

The second person singular of **-er** verbs (and of verbs like **offrir, ouvrir,** and **souffrir,** which conjugate like **-er** verbs) does not take **s** except when followed by **y** or **en.**

Reste à la maison.
Stay home.

Ouvre la fenêtre!
Open the window!

but:

Restes-y.
Stay there.

Cherches-en!
Look for some!

_____
[5] The imperative of reflexive verbs will be treated on pp. 71 .

Irregular imperatives

The verbs **avoir, être, savoir,** and **vouloir** have irregular imperatives.

avoir	être	savoir	vouloir
aie	sois	sache	veuille
ayons	soyons	sachons	veuillons
ayez	soyez	sachez	veuillez

Veuillez is a formal, polite form of *please.*

> **Ayez de la patience!**
> Have patience!

> **Ne soyons pas idiots!**
> Let's not be silly!

> **Veuillez vous asseoir, Mme Deslauriers.**
> Please be seated, Mrs. Deslauriers.

EXERCICE

Traduisez en français.

1. Let's slim down.
2. Don't listen to the feminists!
3. Avoid household chores.
4. Be independent.
5. Don't be too sexy, Brigitte!
6. Work, don't dream!
7. Choose (sing.) your friends with prudence.
8. Don't take that pill!
9. Do (sing.) the cooking tonight, Jean-Pierre.
10. Let's chat in my room.

Related expressions

Some imperatives have become commonplace in the spoken language and are often used as interjections.

Tiens (*from* tenir)

> **Tiens! J'ai une bonne idée!**
> Hey! I've a good idea!

> **Tiens! Le voilà!**
> Look—there he is!

Tiens expresses surprise.

Allons (*from* aller)

> **Allons! Tais-toi!**
> Come on, be quiet!

Allons expresses impatience.

Voyons *or* mais voyons (*from* voir)

> **Mais voyons! Vous savez que c'est impossible!**
> Come now! You know that's impossible!

Voyons or **mais voyons** expresses disapproval or disbelief.

EXERCICE

Remplacez les tirets par **tiens, voyons (mais voyons)** *ou* **allons,** *selon le cas.*

1. _____! Je viens d'avoir une idée exceptionnelle!
2. _____! Vous n'êtes pas Roméo!
3. _____! Sûrement pas avec ma petite amie!
4. _____! Bavardez moins fort!
5. _____! Ce n'était qu'un petit mensonge!
6. _____! Elle sait la réponse!
7. _____! Je n'étais même pas avec lui ce soir-là!
8. _____! Répondez tout de suite!
9. _____! Voilà Maurice!
10. _____! Elle n'est pas si frustrée que ça!

Personal pronouns———————————

A pronoun is a word that replaces a noun. In French a pronoun has the same gender and number as the noun it replaces.

> **Connaissez-vous les Giroud? —Oui, je les connais.**
> Do you know the Girouds? —Yes, I know them.
>
> **Condamnez-vous le divorce? —Oui, je le condamne.**
> Do you condemn divorce? —Yes, I condemn it.
>
> **Parle-t-il avec Adèle? —Oui, il parle avec elle.**
> Is he speaking with Adele? —Yes, he's speaking with her.

Direct and indirect object pronouns, y *and* en

A direct object receives directly the action of the verb.

Il embrasse Brigitte
He kisses Brigitte.

Il l'embrasse.
He kisses her.

An indirect object receives indirectly the action of the verb. It is often preceded by *to*, expressed or understood.

Elle donne la bague à son fiancé.
She gives the ring to her fiancé.

Elle lui donne la bague.
She gives him the ring.

Direct object pronouns

me	me	**nous**	us
te	you	**vous**	you
le	him, it	**les**	them
la	her, it		

Je la traite comme une égale.
I treat her as an equal.

Je te vois demain.
I'll see you tomorrow.

The pronouns **me, te, le,** and **la** adopt the elided forms **m', t', l'** before verbs beginning with a vowel or mute **h.**[6]

Je l'aime beaucoup.
I love her (him, it) very much.

On m'habitue au travail dur.
They are getting me used to hard work.

but: **Il me hait.**
He hates me.

Indirect object pronouns

me	to me	**nous**	to us
te	to you	**vous**	to you
lui	{to him / to her}	**leur**	to them

---

[6] There are two kinds of **h**'s in French, the mute **h** and the aspirate **h**; in pronunciation, both are silent. Elision occurs before a word beginning with a mute **h,** but not before a word beginning with an aspirate **h.** Words beginning with an aspirate **h** are marked with an asterisk in most French dictionaries, as in the end vocabulary of this book.

Sa femme lui parle tendrement.
His wife speaks tenderly to him.

Il me donne le livre.
He gives the book to me.

Keep in mind that very often a French indirect object is not introduced by *to* in English.

Il lui offre une vie parfaite.
He offers her a perfect life.

Ma mère me demande de faire le lit.
My mother asks me to make the bed.

EXERCICES

1. *Remplacez les tirets par* **le, la, les, lui,** *ou* **leur.**

    1. Connaissez-vous cette femme? —Oui, je _____ connais très bien.
    2. Votre père approuve-t-il la liberté sexuelle? —Non, il ne _____ approuve pas.
    3. Comment son ami la traite-t-il? —Il _____ traite comme une véritable égale.
    4. Donne-t-elle la clef à Jean? —Oui, elle _____ donne la clef.
    5. Les féministes dénoncent les stéréotypes féminins. Nous _____ dénonçons aussi.

2. *Traduisez en français.*

    1. They are lying to us!
    2. Her boyfriend is cheating on her.
    3. He offers me a happy life if I marry him.
    4. When I speak to her, she doesn't hear me!
    5. You write us often.

Y *as an adverb and pronoun*

1. As an adverb, **y** means *there*. It refers to a previously mentioned noun preceded by a preposition of place such as **à, dans,** or **chez.** It is almost always used in French, though often it need not be translated in English.

    Je vois Marc dans la rue. Il y fait quelque chose.
    I see Marc in the street. He's doing something there.

    Allez-vous à Paris? —Oui, j'y vais.
    Are you going to Paris? —Yes, I'm going.

If a place has not been previously mentioned, **là** is used instead of **y.**

Mettez-vous là, s'il vous plaît.
Sit there, please.

Où est-elle? —Là.
Where is she? —There.

Note that **y** is not used with the verb **aller** in the future and conditional tenses: **j'y vais,** but **j'irai** and **j'irais.**

2. As a pronoun, **y** refers to things or ideas. It is used as the object of verbs and expressions ending in **à. Y** is not used to refer to persons.

Pensez-vous à la soirée? —Oui, j'y pense.
Are you thinking about the party? —Yes, I'm thinking about it.

S'intéresse-t-elle aux mouvements contre la discrimination sexuelle?
—Oui, elle s'y intéresse énormément!
Is she interested in movements against sexual discrimination?
—Yes, she's very much interested in them.

En *as an adverb and pronoun*

1. As an adverb, **en** means *from there*, expressed or understood.

Viennent-ils d'Allemagne? —Oui, ils en viennent.
Do they come from Germany? —Yes, they come from there.

Reste-t-elle à Paris? —Non, elle en revient demain.
Is she staying in Paris? —No, she's coming back (from there) tomorrow.

2. As a pronoun, **en** usually refers to things or ideas. It replaces nouns in expressions formed with **de:** the partitive **(de l'argent, du pain,** etc.); objects of expressions of quantity **(assez de, beaucoup de,** etc.); and objects of verbs and expressions ending in **de (parler de, capable de,** etc.). Its English equivalents are *some, any, of it,* or *of them,* expressed or understood.

A-t-elle des vêtements chic? —Oui, elle en a.
Does she have any stylish clothes? —Yes, she has some.

A-t-elle beaucoup d'ambition? —Oui, elle en a beaucoup.
Does she have a lot of ambition? —Yes, she has a lot.

Parle-t-elle de son avortement? —Oui, elle en parle.
Does she talk about her abortion? —Yes, she talks about it.

Est-elle capable de poursuivre une carrière? —Oui, elle en est très capable.
Is she capable of pursuing a career? —Yes, she's very capable of it.

En also replaces nouns modified by numbers.

> **Combien de pièces l'appartement a-t-il? —Il en a huit.**
> How many rooms does the apartment have? —It has eight.

En may also replace persons after numbers and expressions of quantity, and with indefinite plural nouns.

> **Combien d'enfants avez-vous? —J'en ai six.**
> How many children do you have? —I have six.
>
> **Combien d'amis ta femme a-t-elle? —Elle en a beaucoup.**
> How many friends does your wife have? —She has a lot.
>
> **A-t-elle des ennemis aussi? —Oui, elle en a.**
> Does she have enemies also? —Yes, she does.
>
> **Avons-nous besoin de jeunes filles pour la soirée? —Oui, nous en avons besoin.**
> Do we need girls for the party? —Yes, we do.

To avoid confusing **y** and **en**, remember that **y** (one letter) is often associated with **à** (one letter), while **en** (two letters) is always associated with **de** (two letters).

EXERCICE

Remplacez les tirets par **y** *ou* **en.**

1. Obéissez-vous aux conseils de votre femme? —Oui, je _____ obéis quand ils sont raisonnables!
2. Avez-vous beaucoup de frères? —Je _____ ai deux.
3. Anne pense-t-elle à son rendez-vous avec Jacques? —Non, elle ne _____ pense pas du tout!
4. Elle vient de voir ses amis en ville. Elle les _____ voit souvent.
5. Vient-elle de France? —Oui, elle _____ vient.
6. Votre sœur a-t-elle trouvé une crèche pour le petit Marc? —Elle a eu de la chance, elle _____ a trouvé deux!
7. Je vais participer à ce mouvement militant. Voulez-vous _____ participer aussi?
8. Avez-vous besoin de patience dans votre travail? —Oui, je _____ ai besoin!
9. Achetez-vous des robes aujourd'hui? —Oui, je _____ achète.
10. J'ai envie de maigrir. _____ avez-vous envie aussi?

Position of pronouns

1. Except in the affirmative imperative, the object pronouns, **y** and **en** directly precede the verb. If there is more than one pronoun with a verb,

the order is as follows:

me		le		lui							
te											
nous	before	la	before	lui leur	before	y	before	en	before	*verb*	
vous		les									
se[7]											

Je vous les recommande.
I recommend them to you.

Il nous en donne.
He gives us some.

Nous les y envoyons.
We send them there.

This order is also observed with infinitives and negative imperatives.

Je vais les leur donner.
I am going to give them to them.

Il veut nous y envoyer.
He wants to send us there.

Ne le lui montrez pas!
Don't show it to him!

Ne m'en donne pas.
Don't give me any.

2. In the affirmative imperative, however, the pronouns follow the verb and are joined to it by hyphens. If there is more than one pronoun with a verb, the order is as follows:

verb	before	*direct object*	before	*indirect object*	before	y	before	en

Donnez-les-leur.
Give them to them.

Envoyons-les-y.
Let's send them there.

The pronouns **me** and **te** change to **moi** and **toi** in final position.

Si vous avez un secret, racontez-le-moi.
If you have a secret, tell it to me.

Explique-toi!
Explain yourself!

---

[7] The reflexive pronoun **se** is treated in Chapter 4.

Note that when **me, te, le,** or **la** elide with **y** or **en,** a hyphen disappears.

Achetez-m'en!
Buy me some!

EXERCICE

Remplacez les mots en italiques par les pronoms convenables.
modèle: Robert a beaucoup *d'amis.*   **Robert en a beaucoup.**

1. Pensez-vous souvent *à votre avenir?*
2. Le matin elle ne fait pas *le lit.*
3. Il y a *des stéréotypes féminins* qui sont justifiés.
4. Je donne souvent *des cadeaux à mon amie.*
5. Je vais vous parler *du Mouvement de libération des femmes.*
6. Il annonce *son mariage à ses amis.*
7. Beaucoup de femmes modernes ont envie de rester *à la maison.*
8. Je veux te montrer *des exemples de discrimination.*
9. Essaie de comprendre *la nouvelle image de la femme moderne.*
10. Elle poursuit deux *carrières.*
11. Jeannine défend *la pilule.*
12. Ne faites pas *de bêtises.*
13. Guy ne songe pas à tromper *Marguerite.*
14. Elle a l'intention *de chercher un poste à Paris.*
15. Je vois *les féministes en ville.*

Disjunctive pronouns

Disjunctive pronouns are personal pronouns that do not form a single word group with the verb (hence the name *disjunctive*).

moi	**nous**
toi	**vous**
lui	**eux**
elle	**elles**
soi	

Lui and **eux** are masculine; **elle** and **elles** are feminine. **Soi** is indefinite, corresponding to the English *oneself* or *itself.*

Use of disjunctive pronouns

1. To respond directly to a question without using a verb:

Qui frappe à la porte? —Moi!

Who's knocking at the door? — I am!

2. After a preposition:

Il part sans elle.
He leaves without her.

Elle va arriver avant vous.
She's going to arrive before you.

But the disjunctive pronoun is used with **à** only after reflexive verbs and a small group of expressions such as **faire attention à, penser à,** and **songer à.** In most cases **à** + *person* is replaced by an indirect object pronoun.

Je pense à lui.　　　　　　　　　**Je m'intéresse à elle.**
I am thinking of him.　　　　　　　　I'm interested in her.

but:

Je lui parle.　　　　　　　　　　　**Je leur obéis.**
I'm speaking to him.　　　　　　　　I obey them.

3. To emphasize the subject:

Toi, tu es toujours contre les nouveaux mouvements.
You are always against new movements.

Moi, je suis pour la libération des femmes.
I am for women's liberation.

Both a disjunctive and a subject pronoun are used, except in the third person, where a disjunctive pronoun may be used alone.

Eux ne vont jamais l'accepter!
They will never accept it!

4. In compound subjects:

Toi et moi ferons le ménage ensemble.
Toi et moi, nous ferons le ménage ensemble.
You and I will do the housework together.

Hélène et moi faisons la vaisselle.
Hélène et moi, nous faisons la vaisselle.
Helen and I do the dishes.

In compound subjects the disjunctive pronouns are often summed up by a personal pronoun (**nous** in the above examples). If both disjunctive pronouns are of the third person, however, they are generally not summed up.

Lui et elle travaillent ensemble.
He and she work together.

5. With comparisons and the expression **ne . . . que** (*only*):

> **Sa sœur est plus honnête que lui.**
> His sister is more honest than he.
>
> **Elle est si amoureuse qu'elle ne voit que lui!**
> She is so in love that she sees only him!

6. After **ni**:

> **Elle n'aime ni lui ni moi.**
> She likes neither him nor me.

7. After **c'est** and **ce sont**:

C'est moi.	**C'est lui.**	**Ce sont eux.**
It is I.	It is he.	It is they.

Note that **ce sont** is used only with the third person plural: **c'est nous, c'est vous,** but **ce sont elles, ce sont eux.**

8. To express the emphatic *myself* (*yourself*, etc.):

> **Je le fais moi-même.**
> I do it myself.
>
> **Eux-mêmes sont féministes!**
> They themselves are feminists!

In this case the disjunctive pronoun is joined by a hyphen to **même,** which takes **-s** in the plural.

9. With indefinite subjects:
The indefinite disjunctive **soi** is used in sentences with indefinite subjects like **on, chacun,** and **tout le monde;** after impersonal verbs; and in fixed indefinite expressions such as **chacun pour soi, en soi,** and **de soi.**

> **Quand on est triste, on a pitié de soi.**
> When one is sad, one pities oneself.
>
> **Il faut être content de soi.**
> One must be content with oneself.
>
> **Le divorce est-il condamnable en soi?**
> Is divorce to be condemned in itself?

EXERCICE

Remplacez les mots anglais par les **pronoms disjoints** (*disjunctive*) *convenables.*

1. Je m'intéresse tellement à _____ (her)!
2. Je n'aime que _____ (you).

3. _____ (*I*) ne vais jamais grossir!
4. Elles n'ont pas confiance en _____ (themselves).
5. Tout le monde a tendance à parler de _____ (himself).
6. _____ (Paul and she) rêvent d'une vie heureuse.
7. Elle et _____ (*I*), nous allons nous marier l'année prochaine.
8. _____ (It is they) qui me demandent de venir.
9. Je pense à _____ (her).
10. Sa femme est plus forte que _____ (he)!
11. Tu tombes amoureuse de lui _____ (yourself).
12. Elle ne trompe ni _____ (them) ni _____ (me).
13. Pour élever mes enfants, chérie, je n'ai que _____ (you).
14. _____ (*I*) dénonce la discrimination; _____ (*you*) l'approuves!
15. Tu es moins naïve que _____ (she).

Related expressions

The neuter pronoun le

Pronouns generally replace nouns. The invariable neuter pronoun **le,** however, is used to replace an adjective or an entire phrase or clause. It is the equivalent of *it* or *so* in English, but often is not translated.

> **Mon père est indépendant mais mes sœurs ne le sont pas.**
> My father is independent but my sisters aren't.
>
> **Croyez-vous qu'elles vont réussir? —Oui, je le crois.**
> Do you think they'll succeed? —Yes, I think so.

EXERCICE

Traduisez en français les mots entre parenthèses.

1. Est-ce que votre sœur est vraiment libérée? —Non, _____ (she isn't).
2. Est-ce que votre fiancée est très intelligente? —Oui, _____ (she is).
3. Les femmes sont-elles quelquefois confuses? — _____ (They are) quelquefois, mais les hommes _____ (are) aussi.
4. Est-elle toujours jalouse? —Non _____ (she isn't).
5. Voulez-vous épouser une femme séduisante? —_____ (I do and I don't).

Exercices d'ensemble

I. *Répondez en remplaçant les mots en italiques par un pronom.*
   modèle: Êtes-vous *féministe?* **Je le suis.**
      ou: **Je ne le suis pas.**

   1. Aimez-vous partager *les travaux ménagers?*
   2. Faut-il accepter ou refuser *les rôles féminins traditionnels?*

3. Qui fait *la cuisine* chez vous?
4. Voulez-vous avoir *des enfants*? Si oui, combien?
5. Aimez-vous *les femmes qui flirtent toujours*?
6. Caractérisez-vous! Êtes-vous *doux*? *séduisant*? *jaloux*? *traditionaliste*? *indépendant*? *frustré*? *confus*? *fidèle*? *féministe*?
7. Avez-vous l'intention *de poursuivre une carrière*?
8. Approuvez-vous *la limitation des naissances*?
9. L'avortement est-il *immoral*?
10. Les hommes que vous connaissez respectent-ils *les femmes*?
11. Bavardez-vous *en classe*?
12. Respectez-vous *les féministes*?
13. Les femmes et les hommes sont-ils *égaux* à votre université?
14. Qui fait *la vaisselle* chez vous?
15. Avez-vous jamais envie *de tromper votre ami(e)*?
16. Avez-vous peur *de votre professeur*?
17. Discutez-vous *vos problèmes personnels* avec *votre ami(e)*?
18. Rêvez-vous quelquefois *d'un amour idéal*?
19. Connaissez-vous *des cas de discrimination socio-économique*?
20. Avez-vous *des amis fidèles*?

II. *Traduisez en français.*

1. My husband and I are equal; we share the household chores.
2. Let's avoid feminine stereotypes because they aren't true.
3. She has just found a good job.
4. Don't go out with her if she's jealous!
5. Let's do the cooking together tonight.
6. Marguerite wants to get married and have a family.
7. But Jeannine refuses traditional feminine roles.
8. How long has she been going out with David?
9. Don't choose a career if you are too confused.
10. She is frustrated because her boyfriend does not treat her like an equal.
11. If that young woman wants to pursue a career, send her to me.
12. She works in Paris, but I don't.

III. *Reliez (link) un verbe de la première colonne à une expression de la deuxième colonne et formulez des phrases en suivant le modèle.*
modèle: condamner l'avortement

    Condamnons l'avortement.
    Condamnons-le.
    Ne le condamnons pas.

1.	abolir	la fidélité
2.	craindre	le divorce
3.	condamner	l'avortement
4.	encourager	le chauvinisme du mâle
5.	avoir peur de	la coquetterie des femmes

6.	décourager	l'égalité des sexes
7.	recommander	les unions libres
8.	dénoncer	la pilule
9.	défendre	la naïveté des jeunes filles
		le mariage
		le mouvement de libération des femmes
		la chasteté
		les vices des jeunes
		les bébés
		la famille

IV. *En employant les deux colonnes de l'exercice III, reliez un verbe de la première colonne à une expression de la deuxième colonne et formulez des phrases en suivant le modèle.*

modèle : recommander   le mariage

Recommandez-vous le mariage?
Oui, je le recommande.
Non, je ne le recommande pas.

Sujets de discussion ou de composition

1. Une féministe essaie de convertir une maîtresse de maison traditionaliste à son opinion. Imaginez les arguments qu'elle va employer.

2. Imaginez que vous êtes parent et que votre fille sort régulièrement avec un jeune homme qu'elle veut épouser. Quels conseils allez-vous lui donner à propos du mariage?

3. Nommez une femme que vous admirez et expliquez pourquoi vous l'admirez.

4. Pour les femmes : Quel rôle féminin voulez-vous adopter maintenant et à l'avenir?

5. Pour les hommes : Quelle sorte de femme préférez-vous?

3
Nouns
and articles

Chapter 3 at a glance

NOUNS

I. *Indiquez le genre* (**masculin** *ou* **féminin**) *sans consulter le dictionnaire.*

1. communication
2. biologie
3. latin
4. Californie
5. promesse
6. travail
7. moment
8. symbolisme

II. *Mettez au féminin.*

1. l'ami
2. l'oncle
3. l'écrivain
4. l'acteur
5. le chat

III. *Remplacez le tiret par* **le** *ou* **la.**

1. Avez-vous vu _____ Tour Eiffel?
2. Je vais faire _____ tour du monde.

IV. *Mettez au pluriel.*

1. la mère
2. l'œil
3. le fils
4. le bijou
5. le journal
6. le grand-père
7. le feu
8. le pique-nique

V. *Remplacez les mots entre parenthèses par la forme convenable de* **gens,** **monde, personnes, peuple** *ou* **on.**

1. _____ (The people) américain respecte la famille.
2. Il y avait vingt _____ (people) à notre réunion de famille.
3. _____ (People) dit qu'il ressemble à sa mère.

ARTICLES

VI. *Traduisez en français les mots entre parenthèses.*

1. _____ (Parents) devraient-ils jouer avec leurs enfants?
2. _____ (Little Robert) est impossible _____ (in the morning)!

VII. *Situez le nom donné.*
modèle: Montréal **Montréal se trouve au Canada.**

1. Paris
2. New York
3. les Champs-Élysées
4. la Nouvelle-Orléans
5. Londres
6. Tokyo

VIII. *Remplacez les tirets par* **les** *ou* **des.**

1. _____ enfants ont-ils _____ obligations envers leurs parents?
2. J'ai _____ tantes qui me donnent toujours _____ cadeaux.

IX. *Remplacez les tirets par l'article partitif* **(du, de la, des)** *ou par* **de** *tout seul.*

1. Il a deux sœurs mais il n'a pas ——— frères.
2. Les Mercier font beaucoup _____ sacrifices pour leurs enfants.
3. Je connais _____ filles qui n'obéissent pas à leurs parents.
4. Ma camarade de chambre a _____ excellents rapports avec sa famille.
5. Avez-vous souvent _____ disputes avec vos parents?

X. *Remplacez les tirets par* **de, des** *ou* **du.**

1. Quand votre famille va-t-elle revenir _____ France?
2. Mon avion part _____ États-Unis la semaine prochaine.
3. Mon camarade de chambre vient _____ Canada.

Vocabulaire du thème: La Famille

MEMBRES DU FOYER

le **foyer** *the home*
les **parents** (m) *parents*
l' **enfant** (m, f) *child*
le, la **gosse** (fam.) *kid*
l' **enfant unique** (m, f) *only child*

l' **aîné** (m), l'**aînée** (f) *the elder, the eldest*
le **cadet**, la **cadette** *the younger, the youngest*
le **jumeau**, la **jumelle** *twin*

RAPPORTS FAMILIAUX

avoir de bons rapports avec *to have an honest relationship with*
s' **entendre avec** *to get along with (someone)*
avoir des liens de famille étroits *to have close family ties*
faire des sacrifices pour *to make sacrifices for*
mériter l'amour de *to deserve, to earn the love of*
respecter *to respect*
soigner *to care for, to take care of*
admirer *to admire*

faire une sortie en famille *to have a family outing*
ensemble *together*

le **fossé entre les générations** *generation gap*
le **manque de communication** *lack of communication*
se **détacher de** *to break away from*
avoir des liens de famille lâches *to have loose family ties*
la **dispute** *quarrel*

l' **éducation** (f) *upbringing*

indulgent *lenient*
négliger *to neglect*
irresponsable *irresponsible*

strict *strict*
exigeant *demanding*
responsable *responsible*

bien élevé *well brought up*
sage *well-behaved*
poli *polite*
obéir à *to obey*

mal élevé *badly brought up*
gâté *spoiled*
ingrat *ungrateful*
désobéir à *to disobey*

LA DISCIPLINE

être juste (injuste) envers *to be fair*
  (unfair) to
corriger *to correct*
punir *to punish*

gronder *to scold*
gifler *to slap*
donner une fessée à *to give a spanking to*

Nouns

A noun is a word used to name a person, place, or thing. Unlike English nouns, all French nouns are either masculine or feminine in gender.

Recognition of gender

The gender of most nouns is arbitrary and must be learned. However, certain indications can be helpful.

Sex

Nouns that refer to persons and animals of the male or female sex are usually masculine and feminine respectively.

le père

le chat

la mère

la chatte

Endings and words usually masculine

1. Nouns ending in **-ail, -eau, -ent, -ier,** and **-isme** are usually masculine.

le travail

le couteau

le classicisme

le gouvernement

le papier

Exceptions: **l'eau** (f), **la peau** (*skin*), **la dent** (*tooth*).

2. The names of languages, trees, metals, days, months, and seasons, and adjectives used as nouns, are usually masculine.

le français	**l'or** *(gold)*	**l'hiver**
le russe	**le mardi**	**le pauvre**
le chêne *(oak)*	**le (mois de) septembre**	**le beau**

Endings and words usually feminine

1. Nouns ending in **-esse, -ette, -ie, -ion, -té,** and **-ure** are usually feminine.

la finesse	**la génération**
la cigarette	**la société**
la copie	**la nourriture**

Exceptions: **le génie, le parapluie** *(umbrella)*.

2. The names of natural and social sciences are usually feminine.

la biologie	**la chimie**
la physique	**la sociologie**

3. The names of continents, countries, provinces, and states ending in unaccented **-e** are usually feminine.

l'Asie	**la France**
la Virginie	**l'Angleterre**
la Bretagne	**la Floride**

Exception: **le Mexique.**

EXERCICE

Indiquez le genre sans consulter le dictionnaire.

1. français	7. vrai	13. manteau	19. octobre
2. partialité	8. eau	14. conception	20. allocation
3. lundi	9. botanique	15. ceinture	21. détail
4. fer *(iron)*	10. peuplier *(poplar)*	16. discernement	22. promesse
5. Louisiane	11. moment	17. latin	23. assiette
6. Afrique	12. communication	18. activité	24. communisme

Formation of the feminine singular

Feminine nouns derived from the masculine

1. French nouns usually form the feminine singular by adding an unaccented **-e** to the masculine singular.

MASCULINE SINGULAR	FEMININE SINGULAR
un ami	**une amie**
un orphelin	**une orpheline**
un Français	**une Française**

2. Nouns with certain endings form the feminine in other ways.

ENDING	MASCULINE	FEMININE
el ⎫ 　　**to elle** **eau** ⎭	**Gabriel** **jumeau**	**Gabrielle** **jumelle**
en to enne	**lycéen**	**lycéenne**
on to onne	**baron**	**baronne**
et to ette	**cadet**	**cadette**
eur to euse	**danseur**[1]	**danseuse**
teur to trice	**acteur**[2]	**actrice**
er to ère	**écolier**	**écolière**
x to se	**époux**	**épouse**
f to ve	**veuf** (*widower*)	**veuve** (*widow*)

Feminine nouns not derived from the masculine

The feminine of some common nouns is not derived regularly from the masculine and must simply be learned.

MASCULINE	FEMININE
le fils	**la fille**
le frère	**la sœur**
le mari	**la femme**
le neveu	**la nièce**
l'oncle	**la tante**
le père	**la mère**
le roi	**la reine**
le dieu	**la déesse**
le héros	**l'héroïne**

---

[1] Like **danseur**: other nouns derived from the present participle (**buvant, buveur**), such as **chanteur, flatteur, menteur, trompeur, travailleur**, etc.

[2] Like **acteur**: other nouns ending in **-teur** that are not derived from the present participle: **auditeur, conducteur, directeur, instituteur**, etc.

Nouns without a separate feminine form

1. Many nouns indicating professions previously associated with males do not have a feminine form.

architecte	diplomate	juge
athlète	écrivain	ministre
auteur	ingénieur	peintre
dentiste	journaliste	professeur

The feminine of these nouns is often indicated by using a feminine personal pronoun in the sentence, or by placing the words **femme** or **femmes** before or after the noun.

J'aime mon professeur parce qu'elle est sympathique.
I like my teacher because she's nice.

Il y a trois femmes écrivains dans la famille.
There are three women writers in the family.

2. Some nouns indicating persons form the feminine by simply using the feminine article **la** or **une**. Many of these nouns end in unaccented **e**.

artiste	enfant	secrétaire
élève	pianiste	touriste

Homonyms

Some nouns, called homonyms (**homonymes**), are identical in sound and spelling, but not in gender and meaning. Their meaning is apparent only from the gender of the article.

le critique *critic*	**la critique** *criticism*
le livre *book*	**la livre** *pound*
le physique *physique*	**la physique** *physics*
le somme *nap*	**la somme** *sum*
le tour *tour*	**la tour** *tower*

EXERCICES

1. *Mettez au féminin.*

1. le menteur	5. le dieu	9. le chanteur	13. le Juif
2. le chien	6. l'aîné	10. le fils	14. l'infirmier
3. l'Italien	7. le cousin	11. le cadet	15. le héros
4. le conducteur	8. le frère	12. le chat	16. le neveu

2. *Identifiez les personnages suivants.*
  modèle: Homère   **Homère était poète.**

1. Le Corbusier
2. Édith Piaf
3. Honoré de Balzac
4. Jane Austen
5. Auguste Renoir

6. Louis XIV
7. Picasso
8. Marie-Antoinette
9. Martha Graham
10. Sarah Bernhardt

3. *Remplacez les tirets par l'article* **le** *ou* **la.**

1. Dites-moi _____ somme qu'il faut payer.
2. Les Dupont vont faire _____ tour du monde.
3. Einstein a fait des découvertes extraordinaires dans le domaine de _____ physique.
4. Cela coûte combien _____ livre?
5. M. Desjardins est _____ critique remarquable qui a écrit cet article.

Formation of the plural

The plural with s

The plural of French nouns is generally formed by adding **s** to the singular. A noun that already ends in **-s** in the singular will not change in the plural.

la fille
le fils

les filles
les fils

Names of families do not take **-s** in the plural.

Je suis allé chez les Janvier hier.
I went to the Janviers' yesterday.

The plural with x or z

1. Nouns with certain endings form the plural in **x** or **z**.

CHANGE	SINGULAR	PLURAL
al to **aux**[3]	le cheval	**les chevaux**
au to **aux**	le noyau *(stone of a fruit)*	**les noyaux**
eau to **eaux**	le couteau	**les couteaux**
eu to **eux**	le neveu	**les neveux**
x no change	le prix	**les prix**
z no change	le nez	**les nez**

---

[3] The nouns **le bal, le récital, le carnaval,** and **le festival** add **s** to form the plural.

2. Seven nouns ending in **-ou** form the plural in **-x.**

le bijou *jewel*	**les bijoux**	le hibou *owl*	**les hiboux**
le caillou *pebble*	**les cailloux**	le joujou *toy*	**les joujoux**
le chou *cabbage*	**les choux**	le pou *louse*	**les poux**
le genou *knee*	**les genoux**		

Irregular plurals

A small group of common nouns have unusual plurals.

SINGULAR	PLURAL
le ciel	**les cieux**
l'œil	**les yeux**
le travail	**les travaux**
madame	**mesdames**
mademoiselle	**mesdemoiselles**

The plural of compound nouns

A compound noun is a noun formed by two or more words connected by a hyphen: **le grand-père, le premier-né.** The formation of the plural depends on the words that make up the compound noun. As a rule, only nouns and adjectives can be made plural, in a compound noun, the other elements—verbs, adverbs, prepositions, pronouns—being invariable. Since this rule has many exceptions, the plural of compound nouns should always be checked in a dictionary. Here are the plurals of some common ones:

le beau-frère *brother-in-law*	**les beaux-frères**	le premier-né *firstborn (child)*	**les premiers-nés**
la belle-sœur *sister-in-law*	**les belles-sœurs**	le dernier-né *last child*	**les derniers-nés**
le beau-père *father-in-law*	**les beaux-pères**	le nouveau-né *newborn child*	**les nouveau-nés**
la belle-mère *mother-in-law*	**les belles-mères**	le pique-nique *picnic*	**les pique-niques**
le grand-père *grandfather*	**les grands-pères**	le réveille-matin *alarm clock*	**les réveille-matin**
la grand-mère *grandmother*	**les grands-mères**		

EXERCICE

Mettez au pluriel.

1. madame
4. le carnaval
7. le fou
10. le ciel
13. le tapis

2. le feu
5. le tableau
8. la grand-mère
11. le pique-nique
14. l'œil

3. le général
6. la croix
9. le beau-frère
12. le manteau
15. le nez

Related expressions

In French, a number of words are used to express *people*.

Les gens

The word **gens** is a collective plural meaning *people*. It is unusual in that it is feminine if an adjective precedes it, but masculine if an adjective follows it.

> **Il faut aider les vieilles gens.**
> One must help old people.

> **Les gens ingrats ont probablement des enfants ingrats.**
> Ungrateful people probably have ungrateful children.

Note also that **jeunes gens** is the plural of **jeune homme** (**jeunes hommes** is rarely used).

> **Ces jeunes gens ont des liens de famille étroits.**
> These young men have close family ties.

Le monde

Le monde refers to people in the collective singular. The expression **tout le monde** (*everybody*) is very common.

> **J'ai invité du monde à dîner ce soir.**
> I invited people to dinner tonight.

> **Tout le monde ici parle français.**
> Everybody here speaks French.

Les personnes

Les personnes (f) usually indicates a small number of people who can be counted (the collective nouns **gens** and **monde** cannot be counted).

> **J'ai rencontré plusieurs personnes intéressantes chez les Pelletier.**
> I met several interesting people at the Pelletiers'.

Le peuple

Le peuple refers to those who constitute a nation. It also has the somewhat pejorative meaning of *the masses, the common people.*

> **Le peuple français a élu un nouveau chef d'état.**
> The French people elected a new leader.
>
> **Sans une presse libre, le peuple est ignorant.**
> Without a free press, the masses are ignorant.

On

On is an indefinite pronoun expressing *people* in the indefinite sense of *they, you, one,* or *we.*

> **On dit que la famille traditionnelle ne va pas durer.**
> People say that the traditional family will not last.

EXERCICE

Remplacez les mots entre parenthèses par la forme convenable de **gens, monde, personnes, peuple** *ou* **on.**

1. ———— (The people) du quartier trouvent cette famille un peu bizarre.
2. Plusieurs ———— (people) m'ont demandé le prix de ce joujou.
3. ———— (The American people) est souvent généreux.
4. ———— (People) dit que les enfants uniques sont souvent gâtés.
5. Il y a des ———— (people) qui détestent les gosses.
6. J'ai invité cinq ———— (people) à dîner.
7. Les vieilles ———— (people) ressemblent souvent aux enfants.
8. Parfois les jeunes ———— (men) font très bien la cuisine.
9. ———— (People) admire les parents qui ont fait des sacrifices pour leurs enfants.
10. Combien de ———— (people) vont venir déjeuner chez nous cet après-midi?

Articles_____

An article is a word placed before a noun to indicate its number and degree of determination. There are three kinds of articles in French: definite, indefinite, and partitive.

The definite article

	SIMPLE FORM	WITH à	WITH de
MASCULINE SINGULAR	le	au	du
FEMININE SINGULAR	la	à la	de la
PLURAL	les	aux	des

The elided form **l'** replaces **le** and **la** before singular nouns and adjectives beginning with a vowel or mute **h: l'enfant, l'hôtel, l'autre gosse.**
The definite article has varied uses in French.

To indicate a particular noun

Here the French definite article is used like *the* in English.

> **La mère a oublié la moutarde et la limonade pour la sortie en famille.**
> The mother forgot the mustard and the lemonade for the family outing.

However, in French the article is generally repeated after each noun in a series, whereas in English often it is not.

> **Je ne peux pas trouver le pain, le vin et le fromage!**
> I can't find the bread, wine, and cheese!

Before nouns used in a general sense

Here usage differs from English, which in generalizations and abstractions uses no article at all.

> **La vie est difficile.**
> Life is difficult.
> **L'histoire me passionne.**
> History excites me.
> **Les enfants adorent imiter les adultes.**
> Children love to imitate adults.·

With temporal expressions

The definite article is used with days of the week, and with the nouns **matin, après-midi,** and **soir,** to indicate habitual recurrence.

> **Papa nous emmène au cinéma le vendredi.**
> Dad takes us to the movies on Fridays.

En été notre famille fait un pique-nique le dimanche.
In the summer our family goes on a picnic on Sundays.

Je fais le lit le matin et elle fait la vaisselle le soir.
I make the bed in the morning and she washes the dishes at night.

Note, however, that the article with the day is omitted when a particular day is indicated.

Ces gosses sont ravis parce que les vacances commencent vendredi.
These kids are delighted because vacation begins Friday.

With proper names

1. The definite article is used with proper names preceded by a title or an adjective.

Le général De Gaulle a gouverné la France.
General De Gaulle governed France.

Dans ce roman de Balzac, le vieux Goriot fait beaucoup de sacrifices pour ses filles ingrates.
In this novel by Balzac, old Goriot makes many sacrifices for his ungrateful daughters.

Otherwise, proper names are used without the article.

Jules est un père juste et raisonnable.
Jules is a fair and reasonable father.

2. The definite article is not used before a title if one is speaking to the person directly.

Général De Gaulle, allez-vous gouverner la France?
General De Gaulle, are you going to govern France?

Docteur Leblond, comment va notre enfant?
Doctor Leblond, how is our child?

With units of weight and measure

Les bonbons coûtent dix francs la livre.
The candy costs ten francs a pound.

Les œufs coûtent cinq francs la douzaine.
Eggs cost five francs per dozen.

But note these related expressions:

1. frequency or amount per unit of time = **par** + *noun*

> **Je vais à New York deux fois par an (mois, semaine, etc.).**
> I go to New York twice a year (month, week, etc.).
> **Nous gagnons trente dollars par jour.**
> We earn thirty dollars a day.

2. money per hour = **de l'heure**

> **Mon fils gagne trois dollars de l'heure pendant les vacances d'été.**
> My son earns three dollars an hour during summer vacation.

3. speed per hour = **à l'heure**

> **La voiture, ma fille au volant, roulait à 130 kilomètres à l'heure!**
> The car, with my daughter at the wheel, was traveling at 130 kilometers per hour!

EXERCICE

Traduisez les mots entre parenthèses.

1. (Professor) Dubonnet vient dîner chez nous _____ (on Mondays).
2. Abraham Lincoln est né _____ (on February 12).
3. _____(Responsible parents) corrigent leurs enfants.
4. _____ (Dr. Janvier) sera absent _____ (Saturday) parce qu'il est malade.
5. Comment! Vous avez payé cette viande quatre dollars _____ (a pound)?
6. _____ (Little Babette) est toujours impossible _____ (in the morning).
7. _____ (Children) sont parfois plus exigeants que leurs parents!
8. Mon frère Robert gagne _____ (five dollars an hour).
9. Vos cousins viennent chez nous _____ (on Monday, April 17).
10. Elle rencontre son ami _____ (on Sundays).

The definite article with geographical names

The definite article is used with most geographical names (continents, countries, provinces, states, mountains, rivers, oceans, etc.): **l'Afrique, la France, la Normandie, le Massachusetts, la Seine, la Nouvelle-Zélande.**

> **La France est riche en agriculture.**
> France is rich in agriculture.
> **La Seine traverse Paris.**
> The Seine crosses Paris.

The definite article is not used with cities unless it forms an integral part of the name: **Le Havre, La Haye** (*The Hague*), **La Nouvelle-Orléans.**

>**Boston est une ville historique.**
>Boston is a historical city.

>**Le Havre est un port important.**
>Le Havre is an important port.

The definite article is sometimes used and sometimes omitted when expressing *to*, *in*, and *from* with geographical names.

To and *in* with geographical names

1. With cities

The preposition **à** alone is used before names of cities.

>**Nous comptons passer nos vacances à Paris.**
>We intend to spend our vacation in Paris.

The names of cities that include the article make the normal contraction with **à.**

>**Demain je vais au Havre.**
>Tomorrow I'm going to Le Havre.

2. With states

En is used before feminine states of the union; **dans** + *definite article*, or the expression **dans l'état de,** is used before masculine states.

>**Si vous avez froid l' hiver, allez en Floride.**
>If you are cold in winter, go to Florida.

>**Elle est née dans l'état d'Indiana.**
>She was born in Indiana.

>**Mon père est né dans le Kentucky.**
>My father was born in Kentucky.

Exceptions: **au Texas, au Nouveau-Mexique.**

3. With countries

En is used before feminine countries, and before masculine singular countries beginning with a vowel.

>**Je l'ai rencontré en France.**
>I met him in France.

>**On peut trouver beaucoup de pétrole en Iran.**
>One can find a lot of oil in Iran.

The preposition **à** + *definite article* is used before plural names of countries, and masculine singular countries beginning with a consonant.

> **Les enfants sont-ils choyés aux Etats-Unis?**
> Are children pampered in the United States?
>
> **Je vais au Portugal.**
> I'm going to Portugal.

4. With continents

En is used with continents.

> **Je vais passer mes vacances en Europe.**
> I'm going to spend my vacation in Europe.
>
> **Il va en Asie.**
> He is going to Asia.

5. With islands

The use of the article to express **to** and **in** with the names of islands is somewhat complex and depends on their gender, size, and distance from France. As a general rule, large feminine islands take **en (en Islande),** many feminine islands take **à la (à la Martinique),** and many masculine islands take **à** alone **(à Cuba).**

From **with geographical names**

In French, **from** is expressed by **de** alone before most feminine singular geographical names, and before islands and cities. **From** is expressed by **du** before masculine singular names, and by **des** before all plural names.

> **D'où venez-vous, des États-Unis ou de France?**
> Where are you coming from, the United States or France?
>
> **Toute ma famille vient du Japon.**
> All my family comes from Japan.
>
> **Je viens de rentrer de Paris.**
> I just returned from Paris.

EXERCICES

1. *Situez le nom donné.*
modèle: Rome—Rome se trouve en Italie.

1.	Tokyo	**7.**	Moscou
2.	la Nouvelle Orléans	**8.**	Houston
3.	Miami	**9.**	la vallée de la Loire
4.	Detroit	**10.**	la Maison Blanche
5.	le Vatican	**11.**	la Chine
6.	les Nations Unies	**12.**	Québec

2. *Remplacez les tirets par* **de, des** *ou* **du.**

1. Mes parents viennent _____ Argentine.
2. Mon oncle revient _____ États-Unis.
3. Quand l'avion partira-t-il _____ New York?
4. Nos voisins reviennent _____ Mexique.
5. Ma tante Marie est arrivée _____ Canada hier.

The indefinite article

	SINGULAR	PLURAL
MASCULINE	un	des
FEMININE	une	des

In the singular, the indefinite article in French expresses the English indefinite articles *a* and *an*. In the plural, the indefinite article in French is identical with the plural of the partitive (discussed below), which is translated by *some* or *any* in English, or often by no word at all.

Nous avons un gosse de quinze ans.
We have a fifteen year old kid.

Mon fils a acheté des pommes et des oranges.
My son bought (some) apples and oranges.

Unlike in English, however, the indefinite article in French is normally repeated after each noun in a series.

Je vois un homme, une femme et un enfant.
I see a man, woman, and child.

The partitive article

	SINGULAR	PLURAL
MASCULINE	du de l'	des
FEMININE	de la de l'	des

As its name indicates, the partitive article designates a part of the whole represented by the noun. English does not possess a partitive article, but expresses the partitive notion by placing *some* or *any* before the noun, or by using the noun alone.

Avez-vous des enfants?
Do you have some children?
or: Do you have any children?
or: Do you have children?

Achetez-moi du pain et du vin, s'il vous plaît.
Buy me some bread and wine, please.
or: Buy me bread and wine, please.

Before an adjective preceding a plural noun

Before an adjective preceding a plural noun, **de** alone expresses the partitive.[4]

Ils ont de beaux enfants.
They have beautiful children.

Des is used, however, if the adjective and the plural noun form a unity: **les petits pois** (*peas*), **les jeunes filles, les jeunes gens.**

Je connais des jeunes filles qui ne veulent pas se marier.
I know some girls who don't want to get married.

Quelques

The adjective **quelques** is the equivalent of the more definite expression *a few.*

Maman, as-tu quelques dollars?
Mom, do you have a few dollars?

EXERCICES

1. *Remplacez les tirets par* **du, de la, des** *ou* **de.**

    1. M. Maquet a _____ fils remarquables.
    2. Notre père a _____ excellents rapports avec nous.
    3. Connaissez-vous _____ jeunes gens responsables?
    4. Nous avons entendu _____ belle musique au concert.
    5. Nos parents ont fait _____ grands sacrifices pour nous.

2. *Traduisez en français.*

    1. I have some friends.
    2. I have a few friends.
    3. I have friends.
    4. Do you have any friends?
    5. I have good friends.

---

[4] Although this rule is followed by most cultivated speakers and writers, the use of **des** + *adjective* + *plural noun* is becoming increasingly popular and is not, in fact, considered incorrect.

The partitive article versus the definite article

The distinction between the partitive article and the definite article, used in the general sense, may sometimes be confusing. A convenient rule of thumb is to insert in the sentence the word *some* or *any* as a test for the partitive, and *all* or *in general* as a test for the definite article. The word that fits most naturally *without changing the sentence's meaning* indicates the appropriate article.

Men are mortal.

all men or *some* men? Clearly, *all* men, since *some* would change the meaning of the sentence. The definite article is therefore appropriate:

Les hommes sont mortels.

Do you have brothers?

All or *any* brothers? Clearly, *any* brothers, since *all* brothers is awkward and does not convey the meaning of the sentence. The partitive article is therefore appropriate:

Avez-vous des frères?

My aunt likes jewels.

Jewels *in general* or *some* or *any* jewels? Clearly, jewels *in general*, since *some* or *any* jewels changes the meaning of the sentence. The definite article is therefore appropriate:

Ma tante aime les bijoux.[5]

EXERCICE

*Remplacez les tirets par la forme convenable de l'*article défini *ou de l'*article partitif.

1. Je déteste _____ disputes.
2. Nos parents ont _____ rapports honnêtes avec nous.
3. Ma mère préfère _____ enfants bien élevés, mais elle nous aime quand même!
4. Les Dupont ont _____ problèmes avec leur aîné.
5. J'aime _____ liens de famille étroits.
6. _____ enfants adorent jouer avec leurs parents.
7. Connaissez-vous _____ enfants parfaits?
8. _____ adolescents ont parfois besoin de se détacher de la famille.
9. Je ne peux pas sortir parce que j'ai _____ travail à faire.
10. Est-ce que _____ jumeaux se ressemblent toujours?

---

[5] After the verbs **aimer, détester,** and **préférer,** the definite article is almost always used.

Omission of the article

Under certain circumstances, nouns may be used in French without any article at all. It is important to note that in all the cases that follow, the noun is understood in a general, indefinite sense.

After certain expressions ending in de

1. After expressions of quantity

   After expressions of quantity such as **beaucoup de, combien de, trop de, peu de, plus de, assez de, une boîte de, un sac de, un million de, une douzaine de,** etc., no article is used.

   > **Beaucoup de mères trouvent que leurs enfants sont parfaits.**
   > Many mothers find that their children are perfect.
   >
   > **Il y avait peu de disputes chez nous.**
   > There were few quarrels at our house.

   However, **de** + *the definite article* (**du, de la, de l', des**) is used after certain expressions: **bien de, la plupart de, la plus grande partie de,** and **la majorité de.**

   > **Bien des enfants admirent leurs parents.**
   > A good many children admire their parents.
   >
   > **La plupart des enfants tiennent de leurs parents.**
   > Most children take after their parents.

2. After **ne . . . pas de** and other general negations

   Like all expressions of quantity, the negative expression of quantity **ne . . . pas de** is followed directly by an indefinite noun without an article. Remember that **ne . . . pas de** may be the negative of both the partitive article (**du, de la, des**) and the indefinite article (**un, une, des**).

   > **Cette pauvre fille a-t-elle des joujoux? —Non, elle n'a pas de joujoux.**
   > Does this poor girl have any toys? —No, she doesn't have any toys.
   >
   > **Avez-vous un frère? —Je n'ai pas de frère.**
   > Do you have a brother? —No, I don't have a brother.

   De without an article is also used after other negative expressions like **ne . . . plus** and **ne . . . jamais.**

   > **Jean a-t-il de l'ambition? —Non, il n'a plus d'ambition.**
   > Does John have ambition? —No, he no longer has any ambition.
   >
   > **Il n'a jamais gagné d'argent.**
   > He has never earned any money.

But the normal partitive forms are used after **être** in the negative.

> **Ce ne sont pas des enfants sages!**
> They are not well-behaved children!
>
> **Ce ne sont pas des bêtises, ce que dit votre père!**
> It's not nonsense, what your father's saying!

3. After verbal and adjectival expressions with **de**

No article is used after verbal and adjectival expressions ending in **de,** such as **avoir besoin de** (*to need*), **avoir envie de** (*to feel like*), **manquer de** (*to lack*), **remplir de** (*to fill with*), **entouré de** (*surrounded by*), and **plein de** (*full of*).

> **Les enfants ont-ils besoin de liberté?**
> Do children need freedom?
>
> **Mon frère manque d'argent.**
> My brother lacks money.

4. After **de** + *noun* used to qualify another noun

In French, when a noun qualifies another noun, it follows that other noun and is joined to it by **de**; no article is used after **de.**

> **une robe de soie**   **un guide de voyage**
> a silk dress   a travel guide
>
> **la maison de campagne**   **des souvenirs d'enfance**
> the country house   childhood memories

After avec *and* sans

After the prepositions **avec** (with abstract nouns only) and **sans**, no article is used.

> **La famille a accueilli l'enfant avec enthousiasme.**
> The family welcomed the child enthusiastically.
>
> **Un ménage sans enfants est incomplet.**
> A household without children is incomplete.

But if the noun with **avec** is not abstract, the partitive is used.

> **Mon frère est allé jouer au tennis avec des amis.**
> My brother went to play tennis with friends.

With languages after parler *and* en

No article is used if the verb **parler** and the preposition **en** are directly followed by a noun of language.

Je parle russe.
I speak Russian.

Je ne peux pas lire cet article écrit en français.
I can't read this article written in French.

When **parler** is followed by **pas**, no article is used. When other adverbial expressions intervene between **parler** and a noun of language, the article may or may not be used.

Elle ne parle pas chinois.
She doesn't speak Chinese.

Ma femme parle couramment (le) portugais.
My wife speaks Portuguese fluently.

Vous parlez très bien (le) japonais!
You speak Japanese very well!

Note that languages do not take a capital letter in French.

With qualifying nouns after être

With nouns designating profession, nationality, political allegiance, religion, social class, etc., after the verb **être,** no article is used.

Mon père est employé de bureau.
My father is an office worker.

Sa grand-mère est américaine.
His grandmother is an American.

Son père est conservateur, mais lui est communiste.
His father is a conservative, but he's a Communist.

Ils sont catholiques.
They are Catholics.

Il est avocat, mais ses amis sont ouvriers.
He is a lawyer, but his friends are workers.

The indefinite article is used, however, when the sentence begins with **C'est** or **Ce sont.** It is also usually used when the noun is modified by an adjective.

C'est un docteur.
He is a doctor.

Le Corbusier était un excellent architecte.
Le Corbusier was an excellent architect.

In this case the article is retained after **être** even in the negative.

Ce n'est pas un docteur.
He is not a doctor.

The article with particularized nouns

Remember that in all the cases just covered, where a noun is used without any article, the noun is understood in a general, indefinite sense. If the noun is particularized in any way, an article must be used.

> **J'ai mangé trop de gâteau!**
> I ate too much cake.

but: **J'ai mangé trop du gâteau que vous m'avez donné!**
> I ate too much of the cake you gave me.

> **Cet enfant a besoin de joujoux.**
> This child needs toys.

but: **Cet enfant a besoin des joujoux de son frère.**
> This child needs his brother's toys.

> **Balzac est auteur.**
> Balzac is a writer.

but: **Balzac est un auteur célèbre.**
> Balzac is a famous writer.

EXERCICES

1. *Remplacez les tirets, si nécessaire, par* **de, du, de la** *ou* **des.**

   1. Mon frère n'a pas _____ intelligence.
   2. Donnez une douzaine _____ bonbons à ces gosses.
   3. Ma nièce fait la cuisine avec _____ soin.
   4. La majorité _____ gens ont l'intention d'avoir _____ enfants.
   5. Nous n'avons pas _____ vacances cette année.
   6. Dans ma famille il y a trop _____ garçons et pas assez _____ filles.
   7. Un père a besoin _____ patience d'une mère quand il joue avec son fils gâté.
   8. Ce ne sont pas _____ parents responsables!
   9. Est-il possible de bien élever des enfants sans _____ discipline?
   10. Travaillez si vous manquez _____ argent!
   11. Votre verre est-il rempli _____ vin?
   12. Il ne vous comprendra pas si vous parlez _____ français.
   13. Il faut traiter les enfants avec _____ amour.
   14. Cette famille est pleine _____ vie!
   15. Mon père a acheté une table _____ marbre à ma mère pour son anniversaire.
   16. La plupart _____ enfants ne comprennent pas les problèmes de leurs parents.
   17. Robert, voudriez-vous acheter une douzaine _____ œufs au supermarché?

18. Il vient d'arriver avec _____ amis.

19. J'ai besoin _____ médicaments du docteur Poulet pour soigner ma grand-mère.

20. Il est venu me voir un soir _____ hiver.

2. _Remplacez les tirets, si nécessaire, par_ **un** _ou_ **une.**

1. J. P. Morgan était _____ banquier bourgeois.

2. Ma mère est _____ républicaine, mais mon père est _____ communiste enragé!

3. Êtes-vous _____ étudiant sérieux?

4. De Gaulle était _____ général.

5. Édith Piaf était _____ très bonne chanteuse.

6. Je veux être _____ professeur, mais mes parents veulent que je devienne _____ médecin!

7. Ce n'est pas _____ très bon professeur!

8. Est-elle _____ protestante?

Exercices d'ensemble

I. _Indiquez le genre sans consulter le dictionnaire._

1. espagnol	**6.** brusquerie	**11.** trompette
2. mariage	**7.** Belgique	**12.** Floride
3. bonté	**8.** culture	**13.** cynisme
4. dimanche	**9.** pin _(pine tree)_	**14.** politesse
5. imagination	**10.** été	**15.** vitrail

II. _Mettez les mots en italiques au pluriel. Faites tous les autres changements nécessaires._

1. Le père a donné une fessée _au jumeau._

2. Mon frère paresseux n'aime pas _le travail manuel._

3. M. Dupuy a mal _au genou._

4. Quand j'étais enfant, j'aimais _le cheval de bois._

5. Ma tante a regardé _le bijou_ de ma mère avec intérêt.

6. Je trouve que ma sœur s'entend très bien avec _ce professeur_!

7. Voulez-vous répéter _le prix_, s'il vous plaît?

8. Invitons _notre beau-frère_ à déjeuner.

9. Vous rappelez-vous _notre pique-nique_ ensemble?

10. Vous êtes trop injuste envers _votre neveu américain_!

III. _Remplacez les tirets, si nécessaire, par la forme convenable de l'article_ (**défini**, **indéfini** _ou_ **partitif**) _ou par_ **de.**

1. _____ membres de ma famille sont faciles à décrire.

2. Ma mère est _____ maîtresse de maison.

3. Mon père est _____ avocat célèbre.
4. Tous les deux sont _____ catholiques et _____ républicains.
5. Ils parlent couramment _____ français et _____ anglais.
6. Mon père est _____ républicain très sérieux; il travaille même pour _____ parti républicain.
7. Et moi? Je suis bien élevé maintenant, mais j'étais _____ enfant très gâté quand j'étais jeune!
8. Quand j'étais petit, mes parents ne me donnaient pas _____ fessées.
9. Puisque mon éducation était négligée, j'étais vraiment _____ enfant impossible!
10. Je fumais _____ cigarettes dans ma chambre à l'âge de treize ans.
11. Je rentrais très tard _____ soir.
12. Quand mon professeur _____ français m'appelait, je dormais!
13. Je sortais avec _____ jeunes gens et _____ jeunes filles très mal élevés.
14. Mes parents ont finalement vu que je manquais _____ respect pour eux et que j'avais besoin _____ discipline.
15. Heureusement, j'avais assez _____ courage pour changer mes mauvaises habitudes.
16. Il n'y a plus _____ manque de communication entre mes parents et moi.
17. Maintenant je suis _____ avocat, _____ catholique et _____ républicain!

IV. *Traduisez en français.*

1. American parents often scold their children.
2. She has cousins who live in Mexico.
3. My family ties are loose, but I have a good relationship with my parents.
4. Many parents do not make sacrifices for their children.
5. The Merciers like to have family outings on Sundays.
6. My brother wants to be a teacher.
7. Doctor Colbert is not fair toward his eldest son.
8. One must correct children with love.
9. She doesn't speak French, but she speaks English very well.
10. Children obey their parents if they respect them.

Sujets de discussion ou de composition

1. Discutez le pour et le contre: le fossé entre les générations est nécessaire.
2. Les parents et les enfants peuvent-ils être de véritables amis?
3. Discutez le pour et le contre: la famille est une institution en train de mourir.

4. Discutez le pour et le contre: un enfant est négligé si ses parents travaillent.
5. Quelles sont les obligations des parents envers leurs enfants et les obligations des enfants envers leurs parents?
6. Décrivez votre famille (membres, rapports, intérêts, etc.)

4

Reflexives, passé composé, and imperfect

Chapter 4 at a glance

REFLEXIVE VERBS

I. *Complétez au* **présent.**

1. je (se laver)
2. tu (se coucher)
3. elle (s'habiller)
4. nous (se parler)
5. vous (s'endormir)
6. ils (se téléphoner)

II. *Mettez au* **négatif.**

1. Asseyez-vous.
2. Dépêche-toi!
3. Marions-nous!

III. *Traduisez en français en employant* **l'un l'autre.**

1. They kiss (*embrasser*) each other.
2. We look at each other.

IV. *Traduisez en français les verbes entre parenthèses en employant* **se rappeler** *ou* **se souvenir de.**

1. _____ (We remember) la pollution à Los Angeles.
2. Oui, _____ (I remember) Geneviève!

THE PASSÉ COMPOSÉ AND IMPERFECT

V. *Mettez les verbes au* **passé composé** *en faisant l'accord du participe passé s'il y a lieu.*

1. nous (visiter)
2. ils (entendre)
3. je (finir)
4. nous (dire)
5. je (faire)
6. tu (prendre)
7. elle (aller)
8. elles (se promener)
9. ils (se parler)
10. Voici les villes que nous _____ (visiter).

VI. *Mettez les verbes à l'*imparfait.

1. je (danser)
2. tu (aller)
3. elle (choisir)
4. nous (être)
5. vous (avoir)
6. elles (nager)

VII. *Traduisez au* **passé composé** *ou à l'*imparfait *les mots entre parenthèses.*

1. Elle _____ (heard) un oiseau chanter dans les arbres.
2. Ils _____ (were talking) de l'atmosphère poétique de Paris.
3. Quand il _____ (was) jeune, il _____ (used to look at) ce lac pendant des heures!
4. Hier le ciel _____ (was) bleu et l'air _____ (was) frais!
5. Oui, nous (did see) _____ un artiste célèbre à Montmartre!
6. Ils _____ (had been waiting) depuis une heure quand ils ont vu le train.

VIII. *Mettez les verbes entre parenthèses au* **passé composé** *ou à l'*imparfait, *selon le cas.*

L'été dernier ma famille et moi, nous _____ (aller) à la campagne. Il _____ (faire) beau et le ciel _____ (être) bleu. Alors nous _____ (décider) de faire un pique-nique dans le bois. Pendant que nous _____ (être) assis, nous _____ (entendre) un bruit étrange derrière nous. Nous _____ (se retourner) et nous _____ (voir) un ours [*bear*] qui _____ (s'approcher) de nous! Il _____ (avoir) l'air méchant! Nous _____(se lever) tout de suite et nous _____ (courir) jusqu'à la voiture. L'ours _____ (manger) les sandwiches et la limonade!

IX. *Traduisez en français les mots entre parenthèses.*

1. Nous _____ (left) du bar à trois heures du matin.
2. Où _____ (did you leave) votre chapeau?
3. Nous _____ (left) la ville à cause de la pollution.

X. *Traduisez en français les mots entre parenthèses.*

1. Ils _____ (had just finished) l'examen quand le professeur a demandé les copies.
2. Nous _____ (had just seen) New York.

Vocabulaire du thème: Ville et Campagne

LA VILLE

LE MILIEU

le **citadin** *city dweller*
le **métro** *subway*
la **voiture** *car*

garer une voiture *to park a car*
la **banlieue** *suburbs*

PLAISIRS

la **vie culturelle** *cultural life*
les **distractions** (f) *entertainment*
la **boîte de nuit** *night club*
le **grand magasin** *department store*
la **boutique** *shop*
faire des courses *to go shopping*
stimulant *stimulating*
dynamique *dynamic*

flâner *to stroll*
se **promener** *to take a walk, to walk*
visiter un endroit *to visit a place*
rendre visite à une personne *to visit a person*
fréquenter (un café, un bar, etc.) *to frequent (a café, a bar, etc.)*
se **perdre** *to get lost*

PROBLÈMES

le **bruit** *noise*
la **circulation** *traffic*
la **pollution** *pollution*
le **voyou** *hoodlum*

attaquer *to attack, to mug*
louche *shady, suspicious*
anonyme *anonymous*
sale *dirty*

LE MILIEU

le **campagnard** *country dweller*
le **paysan** *peasant, hick*
le **fermier** *farmer*
la **ferme** *farm*
le **bois** *woods*

le **champ** *field*
la **rivière** (*small*) *river*
le **lac** *lake*
le **poisson** *fish*

PLAISIRS

faire du camping *to go camping*
faire de la bicyclette *to go bicycle riding*
faire un pique-nique *to have a picnic*
aller à la pêche *to go fishing*

coucher à la belle étoile *to sleep outdoors*
méditer (sur) *to meditate* (*about*)
paisible *peaceful*
isolé *isolated*

PROBLÈMES

s' **ennuyer** *to be bored*
l' **insecte** (m) *insect*
l' **abeille** (f) *bee*
le **moustique** *mosquito*

piquer *to sting*
l' **ours** (m) *bear*
le **serpent** *snake*

Reflexives

Reflexives may express either reflexive action (reflexive verbs) or reciprocal action (reciprocal verbs).

Reflexive verbs

In reflexive action the subject acts on itself. The reflexive action is indicated by a reflexive pronoun. Many verbs that are not inherently reflexive become so if used with a reflexive pronoun.

Je me lave.
I wash myself.

Elle s'admire.
She admires herself.

Il se parle.
He speaks to himself.

Reflexive pronouns

1. The reflexive pronouns **me, te, se, nous,** and **vous** agree in person and number with the subject.

se laver

je me lave	nous nous lavons
tu te laves	vous vous lavez
il / elle / on } se lave	ils / elles } se lavent

The pronouns **me, te,** and **se** change to **m', t',** and **s'** before a verb beginning with a vowel or mute **h: je m'habille, elle s'endort.**

2. Reflexive pronouns used in an infinitive construction must also agree with the subject.

> **Allez-vous vous lever de bonne heure à la campagne?**
> Are you going to get up early in the country?

3. Reflexive pronouns are either direct or indirect, depending on the verb.

> *Direct:* **Elle se voit dans le lac.**
> She sees herself in the lake.

> *Indirect:* **Il se parle quand il est seul dans le bois.**
> He speaks to himself when he's alone in the woods.

Verbs that do not translate as reflexives in English

In all the preceding examples, the reflexive pronouns have a true reflexive value in French, so that the verbs translate as reflexives in English. But in many cases the pronouns have lost their reflexive value in French, and the verbs do not translate as reflexives in English.

> **Je me souviens du bruit du métro.**
> I remember the noise of the subway.

> **Elle s'ennuie à la campagne.**
> She's bored in the country.

> **Ils se rendent compte de cela.**
> They realize that.

Other common verbs that do not translate as reflexives:

se fier à	*to trust*	**se sauver**	*to run away*
se méfier de	*to distrust*	**se suicider**	*to commit suicide*
se moquer de	*to make fun of*	**se taire**	*to be quiet, to shut up*

EXERCICE

Complétez au **présent.**

1. vous (se laver)
2. ils (se réveiller)
3. nous (se regarder)
4. elles (se lever)
5. tu (se coucher)
6. ils (se suicider)
7. nous (se perdre)
8. nous (s'endormir)
9. elles (se méfier)
10. ils (se raser)
11. vous (s'habiller)
12. nous (se parler)
13. elles (se taire)
14. je (se fatiguer)

The imperative

1. In the affirmative imperative the reflexive pronouns follow the verb and are connected to it by a hyphen. The pronoun **te** changes to **toi** in final position.

INDICATIVE	IMPERATIVE
Tu te couches.	**Couche-toi!**
You go to bed.	Go to bed!
Vous vous levez.	**Levez-vous!**
You get up.	Get up!
Nous nous sauvons.	**Sauvons-nous!**
We run away.	Let's run away!

2. In the negative imperative the reflexive pronouns precede the verb.

Ne vous dépêchez pas!
Don't hurry!

Ne vous mariez pas!
Don't get married!

EXERCICES

1. *Répondez en employant à l'*impératif *un des verbes de la colonne de droite.*
   Que dites-vous à votre ami . . .
   1. quand il parle pour parler?   se réveiller
   2. quand il est en retard pour le cinéma?   s'amuser bien
   3. quand il est fatigué après avoir fait de la bicyclette?   se laver
   4. quand il est tout sale parce qu'il pleuvait quand il est
      allé à la pêche?   se raser
   5. quand il va à une discothèque avec sa petite amie?   se lever
   6. quand il s'endort pendant que vous parlez
      brillamment?   se taire
   7. quand il a une grande barbe qui vous fait horreur?   se reposer
   8. quand il fait la grasse matinée?   se dépêcher

2. *Mettez au* **négatif** *les réponses dans l'exercice* 1.

Reciprocal verbs

In a reciprocal action the subjects act on each other. Reciprocal verbs are formed in exactly the same way as reflexive verbs. Since a reciprocal action requires at least two people, reciprocal verbs exist only in the plural.

> **Depuis leur premier rendez-vous, ils s'écrivent tous les jours.**
> Since their first date, they have been writing to each other every day.
>
> **Pourquoi vous regardez-vous avec dédain?**
> Why do you look at each other with disdain?

Since reflexive and reciprocal verbs are identical in form, they can be confused. To avoid such confusion, the expressions **l'un(e) l'autre** and **les un(e)s les autres** are often used with reciprocal verbs.

> **Jean et Marie se regardent.**
> John and Mary are looking at themselves.
> John and Mary are looking at each other.
>
> **Jean et Marie se regardent l'un l'autre.**
> John and Mary are looking at each other.
>
> **Est-ce que les Américaines et les Françaises se comprennent?**
> Do American and French women understand themselves?
> Do American and French women understand one another?
>
> **Est-ce que les Américaines et les Françaises se comprennent les unes les autres?**
> Do American and French women understand one another?

When a reciprocal verb requires a preposition, the preposition is placed between the two parts of **l'un(e) l'autre** or of **les un(e)s les autres: l'un à l'autre, les uns des autres,** etc.

> **Les frères se moquent les uns des autres.**
> The brothers make fun of each other.
>
> **Chaque matin ils se disent bonjour l'un à l'autre.**
> Every morning they say good morning to each other.

EXERCICE

Formulez une phrase employant un verbe réfléchi ou un verbe réciproque. Si nécessaire, pour éviter l'ambiguïté, employez **l'un(e) l'autre** *ou* **les un(e)s les autres** *avec le verbe réciproque.*

modèles: Hélène se maquille le matin et Andréa se maquille le matin.
Elles se maquillent le matin.

Jean regarde Marie et Marie regarde Jean.
Ils se regardent l'un l'autre.

1. Jean se rase et Henri se rase.
2. Groucho frappe Harpo et Harpo frappe Groucho.
3. Napoléon écrit à Joséphine et Joséphine lui écrit.
4. Antoine se suicide et Cléopâtre se suicide.
5. Pierre embrasse tendrement Catherine et Catherine embrasse tendrement Pierre.
6. Elle dit bonsoir à Agnès et Agnès lui dit bonsoir.
7. Sa sœur se fie à lui et il se fie à sa sœur.
8. Maigret se méfie de Sherlock et Sherlock se méfie de Maigret.
9. Le voyou attaque Merlin et Merlin attaque le voyou.
10. Isabelle se couche de bonne heure et Ferdinand se couche de bonne heure.

Related expressions

Se souvenir de *and* se rappeler: *to remember*

1. **Se souvenir** is used with the preposition **de**.

   Je me souviens très bien de cet auto-stoppeur.
   I remember that hitchhiker very well.

   Vous souvenez-vous de la circulation à Rome?
   Do you remember the traffic in Rome?

2. **Se rappeler** is not used with **de**.

   Il se rappelle notre rendez-vous au Quartier Latin.
   He remembers our date in the Latin Quarter.

   Vous rappelez-vous son adresse? —Non, je ne me la rappelle pas.
   Do you remember his address? —No, I don't remember it.

EXERCICE

Employez au temps présent **se souvenir de** *et/ou* **se rappeler,** *selon le cas.*

1. Je _____ la jolie vendeuse du grand magasin *Au Printemps.*
2. Ils _____ leurs excursions au bord de la mer.
3. Elle _____ la vie stimulante et dynamique de New York.
4. Nous _____ nos promenades charmantes au jardin du Luxembourg.
5. Je _____ les gens pittoresques de Bretagne.

The passé composé and imperfect___

The **passé composé** (compound past) and the **imperfect** are treated together here because they are often used together in expressing past actions and states.

Formation of the passé composé

The **passé composé** is composed of two parts:

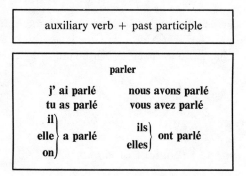

auxiliary verb + past participle

parler

j' ai parlé	nous avons parlé
tu as parlé	vous avez parlé
il elle } a parlé on	ils elles } ont parlé

Formation of the past participle

1. The past participle of regular verbs is formed from the infinitive: parler, **parlé**; finir, **fini**; vendre, **vendu.**

2. The past participles of irregular verbs must simply be learned.

avoir, **eu**			boire, **bu**	
être, **été**			connaître, **connu**	
faire, **fait**			courir, **couru**	
couvrir, **couvert** offrir, **offert**	} -ert		croire, **cru** devoir, **dû**	
rire, **ri** suivre, **suivi**	} -i		falloir, **fallu** lire, **lu** paraître, **paru**	} -u
s'asseoir, **assis** mettre, **mis** prendre, **pris**	} -is		pouvoir, **pu** recevoir, **reçu** savoir, **su** tenir, **tenu**	
construire, **construit** dire, **dit** écrire, **écrit**	} -it		vivre, **vécu** vouloir, **voulu**	

Formation of the auxiliary verb

The auxiliary verb is the present tense of either **avoir** or **être**.

1. **Avoir** is used in the **passé composé** of most verbs.

> **J'ai vécu à New York pendant cinq mois.**
> I lived in New York for five months.
>
> **Ils ont bu de l'eau de source à la campagne.**
> They drank spring water in the country.

2. **Être** is used in the **passé composé** of certain verbs.

a. Reflexive and reciprocal verbs

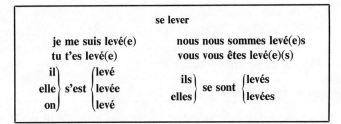

se lever	
je me suis levé(e)	nous nous sommes levé(e)s
tu t'es levé(e)	vous vous êtes levé(e)(s)
il ⎫ ⎧levé elle ⎬ s'est ⎨levée on ⎭ ⎩levé	ils ⎫ se sont ⎧levés elles ⎭ ⎩levées

> **Je me suis amusé dans ce bistro.**
> I had a good time in that bistro.
>
> **Ils se sont téléphoné tous les jours.**
> They telephoned each other every day.

b. Certain intransitive[1] verbs of motion

aller	
je suis allé(e)	nous sommes allé(e)s
tu es allé(e)	vous êtes allé(e)(s)
il ⎫ ⎧allé elle ⎬ est ⎨allée on ⎭ ⎩allé	ils ⎫ sont ⎧allés elles ⎭ ⎩allées

> **Hier nous sommes allés en ville.**
> Yesterday we went downtown.

---

[1] A transitive verb takes a direct object: in the sentence "*She throws the ball*," "*ball*" is the direct object of the transitive verb "*throws*." An intransitive verb does not take a direct object: *She is coming from France; They went out; He died yesterday.*

Other intransitive verbs that take **être:**

arriver	passer
descendre	rester
entrer	retourner
monter	sortir
mourir	tomber
naître	venir
partir	

Ils sont tombés dans la rivière.
They fell in the river.

Elle est morte jeune.
She died young.

Compounds of these verbs also take **être.**

Ils sont redescendus du train.
They got off the train again.

Le voyou est devenu violent.
The hoodlum became violent.

Agreement of the past participle

In certain cases there is agreement of the past participle in the passé composé.

1. Verbs conjugated with **avoir**

   a. The past participle of verbs conjugated with **avoir** generally remains invariable.

      Elle a médité sur la destinée humaine au sommet d'une montagne isolée.
      She meditated about human destiny on top of an isolated mountain.

      Nous avons respiré l'air frais et pur de la campagne.
      We breathed the fresh, pure air of the country.

   b. However, the past participle agrees in number and gender with any **preceding direct object.** The preceding direct object may appear in the form of a personal pronoun, the relative pronoun **que,** or a noun preceded by the adjective **quel.**

      Où avez-vous vu les serpents? —Je les ai vus dans un champ.
      Where did you see the snakes? —I saw them in a field.

      Voici les poissons gigantesques que nous avons attrapés!
      Here are the gigantic fish that we caught!

      Quelles boutiques avez-vous visitées?
      What shops did you visit?

c. But there is no agreement with a preceding indirect object or with the pronoun **en.**

> **Elle leur a dit au revoir à l'aéroport.**
> She said goodbye to them at the airport.
> **Avez-vous vu des jeunes filles au bar? —Oui, j'en ai vu.**
> Did you see any girls in the bar? —Yes, I saw some.

2. Verbs conjugated with **être**

a. Reflexive and reciprocal verbs

If, as is usually the case, the reflexive pronoun is a direct object, the past participle agrees with it. The participle does not agree, however, if the reflexive pronoun is an indirect object.

> **Ils se sont amusés dans une boîte de nuit sur les Champs-Élysées.**
> They had a good time in a nightclub on the Champs-Élysées.
> **Elles se sont regardées au même instant et se sont mises à rire!**
> They looked at each other at the same moment and began to laugh!

but: **Elles se sont parlé au téléphone pendant quatre heures!**
> They spoke to each other on the phone for four hours!
> **Ils se sont dit au revoir les larmes aux yeux.**
> They said goodbye to each other with tears in their eyes.

Note that the past participle remains invariable in the common expression **se rendre compte de** (*to realize*), since the reflexive pronoun is an indirect object.

> **Nous ne nous sommes pas rendu compte des conséquences de la tension raciale.**
> We did not realize the consequences of the racial tension.

b. The intransitive verbs of motion

The past participle agrees in gender and number with the subject of the verb.

> **Nous sommes montés dans l'autobus.**
> We got on the bus.
> **Elles sont passées quatre fois devant la boutique.**
> They passed in front of the shop four times.

Occasionally, some of these verbs are used transitively: that is, they take a direct object. When used transitively, they are conjugated with **avoir,** in which case the past participle does not agree with the subject.

> **Malheureusement nous avons monté la tente sous une ruche!**
> Unfortunately, we put up the tent under a beehive!
>
> **Elles ont passé leurs vacances à Nice.**
> They spent their vacation in Nice.

EXERCICES

1. *Mettez les verbes au* **passé composé** *en faisant l'accord s'il y a lieu.*

1.	elle (aller)	**11.**	ils (se chercher)
2.	nous (courir)	**12.**	elles (se sauver)
3.	je (couvrir)	**13.**	nous (se parler)
4.	nous (flâner)	**14.**	ils (rentrer)
5.	ils (faire)	**15.**	elles (se mentir)
6.	je (offrir)	**16.**	vous (voir)
7.	elle (s'amuser)	**17.**	nous (se téléphoner)
8.	ils (se rendre compte)	**18.**	elle (devenir)
9.	nous (rire)	**19.**	nous (se dire)
10.	elles (visiter)	**20.**	ils (se suicider)

2. *Faites l'accord du* **participe passé** *s'il y a lieu.*

1. Voici la cathédrale que nous avons _____ (visité).
2. Est-elle _____ (allé) à la campagne pour oublier ses ennuis?
3. Ils ont _____ (fait) un pique-nique au bord du lac.
4. Quels champs le fermier a-t-il _____ (cultivé)?
5. Je les ai _____ (vu) dans cette discothèque hier soir.
6. La pollution atmosphérique a _____ (couvert) la ville.
7. Je leur ai _____ (téléphoné) trois fois hier soir.
8. Regardez les poissons malsains que les gens ont _____ (attrapé) dans la Seine.
9. Malheureusement ils ne se sont pas _____ (rendu) compte de l'indifférence des citadins.
10. Nous nous sommes vite _____ (habitué) à la vie en ville.
11. Voici la maison que nous avons _____ (construit).
12. Quelle pollution nous avons _____ (vu) en ville!
13. Ils sont _____ (allé) à la pêche à deux heures du matin!
14. Voici un des grands magasins où nous avons _____ (fait) des courses.
15. Les chauffeurs ont _____ (garé) leurs élégantes voitures dans l'avenue des Champs-Élysées.
16. Pourquoi se sont-ils _____ (moqué) des campagnards?

Formation of the imperfect

The **imperfect** is formed by replacing the **-ons** ending of the first person plural of the present tense with the imperfect endings **-ais, -ais, -ait, -ions, -iez, -aient.**

boire	nous **buvons**
je buv**ais**	nous buv**ions**
tu buv**ais**	vous buv**iez**
il elle on } buv**ait**	ils elles } buv**aient**

Regular and irregular verbs alike follow this rule: nous parlons, **je parlais**; nous finissons, **je finissais**; nous vendons, **je vendais**; nous avons, **j'avais**; nous faisons, **je faisais;** etc.

Note, however, the irregular imperfect stem of the verb être: **j'étais, tu étais,** etc. Note also the spelling changes of the **-cer** and **-ger** verbs:

commencer	nous commen**çons**
je commen**çais**	nous commen**cions**
tu commen**çais**	vous commen**ciez**
il elle on } commen**çait**	ils elles } commen**çaient**

manger	nous mang**eons**
je mang**eais**	nous mang**ions**
tu mang**eais**	vous mang**iez**
il elle on } mang**eait**	ils elles } mang**eaient**

EXERCICES

*Mettez les verbes à l'***imparfait.**

1. elle (tenir)
2. nous (flâner)
3. il (mentir)
4. vous (être)
5. je (avoir)
6. vous (faire)
7. il (piquer)
8. je (sortir)
9. nous (se promener)
10. ils (construire)
11. on (punir)
12. tu (recevoir)
13. je (rendre)
14. vous (pouvoir)
15. nous (courir)
16. elles (se connaître)
17. on (arranger)
18. nous (rire)
19. vous (offrir)
20. ils (avancer)

Use of the passé composé and the imperfect

The passé composé

The **passé composé** is used to express a completed action in the past. The single form of the **passé composé** corresponds to three forms of the English past tense.

$$\textbf{ils ont couru} \begin{cases} \text{they ran} \\ \text{they have run} \\ \text{they did run} \end{cases}$$

Hier j'ai visité quatre musées et trois cathédrales!
Yesterday I visited four museums and three cathedrals!

Avez-vous jamais couché à la belle étoile?
Have you ever slept under the stars?

Avez-vous entendu le bruit de la circulation hier soir?
Did you hear the noise of the traffic last night?

The action expressed is always a completed action. It may have been of short or long duration, or have been repeated a specified number of times.

Ma mère et moi, nous avons vécu à Rome pendant dix ans.
My mother and I lived in Rome for ten years.

Je vous ai téléphoné quatre fois lundi dernier.
I phoned you four times last Monday.

The imperfect

The **imperfect** is used to express past actions or states that were not completed ("imperfect" means, in fact, not completed).

1. It expresses a continuous action in the past (equivalent to *was* + verb + *-ing* in English). The *passé composé* is used to indicate any action that interrupts this continuous action.

   Le fermier cultivait la terre toute la journée.
   The farmer was cultivating the earth all day long.

   Elle traversait la rue quand elle a vu l'accident.
   She was crossing the street when she saw the accident.

   Je rentrais à bicyclette quand il a commencé à pleuvoir.
   I was going home on my bicycle when it began to rain.

2. It indicates a customary action in the past (equivalent to the past tense, or to *used to* or *would* + verb, in English).

   Quand j'étais jeune, je faisais du camping presque tous les mois.
   When I was young, I went (used to go, would go) camping almost every month.

L'année dernière je quittais la ville le vendredi soir et j'y revenais le lundi matin.
Last year I used to leave the city Friday night and come back Monday morning.

3. It is used to describe past conditions or states of mind that have no beginning or end.

Hier le ciel était bleu et la campagne était belle.
Yesterday the sky was blue and the country was beautiful.

Il savait que je n'aimais pas la ville!
He knew I didn't like the city!

However, when verbs denote a *change* in conditions or in a state of mind, they are put into the *passé composé*. Such states have a beginning and end, and are therefore considered completed.

Il a eu peur quand ce type louche s'est approché de lui.
He got scared when that shady character approached him.

Soudain il a fait nuit.
Suddenly it became dark.

4. It is used with **depuis** or **il y avait . . . que,** to express an action that began in the past and continued until another time, also in the past. English uses the progressive form of the pluperfect (*had been* + present participle, or *had been*) to express this idea.

Ils faisaient de la bicyclette depuis cinq minutes quand il a commencé à pleuvoir.
They had been bicycle riding for five minutes when it began to rain.

Il y avait cinq heures qu'elle flânait à Paris quand elle est tombée malade.
She had been strolling in Paris for five hours when she got sick.

Il y avait deux heures qu'il était dans le bois quand il a vu l'ours!
He'd been in the woods for two hours when he saw the bear!

EXERCICES

1. *Traduisez à l'*imparfait *ou au* passé composé *les mots entre parenthèses.*

1. Elle _____ (was meditating) sur la condition humaine quand un méchant moustique l'a piquée!
2. Quand je _____ (was) étudiant à Paris, je _____ (used to frequent) un petit café à côté de Notre-Dame de Paris.
3. Comment! Vous _____ (visited) le Louvre trois fois en une journée?

4. Heureusement, nous _____ (être) dans la tente quand il _____ (began) à pleuvoir.
5. Je _____ (was taking a walk) aux Champs-Élysées quand une femme un peu louche me _____ (said) bonsoir.
6. Parlez-moi de tous les musées, les monuments et les grands magasins que vous _____ (visited) à Paris.
7. Gérard et son amie Nathalie _____ (were having a picnic) à Versailles quand _____ (it got cold).
8. Ils _____ (returned) à la campagne à cause de la pollution et du bruit de la ville.
9. Nous _____ (were sleeping outdoors) quand soudain je _____ (felt) quelque chose dans mon sac de couchage!
10. Nous _____ (could not) garer notre voiture parce que la circulation _____ (was) trop intense.
11. Pendant nos vacances d'été, nous _____ (used to go fishing) tous les matins.
12. Il _____ (was) très chaud ce matin-là, mais nous y _____ (went) quand même.
13. Pendant son séjour à Paris, elle _____ (strolled), anonyme, dans les rues étroites du Quartier Latin.
14. Les campagnards qui _____ (were visiting) Paris _____ (got lost) dans un grand magasin.
15. Il _____ (became frightened) quand il _____ (heard) un bruit étrange dans la rue derrière lui.

2. *Traduisez en français.*

1. She had been shopping for five minutes when she lost her purse (*le sac*).
2. They were walking in the woods when the bees stung them.
3. We'd been strolling in the Latin Quarter for an hour when the hoodlum attacked us!
4. He had been meditating for two days when he found the solution (*la solution*).
5. The farmer had been in the field for two minutes when he saw the snake.

The passé composé *and* imperfect *in narration*[2]

The **passé composé** and **imperfect** appear together in past narrations. The **passé composé**, with its emphasis on completed action, is used to advance the narration: it indicates facts, actions, and events. The **imperfect**, with its emphasis on incompleted actions or states, is used to set the background: it describes outward conditions and inner states of mind.

---

[2] In formal narrations—historical works, novels, short stories, etc.—the *passé simple* (past definite) is normally used instead of the *passé composé* (see p. 11).

EXERCICE

Voici un passage écrit au temps passé. Identifiez (ne traduisez pas) les verbes qu'il faut mettre au **passé composé** *ou à* **l'imparfait**. *Expliquez précisément les raisons de votre choix.*

Yesterday morning I woke up early. I didn't feel well. I got out of bed, walked to the bedroom window, lifted the shade, and looked out. I immediately felt better. It was a beautiful summer day. There were no clouds in the sky and the sun was shining gloriously. I could hear the usual cacophony of city sounds. I went into the kitchen and kissed Barbara, who was already awake. She knew that I wanted to take a walk in the park.

We quickly ate breakfast, left the building, took the subway, got off after a short ride, and began our walk in the Luxembourg Gardens. We were quietly walking along, minding our own business, when we suddenly heard the sound of music behind us. We stopped, turned around, and saw an odd-looking old man who was playing the accordion. Passers-by were throwing coins at his feet while a small monkey was picking them up and putting them in a tin cup. As this one-man show was passing in front of me, I threw a couple of coins at his feet. Barbara barked approvingly. We then continued our walk.

Related expressions

The verbs **partir, sortir, s'en aller, quitter,** and **laisser** all mean *to leave*. The first three are conjugated with **être,** the last two with **avoir.**

Partir: *to leave*

> **À quelle heure est-elle partie hier soir?**
> What time did she leave last night?

When **partir** means to leave a place, it must be followed by **de.**

> **Elles étaient tristes quand elles sont parties de Paris.**
> They were sad when they left Paris.

Sortir: *to leave, to go out*

> **Il est sorti il y a dix minutes, mais il va revenir tout de suite.**
> He left (went out) ten minutes ago, but he'll be back right away.

> **Je suis sorti avec Hélène parce qu'elle adore faire de la bicyclette.**
> I went out with Helen because she adores bike riding.

When **sortir** means to leave or go out of a place, it must be followed by **de.**

> **Ils titubaient quand ils sont sortis du café.**
> They were staggering when they left the café.

Like the English verb *to go out*, **sortir** often implies leaving an enclosed area, such as a room or a restaurant.

S'en aller: *to leave, to go away (the opposite of to stay)*

Le voyou s'en est allé après avoir vu le gendarme.
The hoodlum left (went away) after seeing the policeman.

Allez-vous-en! Vous nous avez assez tourmentés!
Go away! You've bothered us enough!

S'en aller is often synonymous with **partir.**

Quand l'ours est parti ⎫
Quand l'ours s'en est allé ⎬ **nous sommes retournés à la tente.**
When the bear left, we returned to the tent.

Quitter: *to leave someone or something*

Nous avons quitté la ville à cause de la violence et la tension raciale.
We left the city because of the violence and racial tension.

Elle faisait des courses quand je l'ai quittée.
She was shopping when I left her.

Quitter always takes a direct object.

Laisser: *to leave someone or something somewhere*

Zut! J'ai laissé mon parapluie au Louvre!
Darn it! I left my umbrella at the Louvre!

Quand j'ai laissé Hubert à la discothèque, il s'amusait beaucoup.
When I left Hubert at the discothèque, he was having a great time.

Laisser always takes a direct object.

Venir de + *infinitive*

The imperfect tense of **venir de** + *infinitive* indicates that an action had just been completed in the past. The English equivalent is *had just* + past participle.

Elles venaient de visiter le Louvre.
They had just visited the Louvre.

Remember that the present tense of **venir de** + *infinitive* means *have (has) just* + past participle in English.

Je viens de rentrer.
I have just returned home.

EXERCICES

1. *Traduisez en français les mots entre parenthèses.*

    1. Ils _____ (left the city) pour faire un petit séjour à la campagne.

    2. Nous _____ (left Madeleine) à Chartres parce qu'elle voulait y passer toute la journée!

    3. Nous _____ (left the house) parce qu'il faisait beau.

    4. Elle m'a dit qu'elle allait rester avec moi, mais elle _____ (left) quand même.

    5. Quand le paysan _____ (left) le bar, tout le monde s'est mis à rire.

    6. Elle _____ (left her book) sur la littérature romantique au bord d'un lac.

    7. Après avoir passé deux jours à Paris, le campagnard _____ (left).

    8. Quand les abeilles _____ (left), nous avons recommencé notre promenade.

    9. _____ (Leave)! J'ai entendu assez de vos histoires!

    10. Elle avait si peur de faire son exposé qu'elle _____ (left the classroom).

2. *Traduisez en français en employant* **venir de.**

    1. I had just left Robert in the night club.

    2. We had just left the city because there was too much noise.

    3. They have just gone fishing.

    4. They had just left.

    5. They'd just gotten lost when I found them!

Exercices d'ensemble

I. *Répondez en français par une phrase complète.*

    1. Vous coupez-vous quand vous vous rasez?

    2. Êtes-vous de bonne ou de mauvaise humeur quand vous vous réveillez?

    3. Aimez-vous vous coucher tôt ou tard?

    4. Allez-vous vous marier bientôt?

    5. En quoi vous spécialisez-vous à l'université?

    6. Vous intéressez-vous à la vie culturelle de la ville?

    7. Vous fiez-vous aux autres ou vous méfiez-vous des autres?

    8. Êtes-vous né en ville ou à la campagne?

    9. À quelle heure vous êtes-vous couché hier soir?

    10. Vous fâchez-vous souvent?

II. *Répondez précisément en employant deux ou trois phrases complètes.*

    1. Avez-vous peur de vous promener en ville le soir?

    2. Avez-vous jamais fait du camping?

3. Si vous avez visité récemment une grande ville, expliquez comment vous l'avez trouvée et ce que vous y avez fait.
4. Avez-vous jamais rencontré un serpent venimeux (*poisonous*)?
5. Êtes-vous jamais allé en France?
6. Comment comptez-vous vous amuser ce week-end?
7. Qu'est-ce que vous avez fait pendant votre dernier séjour à la campagne?
8. Vous ennuyez-vous en ville?
9. Vous êtes-vous jamais perdu en ville ou à la campagne?
10. Avez-vous jamais couché à la belle étoile?

III. *Traduisez en français.*

1. They had just visited friends in Paris when they got sick (*tomber malade*).
2. We had been waiting for him for two hours when he arrived!
3. We had just returned from the suburbs.
4. We have just visited an interesting shop.
5. We had been bicycling for five days when we finally saw Paris!

IV. *Décrivez au présent une de vos journées typiques en employant les verbes suivants. Arrangez-les par ordre chronologique.*

se raser	se lever
se coucher	se réveiller
se regarder dans la glace	se mettre au travail
se laver	s'habiller
se couper	se mettre à table
s'endormir	se reposer
se maquiller	

V. *Mettez les verbes entre parenthèses au* **passé composé** *ou à l'***imparfait***, selon le cas.*

A. Il _____ (faire) frais et le ciel _____ (être) bleu à Paris. Roger et Suzanne Smith, touristes intrépides et hardis, _____ (prendre) le petit déjeuner, un café crème et des croissants, dans un café. Ils _____ (venir) de se lever. Ils _____ (se parler) et _____ (lire) avec beaucoup d'attention le guide Michelin. Ils _____ (avoir) l'air un peu gênés parce qu'ils _____ (savoir) que la fin de leur tour d'Europe était arrivée et ils ne _____ (avoir) qu'une journée à passer à Paris! Leur avion _____ (aller) partir le lendemain matin.

À 9 h. précises ils _____ (aller) en taxi au musée du Louvre. Ils y _____ (admirer) la Mona Lisa et la Vénus de Milo. Malheureusement, ils n'y _____ (rester) pas longtemps parce qu'il _____ (falloir) se dépêcher! Entre 10 h. et 11 h. ils _____ (courir) dans les galeries de l'Orangerie, le musée des peintres impressionnistes. Les tableaux de Van Gogh les _____ (impressionner). Entre 11 h. et 12 h. 30 ils _____ (se promener) sur les Champs-Élysées, le grand boulevard chic de Paris. Il y _____ (avoir) beaucoup de distractions intéressantes: des boutiques, des cinémas, des boîtes de nuit et le fameux Drugstore. Ils _____ (se promener) depuis une heure quand ils _____ (décider) d'entrer dans un café pour déjeuner. Ils _____ (être) si pressés qu'ils _____ (finir) de déjeuner en un quart d'heure! Pendant le reste de l'après-midi ils _____ (visiter) la cathédrale de Notre-Dame de Paris, la Sainte-Chapelle, les Invalides (le tombeau de Napoléon) et, finalement, le Quartier Latin. À 5 h. ils _____ (rentrer) à l'hôtel où ils _____ (se reposer) un peu. Ils _____ (passer) une soirée aussi magnifique que leur journée. Ils _____ (dîner) dans un restaurant de luxe et puis, ils _____ (aller) voir *Le Bourgeois gentilhomme* de Molière à la Comédie Française. À minuit, pendant que Robert _____ (faire) les valises, Marie _____ (remarquer) qu'ils avaient oublié de visiter la Tour Eiffel. Quel dommage!

B. Quand Brigitte _____ (être) élève à l'école primaire, elle _____ (passer) chaque été en Bretagne chez son oncle Marc et sa tante Agnès. Ils _____ (habiter) une petite ferme à la campagne. Le matin Brigitte _____ (accompagner) son oncle aux champs où il _____ (cultiver) la terre. Elle _____ (aimer) respirer l'air pur et goûter le silence dans cet endroit tranquille et paisible où elle _____ (pouvoir) oublier la pollution, la circulation et le va-et-vient de la ville. L'après-midi elle _____ (avoir) des activités variées. Parfois elle _____ (nager) ou _____ (faire) de la bicyclette avec ses amis, parfois elle _____ (aider) sa tante à faire des crêpes, cette spécialité bretonne. Le soir elle _____ (écouter) le chant des insectes en se reposant sur son lit. À la fin de l'été, elle _____ (avoir) envie de revoir ses parents, mais elle ne _____ (vouloir) pas quitter la ferme.

Sujets de discussion ou de composition

1. On a tendance à stéréotyper la vie en ville et la vie à la campagne. Présentez quelques stéréotypes et expliquez pourquoi ils sont faux.

2. Vous avez l'occasion de passer une semaine à la campagne ou dans une ville de votre choix. Où voudriez-vous aller? Pourquoi?

3. Racontez une histoire amusante ou sérieuse qui vous est arrivée en ville ou à la campagne.

5

Interrogatives and negatives

INTERROGATIVES

I. *Posez une question en employant l'***inversion.**

1. Il sort du ghetto.
2. Une société sans classes est possible.
3. Cette jeune fille a de la classe.
4. Son père a gagné beaucoup d'argent.

II. *Posez des questions avec* **est-ce-que** *et* **n'est-ce pas** *en employant les phrases de l'exercice* **I.**

III. *Formulez une question en employant* **combien, comment, où, pourquoi** *ou* **quand.**

1. Il ira loin parce qu'il est ambitieux.
2. Ce millionnaire est gentil et poli.

IV. *Posez une question en employant les pronoms interrogatifs* **qui, qui est-ce qui, que, qu'est-ce que** *ou* **qu'est-ce qui.**

1. Il est devenu médecin après ses études.
2. Une vie confortable l'intéresse beaucoup!
3. C'est Jeanne qui a une grande fortune.

V. *Traduisez en employant la forme convenable de* **quel** *ou* **lequel.**

1. _____ (What a) mauvaise odeur!
2. _____ (Which one) de ces jeunes filles a de si bonnes manières?

VI. *Traduisez en français en employant* **quelle** *ou* **qu'est-ce que c'est que.**

1. _____ (What is) la bourgeoisie?
2. _____ (What is) la date aujourd'hui?

NEGATIVES

VII. *Mettez au* **négatif** *en employant* **ne . . . pas.**

1. Elle est vendeuse.
2. Jouent-ils au bridge ce soir?
3. J'aime stéréotyper les gens.
4. Pourquoi suis-je né riche?
5. Il est important d'être snob. (*Mettez l'infinitif au négatif.*)

VIII. *Répondez au* **négatif** *en employant* **ne . . . jamais** *ou* **ne . . . plus.**

1. Êtes-vous jamais allé à l'opéra?
2. Avez-vous encore de la bière?

IX. *Répondez au* **négatif** *en employant* **ne . . . personne, personne ne, ne . . . rien** *ou* **rien ne.**

1. Qu'est-ce que ce millionnaire a fait pour aider les pauvres?
2. Qui veut vivre dans la misère?

X. *Substituez l'expression* **ne . . . que** *pour l'adverbe* **seulement.**

1. Elle est vulgaire seulement avec ses amies.
2. Elle aime seulement les gens cultivés.

XI. *Répondez au* **négatif** *en employant* **ne . . . aucun, aucun . . . ne** *ou* **ne . . . ni . . . ni.**

1. Ont-ils l'intention de partir?
2. Quelle classe sociale est parfaite?
3. Qu'est-ce que votre frère veut devenir, médecin ou avocat?

XII. *Traduisez en français.*

1. I don't think so.
2. There is nothing interesting here!
3. Thanks. —It's nothing.

Vocabulaire du thème: Les Classes Sociales

LES CLASSES

la **haute société** *high society*
la **bourgeoisie** *middle class*
la **classe ouvrière** *working class*
le **peuple** *the people*

le **millionnaire** *millionaire*
l' **homme d'affaires** (m) *businessman*
le **patron** *boss*
l' **ouvrier** (m) *worker*

le **chômeur** *unemployed person*
le **chômage** *unemployment*
le **clochard** *bum*

le **bureau** *office*
l' **usine** (f) *factory*
la **profession** *profession*
le **métier** *trade*
le **salaire** *salary*

LE SUCCÈS

l' **ambition** (f) *ambition*
ambitieux *ambitious*
aller loin *to go far*
améliorer sa condition sociale *to improve one's social position*
le **nouveau riche** *nouveau riche*
l' **arriviste** (m, f) *social climber*

le **snob** *snob*
impressionner *to impress*

le **luxe** *luxury*
somptueux *luxurious*
aisé *well-to-do*
propre *clean*

LA PAUVRETÉ

les **taudis** (m) *slums*
la **misère** *misery, distress*
   misérable *miserable*
   malsain *unhealthy*
   pénible *hard (work), painful*
   sale *dirty*

se **révolter contre** *to revolt against*
faire la grève *to go on strike, to strike*
sortir du ghetto *to get out of the ghetto*

MANIÈRES ET GOÛT

les **manières** (f) *manners*
   être bien élevé *to be well-bred*
   avoir bon goût *to have good taste*
   avoir de la classe *to have class*
   comme il faut *proper*
   poli *polite*

raffiné *refined*

être mal élevé *to be ill-bred*
avoir mauvais goût *to have bad taste*
grossier *gross, coarse*
vulgaire *vulgar*

Interrogatives_____

Formation of questions

Inversion of the subject and verb

1. Simple tenses

   a. If the subject is a pronoun, it is inverted with the verb and connected to the verb by a hyphen.

      Voudriez-vous être riche?
      Would you like to be rich?

      Avez-vous l'intention de réussir?
      Do you intend to succeed?

   Verbs ending in a vowel in the third person singular insert **-t-** between the verb and the inverted subject pronoun.

      Travaille-t-elle maintenant comme secrétaire?
      Does she work now as a secretary?

      Admire-t-il vraiment les snobs?
      Does he really admire snobs?

   b. If the subject is a noun, the order is *noun subject + verb + pronoun subject.*

      Marie habite-t-elle une grande maison?
      Does Mary live in a large house?

      Une société sans classes est-elle possible?
      Is a classless society possible?

2. Compound tenses

In compound tenses inversion takes place only with the auxiliary verb. Inversion of the auxiliary verb follows the same rules as simple verbs.

Cet arriviste a-t-il impressionné le patron?
Did that social climber impress the boss?

Avez-vous remarqué ses manières impeccables?
Did you notice his impeccable manners?

Est-ce que

The expression **est-ce que** placed before any sentence transforms it into a question.

Est-ce que vous êtes trop ambitieux?
Are you too ambitious?

Est-ce que les bourgeois respectent les pauvres?
Do members of the middle class respect the poor?

Est-ce que is almost always used when asking a question in the first person singular. However, the expressions **ai-je** (*have I?*), **dois-je** (*must I?*), **puis-je** (*may I?*), and **suis-je** (*am I?*) are often used.

Est-ce que j'ai l'air d'être avare?
Do I look greedy?

Est-ce que je vous embarrasse parce que je ne suis pas comme il faut?
Do I embarrass you because I'm not proper?

Puis-je vous poser une question indiscrète?
May I ask you an indiscreet question?

N'est-ce pas

The expression **n'est-ce pas,** usually placed at the end of a sentence, expresses confirmation or denial. It is equivalent to the expressions *aren't you, didn't you, isn't he, isn't it,* etc., in English.

Vous êtes fauché, n'est-ce pas?
You're broke, aren't you?

Vous cherchez une situation satisfaisante, n'est-ce pas?
You're looking for a satisfying job, aren't you?

Rising intonation

Any sentence can be made interrogative by pronouncing it with a rising intonation. This manner of asking a question is conversational and colloquial; the other interrogative patterns should be used in formal writing.

Salut! Vous avez bien dormi?
Hi! Did you sleep well?

Tu viens à la réunion du syndicat demain?
(Are) you coming to the union meeting tomorrow?

EXERCICES

1. *Transformez en question chacune des phrases suivantes en employant l'*inversion.

   1. Il gagne beaucoup d'argent.
   2. Elle a de la classe.
   3. Les étudiants sont presque toujours à sec (broke).
   4. Les pauvres sont exploités dans une société capitaliste.
   5. L'esprit de compétition est nécessaire dans les affaires.
   6. Cet ouvrier ambitieux a essayé de sortir du ghetto.
   7. Mlle Delphine de la Vigne est un peu snob.
   8. Le pauvre clochard s'est rendu compte de sa condition sociale.
   9. Un millionnaire réussit toujours dans la vie.
   10. Elle est devenue vendeuse dans un grand magasin.

2. *En employant les phrases de l'exercice 1, posez des questions avec* **est-ce que** (*phrases 1–5*) *et* **n'est-ce pas** (*phrases 6–10*).

Interrogative words

The interrogative adverbs

With the common interrogative adverbs **combien** (*how much*), **comment** (*how*), **où** (*where*), **pourquoi** (*why*), and **quand** (*when*), the order *adverb + inverted verb* is always correct.

> **Comment les pauvres vont-ils sortir du ghetto?**
> How are the poor going to get out of the ghetto?

> **Pourquoi les pauvres ne se révoltent-ils pas contre les riches?**
> Why don't the poor revolt against the rich?

> **Quand cessera-t-il de faire ce travail ingrat?**
> When will he stop doing this thankless work?

In short sentences composed only of **combien, comment, où,** or **quand** with a noun subject and a verb, the order *adverb + verb + noun* may be used. The adverb **pourquoi**, however, does not follow this rule.

> **Combien a gagné le patron?**
> How much did the boss make?

Comment vont les ouvriers?
How are the workers?

Où vont les employés?
Where are the employees going?

but: **Pourquoi ce clochard chante-t-il?**
Why is that bum singing?

Note also that **Comment** + **être** asks for a description; it corresponds to
What is (are) . . . like? in English.

Comment est la haute société en France? —Très snob!
What's high society like in France? —Very snobbish!

Comment est ton patron? —Il est poli mais sévère.
What's your boss like? —He's polite but stern.

EXERCICE

Ces phrases sont des réponses. Formulez des questions en employant **combien,
comment, où, pourquoi** *ou* **quand.**

1. Ce paysan s'appelle Grenadou.
2. Il est simple, naïf et sincère.
3. Il habite un petit village.
4. Hier il a soigné les poules et les vaches.
5. Ensuite, il a ramassé les pommes de terre dans le jardin.
6. Il a observé ses plantes parce qu'il les aime comme ses enfants.
7. À deux heures de l'après-midi il est allé au café.
8. Le café était toujours plein le samedi.
9. Il aime le café parce qu'il y rencontre ses amis.
10. Grenadou aime la terre parce qu'il est paysan.

The invariable pronouns

FUNCTION	PERSONS	THINGS
SUBJECT	**qui** or **qui est-ce qui** who	**qu'est-ce qui** what
DIRECT OBJECT	**qui** whom	**que** what
OBJECT OF PREPOSITION	**qui** whom	**quoi** what

As the table shows, the invariable interrogative pronouns are classified according
to their nature (persons, things) and their function (subject, direct object,
object of a preposition). Both factors must be considered in choosing the

proper interrogative pronoun. Note that **qui** referring to persons is correct for all functions.

> **Qui (qui est-ce qui) va travailler dans ce bureau?**
> Who (person, subject) is going to work in this office?

> **Qu'est-ce qui vous empêche d'aller loin?**
> What (thing, subject) is preventing you from going far?

> **Que voulez-vous comme salaire?**
> What (thing, direct object) do you want for a salary?

> **Qui veut-elle impressionner?**
> Whom (person, direct object) does she want to impress?

> **Avec quoi le charpentier réparera-t-il cette maison?**
> With what (thing, object of preposition) will the carpenter repair this house?

> **Contre qui allez-vous vous révolter?**
> Against whom (person, object of preposition) are you going to revolt?

Note that **que** contracts to **qu'** before a vowel or mute *h*.

> **Qu'a-t-il choisi comme profession?**
> What has he chosen as a profession?

1. In sentences beginning with the subject pronouns, the order *pronoun + uninverted verb* is always followed.

> **Qui remplacera notre professeur?**
> Who will replace our teacher?

> **Qu'est-ce qui se passe?**
> What's happening?

2. In sentences beginning with the object pronouns (direct objects and objects of prepositions), the two most common ways of asking questions, **est-ce que** and inversion, are used.

> **Qui a-t-elle embarrassé?**
> **Qui est-ce qu'elle a embarrassé?**
> Whom did she embarrass?

> **Qu'avez-vous trouvé comme emploi?**
> **Qu'est-ce que vous avez trouvé comme emploi?**
> What have you found for a job?

> **De quoi a-t-il besoin pour aller loin?**
> **De quoi est-ce qu'il a besoin pour aller loin?**
> What does he need to go far?

3. However, if a sentence beginning with **que** has a noun subject, inversion of the subject pronoun cannot be used. The order **que + verb + noun subject** must be used instead.

Que veut la classe ouvrière?
What does the working class want?

EXERCICE

Posez une question en employant un **pronom interrogatif invariable.**
modèle: Rousseau a écrit l'ouvrage *Du Contrat social.*
Qui est-ce qui a écrit l'ouvrage *Du Contrat social?*
or: **Qui a écrit l'ouvrage *Du Contrat social?***
or: **Qu'a écrit Rousseau?**
or: **Qu'est-ce que Rousseau a écrit?**

1. Marx a écrit *Le Manifeste du parti communiste.*
2. Notre patron nous a donné une petite augmentation de salaire.
3. M. Lenormand a fait un discours sur les privilèges des riches.
4. Le livre d'Amy Vanderbilt est sur la table.
5. J'ai besoin de tracteurs pour cultiver la terre.
6. Après ses études, il est devenu pilote de guerre.
7. Mes sœurs se plaignaient de leur patron.
8. Mozart a composé cette belle sonate.
9. Guillaume se sent supérieur parce qu'il est riche!
10. Une vie aisée le tentait beaucoup.

The variable pronoun lequel *(which one, which)*

	MASCULINE	FEMININE
SINGULAR	lequel	laquelle
PLURAL	lesquels	lesquelles

Lequel agrees in gender and number with the noun to which it refers.

Ma sœur est en chômage. —Laquelle?
My sister is unemployed. —Which one?

Lequel de ces ouvriers a volé l'argent?
Which (one) of these workers stole the money?

Lequel contracts with the prepositions **à** and **de: auquel, à laquelle, auxquel(le)s, duquel, de laquelle, desquel(le)s.**

J'ai parlé à certains membres du syndicat. —Auxquels?
I spoke to certain members of the union. —To which ones?

Il n'y a que deux classes sociales: la classe moyenne et la classe ouvrière. De laquelle faites-vous partie?

There are only two social classes: the middle class and the working class. Which do you belong to?

The adjective quel *(which, what)*

	MASCULINE	FEMININE
SINGULAR	quel	quelle
PLURAL	quels	quelles

The adjective **quel** agrees in number and gender with the noun it modifies.

Quelle profession a-t-elle choisie?
What (which) profession did she choose?

Quelles conditions de travail existent dans cette usine?
What working conditions exist in this factory?

Quelle est la date de la grève?
What is the date of the strike?

Quel is also used to express the English exclamations *What a . . . !* or *What . . . !*

Quelle maison propre et confortable!
What a clean and comfortable house!

Quelle bêtise!
What nonsense!

Quel culot!
What nerve!

EXERCICE

Traduisez en employant la forme convenable de **quel** *ou* **lequel.**

1. _____ (What) jolies jambes!
2. Diane, je parle de votre ami. —De _____ (which one)?
3. _____ (What) milieux sociaux fréquentez-vous?
4. _____ (Which one) de ces jeunes filles veut devenir médecin?
5. Un de ses fils a dépensé trop d'argent. —_____ (Which one)?
6. _____ (What a) employé ingrat!
7. _____ (What a) odeur!
8. _____ (What) conditions de vie déplorables!
9. Il y a deux usines dans la ville. _____ (Which) voulez-vous visiter?
10. _____ (What a) salaire il gagne!

Related expressions

The interrogative construction *What is . . .?*

1. If the answer to the question *What is . . . ?* is a definition, the expressions **qu'est-ce que** or **qu'est-ce que c'est que** are used. These are fixed forms; they agree in neither gender nor number.

> **Qu'est-ce qu'un arriviste?**
> What is a social climber?
>
> **Qu'est-ce que c'est que la haute société?**
> What is high society?

2. If the answer is anything other than a definition—dates, names, facts, etc.—the adjective **quel** is generally used, agreeing with the noun in question.

> **Quelle est la date de son anniversaire?**
> What is the date of his birthday?
>
> **Quel est son rôle dans l'entreprise?**
> What is his role in the business?

When the adjective **quel** modifies plural nouns, the English equivalent is *What are . . . ?*

> **Quelles sont les règles de la société?**
> What are society's rules?

EXERCICE

Traduisez en français les mots entre parenthèses.

1. _____ (What is) la dignité humaine?
2. _____ (What are) ses conclusions définitives?
3. _____ (What is) le métier de votre père?
4. _____ (What is) la démocratie?
5. _____ (What is) la politesse française?
6. _____ (What is) la date aujourd'hui?
7. _____ (What is) une profession libérale?
8. _____ (What is) sa classe sociale?
9. _____ (What is) une classe sociale?
10. _____ (What are) les plus grandes villes du monde?

Negatives

ne...pas	*not*
ne...guère	*hardly, scarcely*
ne...jamais	*never*
ne...plus	*no longer*
ne...point	*not*
ne...personne	*no one*
ne...rien	*nothing*
ne...que	*only*
ne...aucun	*no, not any*
ne...ni...ni	*neither...nor*

The basic negative: ne...pas

Position

1. With simple verbs

   a. To form the negative, **ne** is normally placed before the verb and **pas** after it.[1] If the sentence contains object pronouns, they are placed between **ne** and the verb.

      Elle ne travaille pas dans ce magasin.
      She doesn't work in this store.

      Ne faites pas attention à ses remarques présomptueuses.
      Don't pay attention to his presumptuous remarks.

      Il ne me les donne pas tout de suite.
      He doesn't give them to me right away.

      Note that **ne** changes to **n'** before a verb beginning with a vowel or mute *h*.

      David n'habite pas dans un appartement somptueux.
      David doesn't live in a luxurious apartment.

      Elle n'aime pas les snobs.
      She doesn't like snobs.

   b. In interrogative sentences, **ne** is placed before the inverted subject pronoun and verb, and **pas** after them. If the sentence contains object

---

[1] The omission of **ne** is frequent in current popular speech: **C'est pas vrai; J'en veux pas; J'étais pas comme ça.**

pronouns, they are placed between **ne** and the inverted subject pronoun and verb.

N'a-t-il pas l'air un peu trop raffiné?
Doesn't he look a little too refined?

Les patrons n'exploitent-ils pas leurs employés?
Don't the bosses exploit their employees?

Ne les préférez-vous pas?
Don't you prefer them?

If the interrogative form **est-ce que** is used, the general rule in section a. preceding is followed.

Est-ce qu'il n'a pas l'air un peu trop raffiné?
Est-ce que les patrons n'exploitent pas leurs employés?

c. In sentences containing a verb followed by a complementary infinitive, only the main verb is made negative.

Ma sœur n'aime pas stéréotyper les gens.
My sister doesn't like to stereotype people.

Ne voulez-vous pas m'accompagner à l'usine?
Don't you want to accompany me to the factory?

2. With compound verbs

The negative of compound verbs is built around only the auxiliary verb: **avoir** or **être**.

Pourquoi n'a-t-il pas remercié le patron?
Why didn't he thank the boss?

Il n'était pas allé loin.
He hadn't gone far.

3. With infinitives

Both parts of the negation precede a negative infinitive. This rule applies to both the present and the past infinitives.

Il est important de ne pas embarrasser les autres.
It is important not to embarrass others.

Je regrette de ne pas avoir réussi.
I regret not having succeeded.

Followed by the partitive

Remember that after ne . . . pas (and other negatives) the indefinite article (un, une) and the partitive article (du, de la, de l', des) generally change to de; they are translated by *not any* or *no*, or sometimes by no word at all (see pp. 59–60).

> **Avez-vous un métier? —Non, je n'ai pas de métier.**
> Do you have a trade? —No, I don't have a trade.
> **Elle n'a pas trouvé de travail.**
> She didn't find any work.
> or: She found no work.
> or: She didn't find work.

Used without ne or a verb, pas de renders *no* with a noun.

> **Pas de travail!**
> No work!
> **Pas de chance!**
> No luck!

EXERCICES

1. *Mettez au* négatif *en employant* ne . . . pas.

   1. Elle se sent supérieure à tout le monde!
   2. Je quitte l'école à l'âge de seize ans.
   3. Le jardinier adore cultiver ses roses.
   4. Ce subordonné gagne beaucoup moins que son patron.
   5. Un paysan traite-t-il les plantes comme les hommes?
   6. Il aura des problèmes à cause de ses mauvaises manières.
   7. Jean-Louis se marie avec une jeune fille comme il faut.
   8. Ce jeune homme grossier crache (*spits*) toujours par terre!
   9. Votre fiancée a de la classe!
   10. Nous avons une maison somptueuse.

2. *Mettez chaque phrase dans l'exercice* 1 *au* passé composé, *puis mettez-la au* négatif *en employant* ne . . . pas.
   modèle: Il impressionne ses supérieurs.
   > **Il a impressionné ses supérieurs.**
   > **Il n'a pas impressionné ses supérieurs.**

3. *Dans les phrases suivantes, mettez seulement les infinitifs au* négatif.

   1. Il est important de stéréotyper les gens.
   2. Je suis content d'être né riche.
   3. Il est étrange d'aimer l'argent.
   4. Elle espère perdre sa fortune.

Other negatives

ne . . . guère, ne . . . jamais, ne . . . plus, ne . . . point

The position of **ne . . . guère** (*hardly, scarcely*), **ne . . . jamais** (*never*), **ne . . . plus** (*no longer, not any more*), and the more literary **ne . . . point** (*not*) is the same as that of **ne . . . pas.**

> **Elle n'est guère bien élevée.**
> She is hardly well bred.

> **Il n'a jamais fait la connaissance d'un millionnaire.**
> He never met a millionaire.

> **Cette famille misérable n'a point perdu sa dignité humaine!**
> This miserable family has not lost its human dignity!

After these negatives, as after **ne . . . pas,** the indefinite article and the partitive generally change to **de.**

> **Ce clochard ne porte jamais de manteau!**
> This bum never wears a coat!

> **Nous n'avons guère d'espoir.**
> We have hardly any hope.

> **Après la révolution, il n'y aura plus de misère!**
> After the revolution there will be no more misery!

EXERCICE

Répondez au négatif en employant **ne . . . jamais** *ou* **ne . . . plus.**

1. Voulez-vous encore du pain?
2. A-t-elle jamais mené une vie aisée?
3. Avez-vous jamais gagné un salaire suffisant?
4. Ces ouvriers font-ils parfois (*sometimes*) la grève?
5. Habitent-ils encore dans le ghetto?
6. Voulez-vous encore de l'argent?
7. Louez-vous quelquefois une maison au bord de la mer?
8. Arrive-t-il de temps en temps à vous persuader qu'il est sophistiqué?
9. Ce millionnaire avaricieux a-t-il quelquefois pitié des pauvres?
10. Avez-vous jamais travaillé dans une ferme?

ne . . . personne *and* ne . . . rien

The negative pronouns **ne . . . personne** (*no one, not anyone*) and **ne . . . rien** (*nothing, not anything*) are placed in the same position as **ne . . . pas** in simple tenses. In compound tenses, **rien** follows the auxiliary verb while **personne** follows the past participle.

> **Cette famille pauvre ne possède rien.**
> This poor family possesses nothing.

> **Elle était fâchée parce qu'il n'y avait personne à la soirée.**
> She was angry because there was no one at the party.

> **Malheureusement, le propriétaire n'a rien compris.**
> Unfortunately, the owner didn't understand anything.

> **Je n'ai vu personne au bureau.**
> I didn't see anyone in the office.

The pronouns **personne ne** and **rien ne** are often used as subjects.

> **Personne ne l'a remercié de ses sacrifices.**
> No one thanked him for his sacrifices.

> **Rien n'a changé dans sa vie.**
> Nothing changed in his life.

Note that **pas** is never used with the negative expressions **ne . . . personne** or **ne . . . rien.**

EXERCICE

Répondez au **négatif** *en employant* **ne . . . personne, personne ne** *ou* **ne . . . rien, rien ne.**

1. De qui avez-vous pitié, des pauvres ou des riches?
2. Qui l'a aidé à réussir?
3. À quoi vous intéressez-vous?
4. Qui avez-vous vu au bal des Dupont-Seymour?
5. Qu'est-ce qui vous embarrasse maintenant?
6. Qu'est-ce que les banquiers ont finalement décidé?
7. Qui va se révolter contre ce régime totalitaire?
8. Qui blâmez-vous pour ces conditions de vie misérables?
9. En qui avez-vous confiance?
10. De quoi avez-vous besoin pour améliorer votre vie?

ne . . . que

In the restrictive expression **ne . . . que** (*only*), **que** is placed directly before the word it modifies.

> **Ce millionnaire n'aimait que l'argent quand il était jeune.**
> This millionaire liked only money when he was young.

Pourquoi le patron n'a-t-il donné une augmentation de salaire qu'à ses amis?
Why did the boss give a raise only to his friends?

Note that the adverb **seulement** may replace **ne . . . que.**

Notre professeur aimait seulement les livres quand il était jeune.

Pourquoi le patron a-t-il donné une augmentation de salaire seulement à ses amis?[2]

Since **ne . . . que** is a restrictive rather than a negative expression, the partitive construction (**du, de la, de l', des**) does not change to **de** after it.

Elle n'a invité que des jeunes gens bien élevés.
She invited only well-bred young men.

EXERCICE

Substituez l'expression **ne . . . que** *pour l'adverbe* **seulement.**

1. Ils ont habité seulement des logements misérables.
2. Il mange beaucoup seulement quand il est nerveux.
3. Elle s'intéresse seulement aux jeunes gens riches et raffinés.
4. Cette dame lit seulement les magazines de mode.
5. Elle est polie seulement devant les adultes.

ne . . . aucun

The adjective **aucun** (*no, not any*) is placed before the noun it modifies. Like all adjectives, it agrees in number and gender with its noun. **Aucun** is almost always used in the singular.

Ces gens-là n'ont-ils aucune envie de réussir?
Don't those people have any desire to succeed?

Il ne peut trouver aucun travail!
He can't find any work!

When **aucun . . . ne** modifies a subject, **aucun** precedes the noun it modifies and **ne** precedes the verb.

Aucun invité n'est venu à l'heure.
No guest arrived on time.

---

[2] Do not confuse the adverb **seulement** (*only*) with the adjective **seul** (*only*): **Il a seulement une ambition** (*He has only one ambition*); **sa seule ambition** (*his only ambition*).

The more literary expression **ne . . . nul, nul . . . ne** may replace **ne . . . aucun, aucun . . . ne** for emphasis.

> **Je n'ai vu nulle robe plus ridicule que la sienne!**
> I saw no dress more ridiculous than hers!
>
> **Nul membre de cette famille n'arrive à l'heure.**
> No member of that family arrives on time.

EXERCICE

Répondez au **négatif** *en employant* **ne . . . aucun, aucun . . . ne.**

1. Cet avocat a-t-il montré un sens de responsabilité?
2. Quel milieu social est tout à fait parfait?
3. Ont-elles l'intention d'aller loin?
4. Est-ce que ce professeur de sociologie stéréotype les riches et les pauvres?
5. Les ouvriers ont-ils compris toutes les nouvelles règles du syndicat?

ne . . . ni . . . ni

The negative adverbs **ni . . . ni** (*neither . . . nor*) precede the words they modify. The indefinite article and the partitive are omitted after **ni . . . ni.**

> **Il n'a ni la formation ni l'expérience qu'il faut pour remplir ce poste.**
> He has neither the background nor the experience necessary to fill this position.
>
> **Un avocat n'est ni ouvrier ni patron.**
> A lawyer is neither a worker nor a boss.
>
> **Ce pauvre clochard n'a ni femme ni enfants ni amis.**
> This poor bum has neither a wife nor children nor friends.

Note that **ni** may be used more than twice.

EXERCICE

Répondez au **négatif** *en employant* **ne . . . ni . . . ni.**

1. Mon cher, allez-vous au théâtre ou à l'opéra?
2. Ce jeune homme est-il poli et sympathique?
3. Allez-vous devenir médecin, avocat ou homme d'affaires?
4. Votre amie a-t-elle visité des musées ou des usines?
5. Avez-vous un bureau et une secrétaire?

Related expressions

Expressions meaning yes and no

1. oui, non, and si

The adverbs **oui** and **non** are most often used to mean *yes* and *no* in French. **Si,** however, is used for *yes* in response to a negative statement or question.

> **Avez-vous de l'ambition? —Oui.**
> Do you have ambition? —Yes.
>
> **N'avez-vous pas d'ambition? —Si!**
> Don't you have any ambition? —Yes! (I do!)

2. Je crois que oui and Je crois que non

The English expressions *I think so* and *I don't think so* are expressed by **Je crois que oui** and **Je crois que non.**

> **Les riches ont-ils des responsabilités envers les pauvres? —Je crois que oui.**
> Do the rich have responsibilities toward the poor? —I think so.

Personne *or* rien + de + *adjective*

The preposition **de** followed by the masculine singular form of the adjective is always used with **personne** or **rien** to express *no one* or *nothing* + *adjective* in English. An adverb like **si, très, plus,** etc., is sometimes placed in front of the adjective for emphasis.

> **Personne d'intéressant n'est venu.**
> No one interesting came.
>
> **N'avez-vous rien d'original à dire?**
> Have you nothing original to say?
>
> **Je n'ai jamais vu personne de si charitable!**
> I never saw anyone so charitable!

1. Note that if **rien** is the direct object of a compound verb, it is separated from **de** and the adjective.

> **Il n'a rien dit d'intéressant.**
> He said nothing interesting.

2. The indefinite pronouns **quelque chose** and **quelqu'un** are also used with **de** + *masculine adjective.*

> **quelqu'un de grossier**   **quelque chose de raffiné**
> someone vulgar   something refined

ne . . . pas du tout

The expression **ne . . . pas du tout** renders the English *not at all*.

> **Je n'ai pas du tout apprécié ses manières grossières!**
> I didn't appreciate his vulgar manners at all!

> **Aimeriez-vous habiter dans un ghetto? —Pas du tout.**
> Would you like to live in a ghetto? —Not at all.

(ni) . . . non plus

Used with an emphatic pronoun, the expression **(ni) . . . non plus** renders the English *neither* in phrases like *neither do I, neither will he*, etc., the exact translation depending on the pronoun and the preceding verb. In spoken French, **ni** is frequently dropped.

> **Je ne veux pas travailler dans cette usine malsaine! —Ni eux non plus!**
> I don't want to work in this unhealthy factory! —Neither do they!

> **Je ne pouvais pas supporter cet arriviste! —Moi non plus!**
> I couldn't stand that social climber! —Neither could I!

Emphatic pronouns are the only ones used in this expression.

De rien *and* il n'y a pas de quoi

The expressions **de rien** and **il n'y a pas de quoi** both translate the English *you're welcome*.

> **Je vous remercie de ce cadeau formidable! —De rien.**
> **—Il n'y a pas de quoi.**
> I thank you for that terrific gift! —You're welcome.

EXERCICES

1. *Traduisez en français.*

   1. Nothing gross happened.
   2. Someone polite answered the phone.
   3. I saw nothing interesting.
   4. We need someone ambitious.
   5. Something strange impressed him.

2. *Donnez une réponse possible en employant* **pas du tout, (ni) . . . non plus, de rien** *ou* **il n'y a pas de quoi.**

   1. Je vous remercie de m'avoir embarrassée devant mon ami!
   2. Je ne suis pas né très riche.
   3. Voulez-vous dire que je suis grossier, vulgaire et ingrat?

4. Quel compliment! Merci!
5. Je ne voudrais pas habiter dans un ghetto!
6. Soyons francs! N'êtes-vous pas un peu snob?

Exercices d'ensemble

I. *Voici les réponses. Quelles sont les questions?*

1. Non, le peuple n'a pas de privilèges.
2. Oui, je veux visiter votre bureau.
3. Un snob est une personne qui cherche à être assimilée aux gens distingués de la haute société en copiant leurs manières, leurs goûts et leurs modes.
4. Ils se sont révoltés contre leurs oppresseurs.
5. J'ai gagné beaucoup d'argent l'année dernière.
6. Si, cette dame élégante fait partie de la haute société!
7. Il n'a pas réussi parce qu'il se sent inférieur.
8. Le conflit entre les riches et les pauvres s'appelle la lutte des classes.
9. Ce clochard habite dans les taudis.
10. Je n'aime pas mon professeur parce qu'il a de mauvaises manières!
11. Les ouvriers sont fâchés parce que le patron ne veut pas augmenter leur salaire.
12. Un homme «arrivé» est une personne qui a réussi à monter l'échelle (*ladder*) sociale jusqu'au rang le plus élevé.
13. Elle a envie d'améliorer sa condition sociale.
14. Si, elle a très bon goût!

II. *Traduisez en français.*

1. Barbara is neither polite nor refined.
2. They lived in the slums last year, but they no longer live there.
3. I have never earned a lot of money.
4. Don't you want to go far?
5. I saw nothing in that film.
6. She doesn't like to impress people.
7. This wealthy family has only one car?
8. That snob has neither good manners nor good taste.
9. No member of that family wants to work.
10. Doesn't he want to be rich? —Yes, he does.
11. She is not well bred. —Neither are you!
12. The unemployed impress no one.
13. Is he late again? —I don't think so.
14. She has never seen any slums.
15. Do you want to be a millionaire? —Not at all!
16. The working class has neither money nor influence.
17. It's cold and that bum doesn't have a hat.

Sujets de discussion ou de composition

1. Le jeu des vingt questions
   Un étudiant imagine une personne ou une chose. Les autres étudiants essaient de deviner quelle personne ou quelle chose en posant des questions. L'étudiant ne répond que par oui ou non. Si les autres étudiants dépassent vingt questions sans deviner la réponse, l'étudiant gagne.

2. Le jeu des métiers
   Un étudiant imagine un métier ou une profession. Les autres étudiants essaient de deviner quel métier ou quelle profession en posant des questions. L'étudiant ne répond que par oui ou non. Si les autres étudiants dépassent vingt questions sans deviner la réponse, l'étudiant gagne.

3. Voulez-vous améliorer votre condition sociale? Pourquoi ou pourquoi pas? Si oui, qu'est-ce que vous allez faire?

4. Une société sans classes est-elle possible?

5. Est-ce que tout le monde a les mêmes possibilités aux États-Unis ou y a-t-il des classes privilégiées?

6
Descriptive adjectives and adverbs

Chapter 6 at a glance

DESCRIPTIVE ADJECTIVES

I. *Mettez les adjectifs au* **féminin singulier.**

1. coupable
2. prémédité
3. dangereux
4. subjectif
5. long

6. blanc
7. gros
8. doux
9. gentil
10. beau

II. *Mettez les expressions au* **pluriel.**

1. l'avocat dangereux
2. le crime prémédité

3. le nouveau juge
4. le témoin principal

III. *Mettez chaque adjectif avant ou après le nom en faisant* **l'accord** *s'il y a lieu.*

1. prémédité; un crime
2. bon; un avocat

3. ancien (former); le prisonnier
4. vieux, algérien; une femme

IV. *Faites* **l'accord** *de l'adjectif s'il y a lieu.*

1. des institutions _____ (social)
2. un juge et une sentence _____ (juste)
3. une robe _____ (bleu foncé)
4. une _____ (demi)-heure

V. *Traduisez en français en employant l'expression entre parenthèses.*

1. The judge seems reasonable. (avoir l'air)
2. Money makes her happy. (rendre)

ADVERBS

VI. *Changez les adjectifs en adverbes.*

1. arbitraire
2. sérieux
3. innocent

4. meilleur
5. bon

VII. *Mettez les adverbes à la place convenable.*

1. On parle du crime passionnel. (beaucoup)
2. On l'a déclarée innocente. (déjà)
3. On est responsable de ses actions. (moralement)

VIII. *Récrivez la phrase en mettant l'expression en italiques au début.*

  1. L'accusé est *peut-être* coupable.
  2. Le criminel a *à peine* compris son crime.

IX. *Remplacez les tirets par* **tout, tous, toute** *ou* **toutes.**

  1. J'ai l'impression que _____ les suspects sont innocents.
  2. Pourquoi _____ les sentences de ce juge sont-elles si indulgentes?
  3. Ce pauvre homme a _____ perdu à cause de cette indiscrétion.
  4. L'avocat était _____ triste parce que le jury avait condamné son client.

X. *Formulez une phrase comparative en employant les expressions* **plus . . . que, moins . . . que** *ou* **aussi . . . que.**

  1. un professeur; un étudiant; sérieux
  2. une prison; ma maison; confortable

XI. *Traduisez en français.*

  1. the youngest father
  2. the most difficult book

XII. *Remplacez les tirets par* **meilleur** *ou* **mieux.**

  1. Mon avocat plaide _____ que le vôtre.
  2. Bien sûr, c'est le _____ avocat de la ville!

Vocabulaire du thème: La Justice et la Loi

LE CRIME

le **criminel** *criminal*
  commettre un crime *to commit a crime*
l' **agent de police** (m) *policeman*
  arrêter *to arrest*

un **crime passionnel** *a crime of passion*
un **crime prémédité** *a premeditated crime*
le **vol** *theft*
le **viol** *rape*
le **meurtre** *murder*

le **procès** *trial*
le **tribunal** *court*
le **droit** *law (the profession, the study);*
   right (moral, legal)
la **loi** *law (rule, statute)*

l' **accusé** (m) *defendant*
   être accusé de *to be accused of*
le **suspect** *suspect*
l' **avocat** (m) *lawyer*
   interroger *to question*
   plaider *to plead*
   prouver *to prove*

le **témoin** *witness*
le **témoignage** *testimony*
le **juge** *judge*
le **jury** *jury*
le **juré** *jury member, juror*
   peser *to weigh*

prononcer le verdict *to pronounce the*
   verdict
acquitter *to acquit*
condamner *to condemn*
innocent *innocent*
coupable *guilty*

la **sentence** *sentence*
le **bénéfice du doute** *benefit of the doubt*
la **circonstance atténuante** *extenuating*
   circumstance
le **préjugé** *prejudice*
arbitraire *arbitrary*
raisonnable *reasonable*
injuste *unfair, unjust*
juste *fair, just*
sévère *stern*
indulgent *indulgent, lenient*
objectif *objective*
subjectif *subjective*

LA PUNITION

la **punition** *punishment*
la **peine de mort** *death penalty*
l' **emprisonnement perpétuel** *life im-*
   prisonment

la **prison** *prison*
le **condamné** *convict*
le **prisonnier** *prisoner*

Descriptive adjectives————————————

An adjective is a word that modifies a noun or a pronoun. If an adjective describes, it is called a descriptive or qualitative adjective.

> **C'est un avocat courageux.**
> He's a courageous lawyer.
> **Elle est coupable.**
> She is guilty.

In English, descriptive adjectives have only one form. French descriptive adjectives have four, since they usually agree in gender (masculine, feminine) and number (singular, plural) with the noun they modify.

	MASCULINE	FEMININE
SINGULAR:	**un procès intéressant** an interesting trial	**une solution intéressante** an interesting solution
PLURAL:	**des procès intéressants** some interesting trials	**des solutions intéressantes** some interesting solutions

Formation of adjectives

Formation of the feminine singular

1. Most adjectives form the feminine singular by adding an unaccented **e** to the masculine singular. If the masculine singular already ends in an unaccented **e**, the masculine and feminine singular are identical.

MASCULINE SINGULAR	FEMININE SINGULAR
prémédité	**préméditée**
injuste	**injuste**

2. Some feminine singular endings are irregular.

CHANGE	MASCULINE SINGULAR	FEMININE SINGULAR
x *to* **se**	heureux	**heureuse**
er *to* **ère**	cher	**chère**
f *to* **ve**	subjectif	**subjective**
c *to* **que**	public	**publique**
g *to* **gue**	long	**longue**
eur *to* **euse**[1]	menteur	**menteuse**
	cruel	**cruelle**
	pareil	**pareille**
double the consonant + **e**	ancien	**ancienne**
	gras	**grasse**
	gros	**grosse**
	coquet[2]	**coquette**

3. Certain common adjectives also have irregular feminine singular forms.

MASCULINE SINGULAR	FEMININE SINGULAR
beau	**belle**
blanc	**blanche**
bon	**bonne**
doux	**douce**
favori	**favorite**
faux	**fausse**
fou	**folle**
frais	**fraîche**
franc	**franche**
gentil	**gentille**

---

[1] Adjectives in **eur** not derived from a present participle change **eur** to **ice**: **destructeur, destructrice.** The pairs **antérieur, postérieur; intérieur, extérieur; mineur, majeur; supérieur, inférieur;** and **meilleur** are regular and add an unaccented **e**.

[2] A small group of common adjectives ending in **et** change to **ète**: **complet, concret, discret, inquiet, secret.**

MASCULINE SINGULAR	FEMININE SINGULAR
malin	**maligne**
mou	**molle**
nouveau	**nouvelle**
sec	**sèche**
vieux	**vieille**

4. Five of the above adjectives have a second masculine singular form, used before nouns beginning with a vowel or mute **h.**

beau	**bel**
fou	**fol**
mou	**mol**
nouveau	**nouvel**
vieux	**vieil**

le vieux juge	**le vieil Arabe**
the old judge	the old Arab

But these adjectives have only one form in the masculine plural.

les vieux juges	**les vieux Arabes**
the old judges	the old Arabs

Formation of the plural

1. Most adjectives form the plural by adding **s** to the masculine or feminine singular.

SINGULAR	PLURAL
un avocat célèbre	**des avocats célèbres**
a well-known lawyer	some well-known lawyers
une circonstance atténuante	**des circonstances atténuantes**
an extenuating circumstance	some extenuating circumstances

2. Masculine singular adjectives with certain endings have irregular plurals.

CHANGE	MASCULINE SINGULAR	MASCULINE PLURAL
x (*no change*)	courageux	**courageux**
s (*no change*)	gris	**gris**
eau *to* **eaux**	nouveau	**nouveaux**
al *to* **aux**	principal	**principaux**

The adjectives **banal, fatal, final,** and **naval** form the masculine plural by adding **s.**

EXERCICES

1. *Faites l'accord de l'*adjectif.

1. une institution _____ (public)
2. ma _____ (vieux) tante
3. des ambitions _____ (sérieux)
4. un _____ (beau) appartement
5. des témoins _____ (courageux)
6. les examens _____ (final)
7. mes romans _____ (favori)
8. une jeune fille _____ (doux et gras)
9. un _____ (vieux) ami
10. une intelligence _____ (supérieur)
11. les suspects _____ (principal)
12. des activités _____ (amoureux)
13. une solution _____ (subjectif)
14. mon actrice _____ (favori)
15. une philosophie _____ (faux)
16. une femme _____ (menteur)

2. *Faites l'accord des* adjectifs *s'il y a lieu.*

Un des mythes les plus _____ (cher) du XVIIIᵉ siècle était la foi dans le bonheur _____ (terrestre) de l'homme. Avant de pouvoir organiser une _____ (nouveau) société où les hommes seraient _____ (heureux), il fallait extirper les injustices et les préjugés _____ (social) qui rendaient _____ (impossible) le bonheur des hommes. Au nom de la raison, des écrivains _____ (militant), que l'on appelle «philosophes», ont fait le procès des institutions _____ (politique, social et religieux) de l'époque. Parmi les philosophes les plus _____ (connu) étaient Montesquieu, Rousseau, Diderot et Voltaire.

Position of adjectives

After the noun

In English, descriptive adjectives precede the noun they modify. In French, on the other hand, they often follow the noun. Adjectives of color, religion, nationality, and class almost always follow the noun.

la façade grise
the gray façade

une société bourgeoise
a middle-class society

une loi française
a French law

l'avocat catholique
the Catholic lawyer

Note that adjectives of nationality are not capitalized in French. Nouns of nationality, however, are capitalized: **un Français, un Russe, un Japonais.**

Before the noun

1. Some short, common adjectives normally precede the noun.

autre	haut	petit
beau	jeune	premier
bon	joli	vieux
gros	mauvais	vilain

2. Certain adjectives have one meaning when they precede the noun and another when they follow it.

un ancien prisonnier
a former prisoner

une maison ancienne
an old (or ancient) house

un brave juré
a good juror

un savant brave
a courageous scientist

un certain succès
a relative success

un succès certain
a sure success

sa chère femme
his dear wife

un livre cher
an expensive book

le même jour
the same day

le jour même
the very day (emphatic)

le pauvre type
the poor fellow
(unfortunate)

un homme pauvre
a poor man (not rich)

sa propre maison
his own house

une maison propre
a clean house

un simple soldat
a mere soldier

un homme simple
a simple man (plain, uncomplicated)

le seul voyageur
the only traveler

un voyageur seul
a traveler alone (by himself)

le dernier témoin
the last witness (in a series)

l'année dernière
last year (the one just passed)

la prochaine question
the next question
(in a series)

l'année prochaine
next year (the one coming)

3. Many descriptive adjectives that normally follow the noun may precede it for special emphasis. In this case the stress is on the adjective, which is often pronounced in a more emphatic tone of voice.

Une magnifique plaidoirie!
A *magnificent* defense!

Quel dangereux criminel!
What a *dangerous* criminal!

Une juste punition!
A *just* punishment!

Two adjectives with one noun

1. If one adjective normally precedes the noun and the other normally follows it, they are placed in their normal order.

Sartre est un grand écrivain engagé.
Sartre is a great committed writer.

2. If both adjectives normally precede the noun, both are placed either before or after the noun, joined by the conjunction **et.**

C'est une longue et belle histoire.
C'est une histoire longue et belle.
It's a long and beautiful story.

3. If both adjectives normally follow the noun, both are placed after it and joined by **et.**

C'est un prisonnier armé et dangereux.
He is an armed and dangerous prisoner.

Two adjectives juxtaposed

Two adjectives may be juxtaposed if the first adjective describes a word group composed of the second adjective and the noun. Both adjectives are placed in their normal position before or after the noun.

Cunégonde est une gentille jeune fille.
Cunégonde is a nice girl.

Il essaie de comprendre le milieu juridique américain.
He is trying to understand American judicial circles.

In the first example, **gentille** describes the word group **jeune fille**; in the second, **américain** applies to the word group **milieu juridique**.

EXERCICES

1. *Mettez les* **adjectifs** *à la place convenable et faites l'accord.*
   modèle: un criminel (jeune, violent)   **un jeune criminel violent**

   1. un tribunal (français)
   2. une prison (laid)
   3. un avocat (riche)
   4. une action (dangereux)
   5. une loi (parfait, juste)
   6. une idée (exceptionnel)
   7. des jeunes filles (amusant)
   8. une femme (vieux, italien)
   9. une fête (grand, juif)
   10. une sentence (subjectif, arbitraire)

2. *Mettez l'***adjectif** *à la place convenable et faites l'accord.*

   1. sa voiture (*propre:* clean)
   2. mon professeur (*ancien:* former)
   3. une vie (*simple:* uncomplicated)
   4. les réponses (*seul:* only)
   5. une injustice (*certain:* sure)
   6. la semaine (*prochain:* the one coming)
   7. les accusés (*pauvre:* not rich)
   8. ses amies (*cher:* dear)
   9. l'histoire (*même:* same)
   10. un juge (*brave:* courageous)

Agreement of adjectives

French adjectives generally agree in number (singular, plural) and gender (masculine, feminine) with the noun or pronoun they qualify.

> **les institutions sociales**
> social institutions
>
> **une femme compatissante**
> a compassionate woman

An adjective with more than one noun

An adjective that modifies more than one noun is plural. If the gender of the nouns is different, the masculine plural form of the adjective is used. If both nouns are of the same gender, the adjective is naturally in that gender.

> **une jeune fille et un garçon courageux**
> a courageous girl and boy
>
> **les premières questions et réponses**
> the first questions and answers

Irregular agreements

1. Most adjectives of color agree with the noun, but color adjectives composed of two words, such as **rouge foncé, châtain clair, bleu ciel, vert pomme,** and **jaune paille** are invariable.

    une robe bleue
    a blue dress

    une robe bleu foncé
    a dark blue dress

    des cheveux châtain clair
    light brown hair

2. **Demi** and **nu** are invariable and are joined to the noun by a hyphen when they precede it. They agree with the noun when they follow it.

une demi-heure	but	**une heure et demie**
a half hour		an hour and a half
nu-tête	but	**la tête nue**
bareheaded		bareheaded

EXERCICE

Faites l'accord des **adjectifs.**

J'ai été témoin dans un procès _____ (célèbre) l'année _____ (dernier). La suspecte, une _____ (jeune) Française était _____ (accusé) de meurtre. Elle semblait _____ (dangereux). J'ai été _____ (impressionné), pourtant, par le juge, une femme _____ (exceptionnel).

Un peu _____ (gras), elle avait les cheveux _____ (châtain clair) et les yeux _____ (bleu). Mais sa description _____ (physique) n'est pas très _____ (important)! Je l'ai admirée à cause de ses qualités _____ (moral et humain). _____ (Brillant et perceptif), elle était _____ (compatissant) sans être _____ (indulgent), et _____ (objectif) sans être _____ (froid). Ceux qui prétendent que les femmes ne sont pas _____ (travailleur et raisonnable) sont _____ (idiot)!

Et la suspecte? On l'a trouvée _____ (innocent).

Related expressions

Avoir l'air + *adjective*

Elle a l'air content.
She looks happy.

Elles ont l'air contentes.
They seem happy.

The adjectives may agree with either the subject or the masculine noun **air.** In modern usage, agreement is made most often with the subject. When, as often happens, **d'être** is added to the expression, agreement is always with the subject.

> **Elles ont l'air d'être contentes.**
> They seem to be happy.

Rendre + *adjective*

> **Le verdict la rend contente.**
> The verdict makes her happy.
>
> **La peur peut rendre intolérants les hommes.**
> Fear can make men intolerant.

The adjective agrees with the direct object of **rendre** (in the above examples, **la** and **les hommes**).

EXERCICE

*Faites l'accord de l'***adjectif*** entre parenthèses.*

1. Ils avaient l'air _____ (fatigué) pendant le procès.
2. Même si on l'a trouvée coupable, elle avait l'air _____ (innocent).
3. Il rend ma vie _____ (heureux).
4. L'injustice rend les juges _____ (triste).
5. Ils ont l'air _____ (fâché) quand je suis en retard.
6. Pourquoi ce crime la rend-il si _____ (furieux)?
7. Le mal dans le monde les rend _____ (pessimiste).
8. Au contraire, le bien les rend _____ (optimiste).
9. Les arguments que le monde n'est ni bon ni mauvais ont parfois l'air _____ (juste et raisonnable).
10. L'humour peut rendre la vie _____ (gai).

Adverbs_____

An adverb is a word that modifies a verb, an adjective, or another adverb.

> **Le juge a interrogé lentement les témoins.**
> The judge questioned the witnesses *slowly.*
>
> **L'accusé était-il totalement responsable de ses actions?**
> Was the defendant *totally* responsible for his actions?
>
> **Il pèse fort bien les faits.**
> He weighs the facts *very well.*

Formation of adverbs

Adverbs formed by adding -ment to the adjective

1. The most common way of forming adverbs is to add the suffix **-ment** to the masculine form of adjectives ending in a vowel, and to the feminine form of adjectives ending in a consonant. The suffix **-ment** frequently corresponds to the English suffix *-ly*.

   arbitraire, **arbitrairement**   doux, **doucement**
   poli, **poliment**   naturel, **naturellement**
   probable, **probablement**   sérieux, **sérieusement**
   vrai, **vraiment**   subjectif, **subjectivement**

2. A small number of adverbs have **é** rather than **e** before **-ment**. Some of the most common are:

   confus, **confusément**   précis, **précisément**
   énorme, **énormément**   profond, **profondément**

3. The adverbs corresponding to the adjectives **gentil** and **bref** are **gentiment** and **brièvement**.

4. Adjectives ending in **-ant** or **-ent** form adverbs ending in **-amment** and **-emment** (both pronounced amã).

   constant, **constamment**   innocent, **innocemment**
   puissant, **puissamment**   patient, **patiemment**

   But the adjective **lent** forms its adverb normally: **lentement**.

Adverbs that do not add -ment to the adjective

1. A small number of very common adjectives form adverbs that do not end in **-ment**.

   bon, **bien**   meilleur, **mieux**
   mauvais, **mal**   petit, **peu**

   Un bon avocat plaide bien.
   A good lawyer pleads well.

   Un mauvais témoin s'exprime mal.
   A bad witness expresses himself badly.

2. Some adjectives are used as adverbs after the verb without changing form.

voler bas to fly low	**chanter faux** to sing off key
sentir bon to smell good	**courir vite** to run fast
voir clair to see clearly	**parler net** to speak clearly
marcher droit to walk straight	**travailler dur** to work hard

Les forçats travaillent dur en prison.
Convicts work hard in prison.

Mon avocat parle net.
My lawyer speaks clearly.

EXERCICE

Changez les adjectifs en **adverbes.**

1. bon	**10.** profond	**18.** courageux
2. sincère	**11.** confus	**19.** principal
3. agréable	**12.** évident	**20.** faux
4. bête	**13.** poli	**21.** énorme
5. mauvais	**14.** objectif	**22.** assuré
6. triste	**15.** stricte	**23.** bruyant
7. sec	**16.** prématuré	**24.** seul
8. naïf	**17.** naturel	**25.** certain
9. long		

Position of adverbs

With verbs

1. As a general rule, adverbs follow verbs in simple tenses in French. In English, on the other hand, adverbs very often precede the verb.

Le juge arrive-t-il enfin?
Is the judge finally arriving?

On l'accuse injustement de vol.
He is unjustly accused of robbery.

Il dit toujours la vérité.
He always tells the truth.

2. In compound tenses, most commonly used adverbs are placed between the auxiliary verb and the past participle.[3] These adverbs include:

assez	peu
aussi	presque
beaucoup	souvent
bien	toujours
déjà	trop
encore	vite
enfin	certainement
mal	complètement
même	probablement
moins	vraiment

Il s'est vite aperçu que son avocat avait fait une erreur.
He quickly noticed that his lawyer had made an error.

A-t-il vraiment manqué à sa parole?
Did he really break his parole?

With adjectives and other adverbs

Like English adverbs, French adverbs precede the adjectives or adverbs they modify.

Je le tiens moralement responsable de ses actions.
I hold him morally responsible for his actions.

La justice ne se révèle pas très vite.
Justice does not reveal itself very quickly.

For emphasis

Some adverbs may exceptionally appear at the beginning of a sentence for emphasis. Most common are the adverbs **généralement, heureusement, malheureusement,** and adverbs of time and place.

Heureusement, elle n'a pas encore entendu les mauvaises nouvelles.
Luckily, she hasn't yet heard the bad news.

Aujourd'hui, le jury va prononcer le verdict!
Today, the jury is going to pronounce the verdict!

---

[3] Some adverbs, generally ending in **-ment** may appear after the past participle, or even at the end of the sentence: **Il est arrivé lentement au tribunal; Il a prouvé son innocence facilement.** Usage or style dictate their position.

EXERCICE

Mettez les **adverbes** *à la place convenable.*

1. Je lui donne le bénéfice du doute. (toujours)
2. Le juge a expliqué ses droits au prisonnier. (bien)
3. L'accusé proteste-t-il de son innocence? (encore)
4. Le tribunal a condamné le suspect. (certainement)
5. Ce politicien va-t-il en prison? (vraiment)
6. Mon avocat a posé des questions importantes! (enfin)
7. Le juge a pesé le pour et le contre de l'affaire. (bien)
8. Selon l'existentialisme de Sartre, chacun crée ses propres règles de conduite. (constamment)
9. Cet étudiant va devenir un avocat célèbre. (probablement)
10. Accepter ses responsabilités n'est pas toujours facile. (complètement)
11. Il aime gagner. (trop)
12. Elles espèrent prouver qu'il est innocent. (aujourd'hui)
13. Mon fils, je crois que tu t'es amusé. (beaucoup)
14. Il ment trop! (malheureusement)
15. On a acquitté l'accusé. (vite)

Related expressions

À peine, aussi, peut-être

1. When **à peine** (*hardly*), **aussi** (*therefore, consequently*), and **peut-être** (*perhaps*) introduce a statement, the subject and verb are inverted.

   > **À peine le chef du jury a-t-il pu prononcer le verdict.**
   > The jury foreman was hardly able to pronounce the verdict.

   > **Aussi est-il allé en prison.**
   > Consequently he went to prison.

   > **Peut-être était-il innocent.**
   > Perhaps he was innocent.

2. **Peut-être** has an alternate expression, **peut-être que,** which does not require inversion of subject and verb.

   > **Peut-être qu'il était innocent.**
   > Perhaps he was innocent.

3. If placed at the beginning of a statement, **aussi** always means *therefore* or *consequently*. When, as is most often the case, **aussi** means *also* or *too*, it is placed within the sentence following the normal rules of position.

Attendez! Je viens aussi!
Wait! I'm coming too!

Il m'a aussi accusé de meurtre!
He also accused me of murder!

EXERCICES

1. *Récrivez la phrase en employant* **à peine** *ou* **peut-être** *au début.*
   modèle: Elle était peut-être innocente.   **Peut-être était-elle innocente.**

   1. Elle était peut-être coupable.
   2. Le voleur a à peine vu sa victime.
   3. Elle ne sait peut-être pas la réponse.
   4. Le témoin a à peine compris la question.
   5. On l'accusera peut-être de viol.

2. *Refaites les phrases 1, 3 et 5 de l'exercice précédent en employant* **peut-être que** *au début.*

3. *Remplacez* **donc** (therefore) *par* **aussi** *en faisant tous les changements nécessaires.*
   modèle: Il a dit la vérité, donc il est allé en prison.
              Il a dit la vérité, aussi est-il allé en prison.

   1. Il n'approuve pas cette loi, il l'a donc violée.
   2. Il veut réussir, il travaille donc sérieusement.
   3. Le jury la croyait, elle était donc très contente!
   4. Il a marché trop lentement, donc il est arrivé en retard.
   5. Son avocat était raciste, donc elle s'est fâchée.

Tout *as an adjective, adverb and pronoun*

1. The adjective **tout**

	MASCULINE	FEMININE
SINGULAR	**tout**	**toute**
PLURAL	**tous**	**toutes**

The adjective **tout** often means *all* or *every*. It agrees in number and gender with the noun it modifies.

   Il travaille toute la journée.
   He works all day.

   Qui est responsable de tous ces vols?
   Who's responsible for all these thefts?

   Il est arrêté tous les mois!
   He is arrested every month!

When used before a singular noun without an article, **tout (toute)** means *every*, *any*, or *all*.

> **Tout agent de police devrait être honnête.**
> Every policeman should be honest.
>
> **Toute justice a disparu du pays.**
> All justice has disappeared from the country.

2. The adverb **tout**

The adverb **tout,** meaning *all* or *quite*, is invariable except when it appears before a feminine adjective beginning with a consonant or aspirate **h**. The feminine singular or plural forms **(toute** and **toutes)** must then be used.

> **Pourquoi les amis du condamné sont-ils tout contents?**
> Why are the convict's friends quite happy?
>
> but: **C'est dégoûtant! La prison est toute remplie de rats!**
> It's disgusting! The prison is all full of rats!

3. The pronouns **tous, toutes, tout**

The masculine and feminine plural pronouns **tous** and **toutes** mean *all*; the invariable pronoun **tout** usually means *everything*. Note that the final **s** of **tous** is pronounced when it is used as a pronoun, but silent when it is used as an adjective.

> **Tous ont l'air d'être raisonnables.**
> All seem reasonable.
>
> **Elles sont toutes accusées de vol.**
> They are all accused of theft.
>
> **Elle a tout perdu à cause des préjugés du jury.**
> She lost everything because of the jury's prejudices.

EXERCICE

Remplacez les tirets par **tout, tous, toute** *ou* **toutes.**

1. On ne savait pas _____ les circonstances du crime.
2. Pourquoi sont-elles _____ tristes?
3. _____ les lois ne sont pas justes parce que _____ les hommes ne le sont pas.
4. _____ criminel dangereux doit être emprisonné.
5. Elles sont _____ arrivées à l'heure.
6. _____ les étudiants ont trouvé le professeur coupable d'indulgence.
7. Elle était _____ heureuse d'apprendre qu'il était innocent.
8. Les jurés se sont _____ levés pour prononcer le verdict.

9. Avez-vous _____ préparé pour le procès?

10. Est-ce que _____ les hommes ont les mêmes droits aux États-Unis?

11. _____ ont réussi à convaincre le jury.

12. Le juge a perdu _____ objectivité!

Comparative and superlative of adjectives and adverbs

The comparative

The comparative is used to compare two things. There are three comparative expressions used with both adjectives and adverbs:

comparison of superiority: **plus . . . que** _more . . . than_
comparison of inferiority: **moins . . . que** _less . . . than_
comparison of equality: **aussi . . . que** _as . . . as_

> **Son avocat parle plus confusément que le mien!**
> His lawyer speaks more confusingly than mine!

> **Votre interprétation est moins subjective que la mienne.**
> Your interpretation is less subjective than mine.

> **La musique est aussi intéressante que le droit.**
> Music is as interesting as law.

1. The adverbs **bien** and **beaucoup** are used to emphasize the comparatives **plus . . . que** and **moins . . . que.** The English equivalent is _much_ or _a lot_.

> **Votre interprétation est bien moins subjective que la mienne.**
> Your interpretation is a lot less subjective than mine.

> **Son avocat parle beaucoup plus confusément que le mien!**
> His lawyer speaks much more confusingly than mine!

2. The expression **si . . . que** may be substituted for **aussi . . . que** in negative sentences.

> **La musique n'est pas si intéressante que le droit.**
> Music is not as interesting as law.

3. _Than_ is expressed by **de** when it is followed by a number.

> **Il a passé plus de cinq ans en prison.**
> He spent more than five years in prison.

> **Je lui ai prêté plus de cinquante dollars.**
> I lent him more than fifty dollars.

EXERCICE

Formulez une **phrase comparative** *avec les mots donnés.*

modèle: votre tête; votre nez; grand **Ma tête est (bien) plus grande que mon nez.**

1. une prison; un hôtel de luxe; confortable
2. votre maison; un château; somptueux
3. un juge; un criminel; sage
4. un crime passionnel; un crime prémédité; révoltant
5. vous; votre professeur de français; sévère
6. vous; votre meilleur ami; raisonnable
7. un meurtre; un vol; choquant
8. votre école secondaire; votre université; difficile
9. vous; votre père; indulgent
10. un lion; un chat; dangereux

The superlative

The superlative is used to compare three or more things. The superlative of adjectives is formed by placing the articles **le, la,** or **les** before the comparative. If the adjective follows the noun, the articles must be used twice: once before the noun and once before the superlative.

> **C'est la plus petite prison de l'état.**
> It's the smallest prison in the state.
>
> **Henri est l'étudiant en droit le plus doué de l'université.**
> Henry is the most talented law student in the university.

The superlative of adverbs is formed by placing **le** before the comparative.

> **Ce témoin a répondu le plus courageusement à la question.**
> This witness answered the question most courageously.

1. The expression **de** + *article* is always used to mean *in, of,* or *on* after the superlative. (Do not use **dans**.)

> **le procès le plus célèbre de la région**
> the most famous trial in the area
>
> **l'athlète le plus fort de l'équipe**
> the strongest athlete on the team

2. If more than one comparative or superlative is used in a sentence, the comparative or superlative words are repeated before each adjective or adverb.

> **Le témoin était plus timide et plus discret que l'avocat.**
> The witness was more timid and discreet than the lawyer.

C'est l'étudiant en droit le plus sensible et le plus travailleur de la classe.
He is the most sensitive and hard-working law student in the class.

3. **De beaucoup** and **de loin** are used to emphasize the superlative. The English equivalent is *by far*.

de loin le juge le plus juste de la ville
by far the fairest judge in the city

le prisonnier de beaucoup le moins dangereux de la prison
by far the least dangerous prisoner in the prison

EXERCICE

Traduisez en français.

My name is Dédé. I am not the nicest fellow (*le type*) in the world. In fact, the police would probably say that I am the least likeable person in Paris. I am certainly the least modest! I am a criminal, the meanest and most dangerous criminal in the city. I commit only the most violent and the most daring (*osé*) crimes. I am also intelligent, a lot more intelligent than most of the detectives at Interpol. You probably want to know what the most intelligent criminal in Paris is doing in this dirty prison. Well (*Eh bien*), nobody's perfect!

Bon, mauvais, petit

Certain forms of the adjectives **bon, mauvais,** and **petit** are irregular.

	COMPARATIVE	SUPERLATIVE
bon	**meilleur** **moins bon** **aussi bon**	**le meilleur** **le moins bon**
mauvais	**plus mauvais, pire**[4] **moins mauvais** **aussi mauvais**	**le plus mauvais, le pire** **le moins mauvais**
petit	**plus petit** **moins petit, moindre** **aussi petit**	**le plus petit** **le moins petit, le moindre**[5]

Certains prétendent que Voltaire était le meilleur écrivain du dix-huitième siècle.
Certain people claim that Voltaire was the best writer in the eighteenth century.

---

[4] **Pire** and **plus mauvais** are used interchangeably.
[5] **Moindre** is used most often in the superlative and in abstract situations: **Henri est le moins petit,** but **Il n'y a pas le moindre espoir.**

Il a réussi sans faire le moindre effort.
He succeeded without making the slightest effort.

Bien *and* mal

Certain forms of the adverbs **bien** and **mal** are irregular.

	COMPARATIVE	SUPERLATIVE
bien	**mieux** **moins bien** **aussi bien**	**le mieux** **le moins bien**
mal	**plus mal, pis**[6] **moins mal** **aussi mal**	**le plus mal, le pis** **le moins mal**

C'est mon avocat qui interroge le mieux les témoins!
My lawyer questions the witnesses the best!

Cet avocat plaide moins mal que l'autre.
This lawyer pleads less badly than the other.

EXERCICES

1. *Traduisez en français les mots entre parenthèses en employant la forme correcte de* **meilleur** *ou* **mieux.**

   1. Qui est _____ (the better) détective, Sherlock Holmes ou Maigret?
   2. Accepte-t-il _____ (better) ses responsabilités maintenant que dans le passé?
   3. Les arguments de mon avocat étaient _____ (better) que ceux de la défense.
   4. Il travaille _____ (the best)!
   5. Cet immigrant connaît l'histoire américaine _____ (better) que la plupart des Américains.

2. *Traduisez en français les mots entre parenthèses en employant la forme correcte de* **mauvais, pire** *ou* **mal.**

   1. C'est _____ (the worst) procès que j'aie jamais vu!
   2. Un crime prémédité est-il _____ (worse) qu'un crime passionnel?
   3. Mon avocat s'habille _____ (worse) que moi!
   4. Une sentence arbitraire, est-ce _____ (the worst) chose?
   5. Je parle beaucoup _____ (worse) que mon frère.

---

[6] **Plus mal** is used more often than **pis**.

Exercices d'ensemble

I. Le texte suivant résume l'intrigue (plot) de *Candide*, un très célèbre conte philosophique de Voltaire.

A. *Faites l'accord, si nécessaire, des **adjectifs** entre parenthèses et répondez aux questions.*

Candide, le personnage _____ (principal), est un _____ (jeune) homme _____ (naïf, courageux et sympathique). Il habite dans le château d'un baron _____ (allemand). _____ (Honnête et ignorant), il croit complètement les préceptes de son maître Pangloss, un philosophe «optimiste» qui croit que tout est bien dans le monde. Cunégonde, la fille du baron, est _____ (doux, frais et gras). Trouvant qu'elle a l'air _____ (séduisant), Candide tombe _____ (amoureux) d'elle. Le baron n'apprécie pas les activités _____ (amoureux) de Candide et Cunégonde et, _____ (fâché), il chasse Candide du château.

Rejeté de ce paradis _____ (terrestre), Candide fait des voyages et est témoin de _____ (nombreux) désastres _____ (naturel) et d'injustices _____ (humain)—une guerre, une tempête, un tremblement de terre, exécutions, viols, meurtres, cas d'exploitation des hommes, etc. Il est si scandalisé qu'il commence à mettre en doute «l'optimisme» de Pangloss. Ses doutes s'intensifient quand il fait la connaissance du _____ (vieux) savant Martin pendant un de ses voyages. Bien plus _____ (pessimiste) que Pangloss, Martin affirme que les hommes sont _____ (rusé, méchant, menteur et lâche). Mais son plus grand malheur arrive lorsque Candide retrouve sa _____ (cher) Cunégonde. Elle n'a plus l'air _____ (joli et gentil); elle est devenue _____ (laid et désagréable)! Le pauvre Candide est _____ (angoissé).

À la fin du conte, Candide décide de rejeter les idées _____ (faux et extrême) de Pangloss et de Martin. À la place, il trouve sa _____ (propre) solution _____ (pratique et réaliste): il faut mener une vie _____ (utile) avec les autres sans penser aux _____ (vain) questions _____ (moral et métaphysique). Ces questions sont _____ (insoluble). «Il faut cultiver notre jardin» est la conclusion _____ (final) de Candide.

B. *Questions*

1. Pourquoi Candide tombe-t-il amoureux de Cunégonde?
2. Pourquoi Candide commence-t-il à mettre en doute «l'optimisme»?
3. Comparez l'attitude de Martin avec celle de Pangloss.
4. Comment Cunégonde a-t-elle changé?
5. À la fin du conte, pourquoi Candide décide-t-il de rejeter les philosophies de Martin et de Pangloss?
6. Quelle est la conclusion de Candide?

II. *Trouvez les* **antonymes** *des mots de la liste 1 dans la liste 2.*

1	2
bon	beau
brillant	coupable
content	courageux
idéaliste	bête
innocent	hypocrite
insupportable	injuste
juste	tolérable
lâche	mauvais
laid	pessimiste
objectif	prémédité
optimiste	réaliste
passionnel	subjectif
sincère	triste

III. *Complétez les phrases avec imagination en employant des* **adjectifs** *variés.*

1. Je crois que la peine de mort est . . .
2. Pendant un procès l'accusé a besoin d'un juge . . . et d'un avocat . . .
3. À mon avis, le système capitaliste est . . .
4. Quand je pense aux injustices actuelles, j'ai l'air . . .
5. Mon écrivain favori est _____ (citez un nom). Je l'aime parce qu'il est . . .
6. Je trouve le mouvement pour la libération des femmes . . .
7. Les annonces publicitaires me rendent . . .
8. Je crois que le mariage est . . .
9. Quand je suis avec mon meilleur ami (ma meilleure amie), j'ai l'air. . .
10. L'actrice (l'acteur) que je préfère est _____ (citez un nom). Je la (le) préfère parce qu'elle (il) est . . .

IV. *Traduisez en français.*

1. Why does he always accuse me?
2. He probably heard the testimony this morning.
3. All men are morally responsible for (*responsable de*) their actions.
4. In my opinion, the suspect was unjustly accused!
5. His lawyer pleaded much better today than yesterday.
6. He easily proved that the defendant was guilty of theft.
7. Is it humanly possible to (*de*) obey all laws?
8. The judge spoke slowly and softly when he pronounced his verdict.
9. She really thinks that her father was unfair.
10. He even questioned the judge!
11. Did the press act (*agir*) more or less reasonably than the president?
12. Who is the worst prisoner in the prison?
13. John is a better juror than Paul.
14. Who has the best lawyer, you or your father?
15. She is more courageous than he.

Sujets de discussion ou de composition.

Employez beaucoup d'adjectifs et d'adverbes dans les réponses.

1. Vous êtes un juré dans un procès célèbre (le procès d'un assassin politique, par exemple). Quelles sont les qualités nécessaires pour être un bon juré?

2. Organisez un débat pour et contre la peine de mort.

3. Décrivez brièvement les petites (ou grandes) injustices qui existent dans votre université.

4. Tout le monde sait que l'injustice n'est pas rare. À votre avis, quelle est la plus grande injustice actuelle? Pourquoi?

5. Si vous avez jamais assisté à (*been present at*) un procès, expliquez-le à toute la classe: le crime; les actions du juge, des avocats, du jury, des témoins; le verdict; etc.

7

Future, conditional, pluperfect; devoir

Chapter 7 at a glance

FUTURE, CONDITIONAL, PLUPERFECT

I. *Mettez les verbes au* **futur** *et au* **conditionnel.**

1. je (voter)
2. tu (applaudir)
3. elle (perdre)
4. nous (faire)
5. vous (être)
6. elles (avoir)

II. *Mettez les verbes au* **futur antérieur** (*future perfect*), *au* **conditionnel passé** *et au* **plus-que-parfait.**

1. je (gagner)
2. tu (mentir)
3. il (attendre)
4. nous (promettre)
5. vous (venir)
6. ils (partir)

III. *Traduisez les verbes en français en employant le* **futur** *ou le* **futur antérieur.**

1. Je suis sûr que notre candidat _____ (will win)!
2. Quand je _____ (am) dix-huit ans, je _____ (will be able) voter aux élections présidentielles.
3. Il _____ (will have lost) l'élection avant la fin de la campagne!

IV. *Traduisez les verbes en français en employant le* **plus-que-parfait,** *le* **conditionnel présent** *ou le* **conditionnel passé.**

1. Si j'étais à votre place, je _____ (would not go).
2. Le public ne savait pas que le président _____ (had already lied) mille fois.
3. Si nous _____ (had done) cela, nous _____ (would have won).

V. *Traduisez les verbes en français en employant le* **conditionnel présent** *ou* **l'imparfait.**

1. Quand le sénateur était jeune, il _____ (would think) toujours à la politique.
2. Tous les candidats ont dit qu'ils _____ (would make) des réformes.

DEVOIR

VI. *Traduisez les verbes en français en employant le verbe* **devoir.**

1. Non, elle n'est pas obligée de voter, mais elle _____ (should) le faire!
2. Ce politicien _____ (used to have to) faire beaucoup de voyages à Washington.
3. Il _____ (had to) déclarer la guerre à cause de la crise politique.
4. Un politicien honnête _____ (should not) accepter de l'argent.

5. Ce journaliste _____ (should not have) écrire cet éditorial injuste.

6. Tiens! Il a refusé cette sinécure! Il _____ (must) être honnête!

7. Le gangster _____ (was to) assassiner le président, mais on l'a arrêté.

VII. *Traduisez les verbes en français en employant les expressions* **être obligé de** + infinitif *ou* **être censé** + infinitive.

1. Il _____ (had to) voter pour son frère.

2. Un politicien dynamique _____ (is not supposed to) dire cela.

Vocabulaire du thème : La Politique

SYSTÈMES

la **démocratie** *democracy*
le **communisme** *communism*
le **socialisme** *socialism*
la **dictature** *dictatorship*
la **monarchie** *monarchy*

le **président** *president*
le **dictateur** *dictator*
le **roi** *king*
le **conseiller** *adviser*

le **ministre** *minister*
le **communiste** *communist*
le **socialiste** *socialist*

le **parti** *party*
le **libéral** *liberal*
le **conservateur** *conservative*
le **réactionnaire** *reactionary*
de **gauche** *leftist*
de **droite** *rightist*

ÉLECTIONS

le **politicien** *politician*
se **jeter dans la politique** *to go into politics*
poser sa candidature *to run for office*
faire de la publicité *to advertise*
embrasser les enfants *to kiss babies*
faire un discours *to make a speech*
être élu *to be elected*

le **programme** *program, platform*
faire des réformes *to make reforms*

maintenir le statu quo *to maintain the status quo*
le **citoyen** *citizen*
le **partisan** *supporter*
applaudir *to applaud*
l' **adversaire** (m) *opponent*
huer *to boo*
avoir le droit de voter *to have the right to vote*

LA CRISE ET LA CORRUPTION

la **crise** *crisis*
le **scandale** *scandal*
le **pot de vin** *bribe*
la **sinécure** *sinecure*
abuser de son autorité *to abuse one's authority*
opprimer *to oppress*
la **manifestation** *demonstration*

démissionner *to resign*

l' **assassin** (m) *assassin*
assassiner *to assassinate*
le **terroriste** *terrorist*
l' **espion** (m) *spy*
espionner *to spy*

Future, conditional, pluperfect_____

Formation of the simple future and conditional

Regular verbs

The simple future and conditional of most verbs are formed by adding the future and conditional endings to the infinitive.

> FUTURE ENDINGS: **-ai, -as, -a, -ons, -ez, -ont**
> CONDITIONAL ENDINGS: **-ais, -ais, -ait, -ions, -iez, -aient**

Note that the conditional and imperfect endings are identical.

<table>
<tr><td colspan="4" align="center">gagner (stem, gagner)</td></tr>
<tr><td align="center">FUTURE</td><td></td><td align="center">CONDITIONAL</td><td></td></tr>
<tr><td>je gagnerai</td><td>I will win</td><td>je gagnerais</td><td>I would win</td></tr>
<tr><td>tu gagneras</td><td></td><td>tu gagnerais</td><td></td></tr>
<tr><td>il
elle } gagnera
on</td><td></td><td>il
elle } gagnerait
on</td><td></td></tr>
<tr><td>nous gagnerons</td><td></td><td>nous gagnerions</td><td></td></tr>
<tr><td>vous gagnerez</td><td></td><td>vous gagneriez</td><td></td></tr>
<tr><td>ils
elles } gagneront</td><td></td><td>ils
elles } gagneraient</td><td></td></tr>
<tr><td colspan="4" align="center">applaudir (stem, applaudir)</td></tr>
<tr><td align="center">j' applaudirai</td><td></td><td align="center">j' applaudirais</td><td></td></tr>
<tr><td colspan="4" align="center">perdre (stem, perdr)</td></tr>
<tr><td align="center">je perdrai</td><td></td><td align="center">je perdrais</td><td></td></tr>
</table>

-er verbs with spelling changes

Regular **-er** verbs with certain endings undergo spelling changes before adding the future and conditional endings.

1. Verbs ending in **e** + *consonant* + **er** (e.g., **mener, élever, peser**) change e to è: **je mènerai, je mènerais; nous élèverons, nous élèverions.**

2. Verbs ending in **-eler** and **-eter** (e.g., **appeler, jeter**) double the **l** and the **t**: **j'appellerai, j'appellerais; elles jetteront, elles jetteraient.**
   Note that **acheter** and **geler** change **e** to **è** instead of doubling the **l** and **t**: **j'achèterai, j'achèterais; nous gèlerons, nous gèlerions.**

3. Verbs ending in **-yer** (e.g., **employer, envoyer, essayer, essuyer, payer**) change **y** to **i**: **j'emploierai, j'emploierais; nous paierons, nous paierions.**
   Verbs ending in **-ayer** may retain the **y**: **je paierai, je payerai.**

Irregular verbs

Many common verbs have unusual future and conditional stems.

aller: **j'irai, j'irais**
avoir: **j'aurai, j'aurais**
courir: **je courrai, je courrais**
devoir: **je devrai, je devrais**
être: **je serai, je serais**
recevoir: **je recevrai, je recevrais**
savoir: **je saurai, je saurais**
tenir: **je tiendrai, je tiendrais**

venir: **je viendrai, je viendrais**
voir: **je verrai, je verrais**
faire: **je ferai, je ferais**
falloir: **il faudra, il faudrait**
mourir: **je mourrai, je mourrais**
pleuvoir: **il pleuvra, il pleuvrait**
pouvoir: **je pourrai, je pourrais**
vouloir: **je voudrai, je voudrais**

EXERCICE

Complétez au **futur** *et au* **conditionnel.**

1. je (être)
2. nous (aller)
3. elle (perdre)
4. nous (essayer)
5. ils (participer)
6. elle (mener)
7. ils (appeler)
8. nous (savoir)
9. vous (mener)

10. je (diriger)
11. il (jeter)
12. je (voir)
13. je (acheter)
14. tu (venir)
15. elle (huer)
16. nous (voter)
17. elle (mourir)
18. nous (devoir)

Formation of the future perfect, past conditional, and pluperfect

Like the **passé composé,** these three tenses are compound tenses, composed of an auxiliary verb **(avoir** or **être)** and a past participle.

COMPOUND TENSE	TENSE OF AUXILIARY	
future perfect **(futur antérieur)**	future	
past conditional **(conditionnel passé)**	conditional	+ *past participle*
pluperfect **(plus-que-parfait)**	imperfect	

future perfect	**j'aurai voté** / **elle sera partie**	*I will have voted* / *she will have left*
past conditional	**j'aurais voté** / **elle serait partie**	*I would have voted* / *she would have left*
pluperfect	**j'avais voté** / **elle était partie**	*I had voted* / *she had left*

EXERCICE

Complétez au **futur antérieur,** *au* **conditionnel passé** *et au* **plus-que-parfait.**

1. nous (opprimer)
2. elles (partir)
3. je (venir)
4. il (rendre)
5. tu (promettre)

6. ils (devenir)
7. je (devoir)
8. vous (faire)
9. elle (aller)
10. il (applaudir)

Use of the simple future and future perfect

Future action

1. The future tenses express future action. The French simple future tense is the equivalent of the English future *will* + verb.

> **Je ne pourrai pas voter pour le candidat libéral.**
> I will not be able to vote for the liberal candidate.
>
> **Elles parleront politique toute la soirée!**
> They'll talk politics all evening!

2. The future perfect corresponds to the English form *will have* + past participle.

> **Il aura fait dix discours en une journée!**
> He will have made ten speeches in one day!
>
> **Le président sera parti pour Paris à neuf heures.**
> The President will have left for Paris at nine o'clock.

3. The immediate future in French is often expressed by **aller** + *infinitive.*

> **Il va bientôt faire son discours.**
> He's soon going to make his speech.

After quand, lorsque, dès que, aussitôt que, tant que

The future tenses must be used after **quand** and **lorsque** (*when*), **dès que** and **aussitôt que** (*as soon as*), and **tant que** (*as long as*) in subordinate clauses, if a future idea is implied. This tense usage differs from English.

> **Dès qu'elle descendra de l'avion, je prendrai la photo.**
> As soon as she gets off the airplane, I will take the picture.
>
> **Quand il sera prêt, il annoncera sa décision.**
> When he's ready, he'll announce his decision.

Quand il sera de retour, téléphonez-moi.
When he's back, call me.

Il prendra des vacances aussitôt qu'il aura démissionné.
He will go on vacation as soon as he has resigned.

Ce politicien continuera à parler tant que vous l'écouterez!
This politician will continue to talk as long as you listen to him!

Note that the main verb in such sentences will be in either the simple future or imperative.

EXERCICE

Mettez les verbes entre parenthèses au **futur** *et traduisez les phrases en anglais.*

1. Silence! Le candidat libéral _____ (prononcer) son discours!
2. Quand je _____ (être) président, je _____ (améliorer) la condition sociale de tous nos citoyens!
3. Je _____ (abolir) la pauvreté et la misère!
4. Je _____ (assurer) la stabilité du franc!
5. Je _____ (maintenir) la paix!
6. Quand je _____ (tenir)[1] mes promesses, vous _____ (avoir) confiance en moi!
7. En réalité, dès qu'il _____ (être) élu, il _____ (abuser de) son autorité.
8. Quand on _____ (aller) le voir dans son bureau, il _____ (avoir) l'air de ne rien comprendre.
9. Lorsqu'il _____ (terminer)[1] ce projet, il _____ (être) probablement riche.
10. Aussitôt qu'il _____ (prendre)[1] sa retraite, il _____ (acheter) un château!

Use of the pluperfect

The pluperfect is used to indicate an action that took place before another past action. It is aptly described by its French name, le **plus-que-parfait**: more in the past than the past. Its English equivalent is either the pluperfect *had* + past participle (*I had spoken*), or the past tense (*I spoke*).

Il ne savait pas qu'elle avait déjà voté.
He didn't know that she had already voted.

Ne vous ai-je pas dit qu'elle était venue?
Didn't I tell you that she had come?
Didn't I tell you that she came?

French usage regarding verb tenses is generally more rigid and precise than English usage; thus the French pluperfect has two possible English equivalents.

------

[1] Use the future perfect.

EXERCICES

Mettez les verbes entre parenthèses au **plus-que parfait** *et traduisez les phrases en anglais.*

1. Ils se sont demandé comment elles _____ (arriver) à cette conclusion.
2. Je ne savais pas que vous me _____ (trouver) si charmant!
3. Le professeur a déclaré que la crise économique _____ (commencer) en Belgique.
4. Le maire a dit que son parti le _____ (blâmer) pour avoir perdu l'élection.
5. Comment pouvaient-ils savoir que l'assassinat _____ (avoir) lieu hier soir à cinq heures?
6. Il a déclaré tristement que sa meilleure amie _____ (ne pas revenir).
7. Le député a juré qu'il _____ (ne pas accepter) le pot de vin!
8. Elle ne savait pas que le ministre _____ (écrire) un livre sur l'art.
9. Comment! Vous a-t-il avoué qu'on le _____ (huer)?
10. Il a dit qu'elle _____ (devenir) membre du parti communiste en 1961.

Use of the conditional

Conditional sentences

1. The conditional tenses are used to indicate a possible or hypothetical fact that is the result of a condition. Their English equivalents are *would* + verb (the simple conditional: *I would vote*) and *would have* + past participle (the past conditional: *I would have voted*).

> **Si j'étais à votre place, je poserais ma candidature.**
> If I were you, I would run for office.

> **Si le président avait consulté ses conseillers, il n'aurait pas déclaré la guerre.**
> If the President had consulted his advisers, he would not have declared war.

2. The conditional tenses are used in conditional sentences (sentences containing *if*-clauses). The following table contains the most common tense sequences used in conditional sentences. The same tense sequences exist in English.

If-CLAUSE	MAIN CLAUSE
present	present, future, imperative
imperfect	present conditional
pluperfect	past conditional

> **Si elle entre, je sors!**
> If she enters, I leave!

Si elle est élue, elle maintiendra le statu quo.
If she is elected, she will maintain the status quo.

Si ce candidat vous gêne tellement, ne l'écoutez pas!
If this candidate bothers you so much, don't listen to him!

S'il lisait *L'Express*, il serait au courant des affaires politiques.
If he read *L'Express*, he would be up-to-date on political affairs.

Si elle avait regardé la télévision, elle aurait su les résultats.
If she had watched television, she would have known the results.

Note that the conditional tenses are used in the main clause, but not in the *if*-clause.

The future of the past

The conditional also expresses the future of the past.

Future of the present: **Il dit qu'il fera un compromis.**
He says he will compromise.

Future of the past: **Il a dit qu'il ferait un compromis.**
He said he would compromise.

Here French and English usage corresponds.

The conditional of politeness

The conditional is used to attenuate questions and requests by making them more courteous and polite.

Present: **Je veux cinquante dollars, papa.**
I want fifty dollars, Dad.

Conditional: **Je voudrais cinquante dollars, papa.**
I would like fifty dollars, Dad.

EXERCICES

1. *Mettez les verbes entre parenthèses au* **temps convenable.**

Si j'étais un réactionnaire fanatique, je _____ (se jeter) dans la politique.
Je _____ (poser) ma candidature comme président et, bien sûr, je _____
(être) élu! Je _____ (commencer) tout de suite un programme de réforme
morale. Je _____ (interdire: *to ban*), par exemple, le maquillage aux
femmes, les barbes et les cheveux longs aux hommes, le chewing gum aux
enfants, et les cigarettes et l'alcool à tout le monde! Je _____ (défendre:
to forbid) même les relations amoureuses! Le vice et le crime _____
(disparaître). La police ne _____ (avoir) rien à faire. La vie _____ (être)
peut-être très monotone, mais cela n' _____ (avoir) aucune importance.

2. *Mettez les verbes entre parenthèses au* **temps convenable.**

1. Si vous en avez l'occasion, _____ (venir) me voir.
2. Si le candidat avait embrassé plus d'enfants, il _____ (gagner).
3. Elle serait au courant de la politique internationale si elle _____ (lire) *Le Monde.*
4. Il _____ (être) en liberté s'il n'abusait pas de son autorité.
5. Il _____ (ne pas déclarer) la guerre s'il avait suivi les conseils de ses ministres.
6. Si les journalistes _____ (vouloir) une interview, ne l'accordez pas!
7. Le candidat de gauche _____ (gagner) si la crise économique avait été plus sévère.
8. Les femmes n'auraient pas aujourd'hui le droit de voter si elles _____ (ne pas se révolter) hier.
9. Je gagnerai sûrement si je _____ (faire) de la publicité!
10. On le _____ (prendre) plus au sérieux s'il était plus honnête et réaliste.

3. *Mettez les phrases au* **passé.**

modèle: De Gaulle dit qu'il sera président de la République.
   De Gaulle a dit qu'il serait président de la République.

1. Il dit qu'un dictateur opprimera le peuple.
2. Elle déclare brusquement que le candidat ne fera pas son discours.
3. Il dit que sa femme se jettera dans la politique.
4. Il affirme qu'il n'acceptera pas de pots de vin.
5. Elle dit qu'il détestera cette sinécure.

Related expressions

The imperfect and conditional "would"

Both the imperfect and conditional tenses may be translated by *would* in English. If *used to*, indicating a customary or repeated action, can be substituted for *would*, the imperfect tense is called for. If not, the conditional tense is used.

Quand j'avais dix-sept ans, je lisais le journal satirique *Le Canard enchaîné* toutes les semaines.
When I was seventeen, I would (used to) read the satirical newspaper *Le Canard enchaîné* every week.

Si vous étiez plus honnête, je voterais pour vous.
If you were more honest, I would vote for you.

EXERCICE

Traduisez en français les verbes entre parenthèses.

1. Quand il était ministre, il _____ (would work) tous les jours.
2. Je _____ (would accept) ce point de vue s'il était plus cohérent!

3. Quand il était plus jeune, il _____ (would vote) toujours pour les politiciens démocrates.

4. Avant chacune de ses campagnes, il _____ (would promise) de faire des réformes.

5. _____ (Would you like) voter pour ce beau candidat républicain?

Devoir

The very common verb **devoir** has multiple meanings. When followed by an infinitive, it expresses one of three notions: necessity or moral obligation, probability, or supposition. When used with a direct object, it means *to owe*.

Necessity or moral obligation

The expression of necessity or moral obligation is perhaps the most common function of **devoir.** The tenses are translated variously.

Present: must, have to

> **Chéri, vous devez refuser immédiatement ce pot de vin!**
> Dear, you must refuse that bribe at once!
> *or:* Dear, you have to refuse that bribe at once!

Imperfect: had to,[2] used to have to

> **Le parti républicain devait travailler plus dur pour remporter la victoire.**
> The Republican Party had to work harder to win.
>
> **Quand j'étais jeune, je devais faire mon lit tous les matins.**
> When I was young, I used to have to make my bed every morning.

Passé composé: had to[2]

> **J'ai dû prendre l'avion parce que j'ai raté le train.**
> I had to take the plane because I missed the train.
>
> **À cause de la crise politique, le président a dû prononcer un discours à la télévision.**
> Because of the political crisis, the President had to make a speech on television.

---

[2] Whether the imperfect or the passé composé is used to render *had to* depends on the use of *had to* in the sentence. See Chapter 4, pp. 80–82.

Present conditional: *should, ought to*

M. le Président, vous devriez agir tout de suite!
Mr. President, you should act right away!

Henri, vous devriez avoir honte!
Henry, you ought to be ashamed!

Past conditional: *should have, ought to have*

J'aurais dû l'avouer plus tôt. Je suis un espion!
I should have admitted it sooner. I'm a spy!

Future: *will have to*

Ils devront adopter le programme du parti.
They will have to adopt the party platform.

EXERCICE

Traduisez en français les verbes entre parenthèses en employant le verbe **devoir.**

1. Les politiciens _____ (must) se tenir au courant des activités de l'opposition.
2. Il _____ (should have) embrasser plus d'enfants!
3. Le président _____ (has to) servir de modèle moral.
4. Le roi _____ (had to) discuter ce problème avec ses conseillers pendant cinq heures.
5. _____ (Should they) servir des hamburgers à la reine?
6. Elle _____ (had to) accorder une interview à la presse tous les jours.
7. Nous _____ (should) faire plus de compromis.
8. Le président _____ (will have to) rétablir la confiance publique.
9. Elle _____ (must) commencer à se créer une nouvelle image.
10. Vous _____ (should not have) le dire!
11. Ses partisans _____ (should) faire de la publicité.
12. _____ (Must you) promettre des choses tout à fait impossibles?
13. Vous _____ (should have) enlever ce ridicule chapeau.
14. Si le dictateur continue à opprimer le peuple, nous _____ (will have to) nous révolter!
15. On _____ (should) toujours applaudir un politicien honnête.

Probability

Devoir commonly expresses probability in three tenses.

Present: *must* meaning *is probably*

Il doit être communiste!
He must be a Communist!
or: He's probably a Communist!

Imperfect: **must have** meaning *was probably, probably used to*

Ses partisans devaient contribuer beaucoup à sa campagne.
His supporters probably used to contribute a lot to his campaign.

Le sénateur devait avoir soixante-dix ans quand il est mort.
The senator must have been (was probably) seventy when he died.

Passé composé: **must have** meaning *have (has) probably*

Le candidat est en retard. Il a dû manquer l'avion.
The candidate is late. He must have (has probably) missed the plane.

EXERCICE

Traduisez en français les verbes entre parenthèses en employant le verbe **devoir.**

1. D'après les résultats, je _____ (must have) gagner!
2. Ils _____ (are probably) être républicains!
3. Elle _____ (must have) se moquer des candidats radicaux tout le temps.
4. Le président a l'air anxieux. Il _____ (has probably) déclarer la guerre!
5. Elle _____ (must) être très contente.
6. Ils _____ (probably used to) voter pour des réactionnaires.

Supposition

Devoir commonly expresses supposition in two tenses.

Present: meaning *am (is, are) supposed to*

Le ministre doit arriver sous peu.
The minister is (supposed) to arrive very soon.

Imperfect: meaning *was (were) supposed to*

Giscard devait prononcer son discours, mais il a commencé à pleuvoir.
Giscard was supposed to make his speech, but it began to rain.

EXERCICE

Traduisez en français les verbes entre parenthèses en employant le verbe **devoir.**

1. Je _____ (was supposed to) voter à la mairie du quartier.
2. Nous _____ (were to) nous lever à cinq heures, mais notre réveille-matin n'a pas sonné.
3. _____ (Are they to) arriver les premiers à la réunion politique?

4. Le professeur _____ (was supposed to) faire une conférence sur les rapports entre l'Église et l'État.

5. Comment _____ (is he to) gagner quand il refuse de discuter le programme de l'opposition?

Meaning to owe

Devoir means *to owe* when it is used with a direct object.

> **Malheureusement, le candidat doit trop d'argent.**
> Unfortunately, the candidate owes too much money.
> **Vous lui devez beaucoup de reconnaissance.**
> You owe him a lot of gratitude.

Related expressions

Être obligé de + infinitive: *to be obliged to, to have to, must*

> **Elle a été obligée de dire à son mari qu'il avait perdu l'élection.**
> She was obliged to tell her husband that he had lost the election.

> **Ils seront obligés de passer la nuit à la belle étoile.**
> They will have to sleep under the stars.

Être obligé de is the equivalent of **devoir** expressing necessity or moral obligation.

Être censé + infinitive: *to be supposed to*

> **Ils sont censés être ici maintenant!**
> They are supposed to be here now!

Être censé is the equivalent of **devoir** expressing supposition.

EXERCICE

Remplacez le verbe **devoir** *par la forme convenable de* **être censé** *ou de* **être obligé de.**

1. Elle devait arriver à huit heures, mais son avion a eu du retard.

2. Mon professeur a insisté! Je dois regarder ce programme à la télévision!

3. Comment ses collègues devaient-ils savoir que le sénateur était un espion?

4. Le candidat a dû passer la nuit à l'aéroport parce qu'il neigeait trop.

5. Il devait faire un discours, mais il est tombé malade.

6. À mon avis, on doit rendre visite à sa mère quand elle est malade.

7. Oui, nous sommes toujours amies. En fait, elle devait me téléphoner ce soir.

8. Est-ce que je dois faire le choix entre le socialisme et la démocratie?

9. Après des manifestations violentes, le gouvernement a dû démissionner.

10. Avez-vous vu Jean récemment? —Non, mais je dois le voir demain.

Exercices d'ensemble

I. *Complétez les phrases avec imagination en employant le vocabulaire du thème.*

    1. Le candidat s'est étonné quand ses partisans . . .

    2. Si les communistes gagnent l'élection, je suis sûr que . . .

    3. Idiot! Si vous étiez un vrai dictateur, vous . . .

    4. Si ce candidat malhonnête devient ministre, je . . .

    5. Les citoyens ne veulent pas de réformes. Le président sera obligé de . . .

    6. Je crois que Jean est un espion parce qu'il . . .

    7. Si ce terroriste avait vraiment du courage, il . . .

    8. Le candidat a l'air triste parce que . . .

    9. Mon vieux, vous êtes un homme sérieux et intelligent. Vous devriez . . .

    10. Si on m'offrait un pot de vin, je . . .

II. *Traduisez en français.*

    1. When will you vote?

    2. If he had been honest, he would have denounced the scandal.

    3. If I were less pessimistic, I would go into politics.

    4. The demonstration will begin as soon as the conservative candidate has given his speech.

    5. If he had become a minister, he would have maintained the status quo.

    6. The citizens will applaud him when he announces some reforms.

    7. He will be a republican as long as he is rich.

    8. He will stop (*cesser de*) kissing babies as soon as he is elected.

    9. The ministers will resign when the President has declared war.

    10. The leftist candidate will be surprised if his supporters begin to boo!

    11. If the party adopts this platform, it will probably lose the election.

    12. If the spy leaves, follow him!

III. *Traduisez en français en employant le verbe* **devoir.**

    1. Women should have had the right to vote.

    2. The assassin was to act (*agir*) before the election.

    3. Those reactionaries must have oppressed the people!

    4. We really should vote against the Communists!

    5. Their opponents must be furious.

    6. They shouldn't have booed him.

    7. She owes me fifty dollars.

8. The Democratic candidate should have created a better image.
9. A liberal president should not maintain the status quo.
10. That old man must have been honest.

Sujets de discussion ou de composition

1. Si vous étiez président, que feriez-vous au cours d'une journée typique?

2. Imaginez que vous êtes un politicien qui vient de perdre une élection. Qu'est-ce que vous auriez dû faire pour gagner?

3. Le terrorisme politique est-il jamais justifié? Si non, pourquoi pas? Si oui, dans quelles circonstances?

4. Pourquoi voudriez-vous être politicien? Pourquoi pas?

5. Imaginez que vous êtes un des personnages suivants, et que vous vous présentez comme candidat présidentiel dans un pays démocratique. Écrivez un discours et prononcez-le devant la classe.
   a. un communiste enragé
   b. un conservateur rusé
   c. une femme libérée
   d. un réformateur sincère mais naïf
   e. un militaire qui rêve de devenir dictateur
   f. un fou

8

Relative pronouns and demonstratives

Chapter 8 at a glance

RELATIVE PRONOUNS

I. *Remplacez les tirets par* **qui** *ou* **que.**

1. Comment! Nous avons perdu les chèques de voyage _____ étaient dans vos valises?
2. Voilà la belle étrangère _____ nous avons déjà vue à Versailles.

II. *Remplacez les tirets par* **ce qui** *ou* **ce que.**

1. Expliquez-nous _____ vous avez vu à Haïti.
2. Quel gourmand! La cuisine française est tout _____ l'intéresse!

III. *Remplacez les tirets par* **qui** *ou une forme de* **lequel.**

1. Je vous présente Babette, la femme avec _____ je compte visiter le Sénégal.
2. Il est sorti de la banque à côté de _____ se trouvait l'agence de voyages.

IV. *Remplacez les tirets par* **où** *ou* **quoi.**

1. Je suis fatiguée et il n'y a rien sur _____ je puisse m'asseoir!
2. Elle m'a dit «Bonjour» au moment _____ elle m'a vu.

V. *Remplacez les tirets par* **dont** *ou* **ce dont.**

1. Voici le touriste désagréable _____ je parlais.
2. C'est _____ il est si fier!

VI. *Traduisez en français les mots entre parenthèses en employant le* **pronom interrogatif** *ou le pronom* **relatif** *convenable.*

1. Il est francophone? _____ (What) cela signifie?
2. Voici _____ (what) on a trouvé dans sa chambre!
3. Voilà cette femme bizarre _____ (whom) j'ai rencontrée au Louvre.
4. _____ (Whom) avez-vous vu pendant les vacances?

VII. *Remplacez les tirets par* **n'importe qui** *ou* **n'importe quoi.**

1. Idiot! _____ pourrait lire cette carte!
2. Ce francophile ferait _____ pour visiter la Martinique.

DEMONSTRATIVES

VIII. *Remplacez les tirets par* **ce, cet, cette** *ou* **ces.** *Employez* **-ci** *et* **-là** *s'il y a lieu.*

1. _____ dame
2. _____ étranger
3. _____ livre
4. _____ maisons
5. _____ coutumes nous sont familières tandis que _____ coutumes nous sont étrangères.

IX. *Remplacez les tirets par* **celui, celle, ceux** *ou* **celles.** *Employez* **-ci** *ou* **-là** *s'il y a lieu.*

1. _____ qui a l'esprit ouvert n'aura pas de problèmes.
2. Geneviève et Marguerite sont des touristes opposées; _____ est gentille tandis que _____ est insolente!
3. Quelles photos préférez-vous, _____ sur la carte postale ou _____ de Marc?

X. *Remplacez les tirets par* **ceci** *ou* **cela (ça).**

1. _____ m'est égal.
2. Faisons un échange! Si vous me donnez _____, je vous donne _____!

XI. *Remplacez les tirets par* **ce, il, elle, ils** *ou* **elles.**

1. Sont- _____ Françaises ou Canadiennes?
2. _____ est une excursion qu'il faut faire!
3. _____ sont les pays exotiques dont nous avons parlé.

XII. *Remplacez le premier tiret par* **c'est** *ou* **il est** *et le deuxième par* **à** *ou* **de.**

1. _____ intéressant _____ comparer deux cultures différentes.
2. Vous êtes-vous jamais senti tout seul? —Oui, et _____ difficile _____ supporter!

XIII. *Complétez en traduisant l'expression entre parenthèses.*

1. Nous avons rendu visite à nos parents _____ (*that morning*).
2. Nous passons _____ (*this month*) à la Guadeloupe.
3. Il est parti _____ (*the next day*).
4. Moi, je pars _____ (*tomorrow*).

Vocabulaire du thème: Le Voyage à l'étranger

TOURISTES ET VOYAGEURS
PRÉPARATIFS

rêver de *to dream of*	le **passeport** *passport*
faire des projets *to make plans*	**faire les préparatifs** *to make prepara-*
l' **agence de voyages** (f) *travel bureau*	*tions*
l' **agent de voyages** (m) *travel agent*	**faire la malle, la valise** *to pack the*
le **chèque de voyage** *traveler's check*	*trunk, the suitcase*

LA DOUANE

passer la douane *to pass through customs*	**fouiller** *to search (a person, a suitcase, etc.)*
le **douanier** *customs officer*	

faire un voyage *to take a trip*
faire une excursion accompagnée *to make a guided tour*
prendre des photos *to take pictures*
rendre visite à *to visit (a person)*
visiter *to visit (a place)*

l' appareil (appareil-photo) (m) *camera*
la carte *map, menu*
le guide *guide, guidebook*
le séjour *stay*
le souvenir *souvenir*

ÉTRANGERS ET INDIGÈNES

l' étranger (m) *foreigner*

l' indigène (m, f) *native*

ASPECTS POSITIFS

agréable *pleasant*
complaisant *accommodating*
avoir l'esprit ouvert *to have an open mind*
accueillir chaleureusement *to welcome warmly*
être bien reçu *to be well received*

s' adapter aux coutumes (aux habitudes) d'un peuple *to adapt to the customs (habits) of a people*
se débrouiller *to get along, to manage*
se fier à *to trust*
se sentir à l'aise *to feel at ease*

ASPECTS NÉGATIFS

désagréable *unpleasant*
dépaysé *lost, homesick*
exigeant *demanding*
hautain *condescending*
être mal reçu *to be badly received*

manquer d'égards envers quelqu'un *to be inconsiderate of someone*
se méfier de *to mistrust*
se sentir mal à l'aise, dépaysé, etc. *to feel ill at ease, lost, etc.*

Relative pronouns

A relative pronoun is a word that joins (relative = relates) a noun or pronoun to a subordinate clause. A subordinate clause that begins with a relative pronoun is called a relative clause. The English relatives are *who, whom, whose, that, which, what.*

> **L'étudiant qui a perdu son passeport a l'air dépaysé.**
> The student who lost his passport seems lost.
>
> > *relative clause:* **qui a perdu son passeport**
>
> **L'étranger que j'ai rencontré à Paris s'appelle Paul.**
> The foreigner whom I met in Paris is named Paul.
>
> > *relative clause:* **que j'ai rencontré à Paris**

The noun or pronoun that precedes the relative pronoun, and to which the relative pronoun refers, is called the antecedent. In the above examples,

l'étudiant and **l'étranger** are antecedents of **qui** and **que** respectively. Relative pronouns may be used as the subject or direct object of a relative clause, or as the object of a preposition.

Relatives used as subject or direct object of a relative clause

ANTECEDENT	SUBJECT		DIRECT OBJECT	
PERSON	qui	*who*	que[1]	*whom*
THINGS	qui	*that, which*	que[1]	*that, which*
INDETERMINATE	ce qui	*what*	ce que[1]	*what*

To determine whether a relative pronoun is the subject or the direct object of a relative clause, it is first necessary to recognize the verb of the relative clause, as distinguished from that of the main clause.

Sentence 1: **Le touriste qui habite chez nous vient de la Martinique.**
The tourist who lives at our house comes from Martinique.

Sentence 2: **L'île que nous avons explorée était très exotique.**
The island that we explored was very exotic.

In these two sentences, the verbs in the relative clauses are **habite** and **avons explorée.** Knowing this, one must then determine whether the relative pronouns are used as subject or direct object of these verbs. In sentence 1, **qui** is the subject of the verb **habite.** In sentence 2, **que** is the direct object of the verb **avons explorée** (whose subject is **nous**).

Qui *and* que

Qui is the subject and **que** is the direct object, when the antecedent is a person or a specified thing.

Comment s'appelle la jeune fille qui nous a accueillis?
What is the name of the girl who welcomed us?

L'agent de voyages qui a tout arrangé était compétent.
The travel agent who arranged everything was competent.

Tahiti est l'île que je trouve la plus charmante.
Tahiti is the island (that) I find the most charming.

Voilà un pays que j'aimerais visiter!
There's a country (that) I would like to visit!

---

[1] **Que** changes to **qu'** before a vowel or mute **h.**

Note that although the direct object relative pronoun is often omitted in English, its counterpart **que** must always be used in French.

Ce qui *and* ce que

Ce qui is the subject and **ce que** is the direct object when the antecedent is indeterminate: that is, something other than a person or a specified thing (e.g., an idea or an unspecified thing).

> **Dites-moi tout de suite ce qui vous gêne!**
> Tell me right away what is bothering you!
>
> **Le guide ne sait pas ce que les touristes veulent visiter.**
> The guide doesn't know what the tourists want to visit.

Note that **tout ce qui** and **tout ce que** must be used to mean *all that* or *everything that*.

> **L'étude de la poésie africaine est tout ce qui l'intéresse.**
> The study of African poetry is all that interests her.
>
> **Montrez-moi tout ce que vous avez acheté pendant votre voyage.**
> Show me everything that you bought during your trip.

EXERCICE

Remplacez les tirets par **qui, que, (tout) ce qui** *ou* **(tout) ce que.**

1. Comment s'appelle cet étranger bizarre _____ vient d'entrer?
2. L'étudiante _____ parle si bien français est africaine.
3. Savez-vous _____ nous allons faire en Suisse?
4. Les gens _____ parlent deux langues sont bilingues.
5. L'hôtel _____ elle a recommandé est vraiment remarquable!
6. Dites-moi _____ vous avez vu au Canada!
7. C'est un poète célèbre _____ est aussi un homme politique au Sénégal.
8. Cette touriste ne peut pas faire _____ vous avez fait parce qu'elle ne passe qu'une semaine à Paris.
9. Le pays _____ il choisira sera certainement un pays francophone (*French-speaking*).
10. Où avez-vous mis la carte _____ je vous ai donnée?

Relatives used with prepositions

There are two groups of relatives that are used with prepositions: one group is used with all prepositions and the other only with the preposition **de.**

Relatives used with prepositions

ANTECEDENT	RELATIVE	
PERSON	qui, lequel[2]	*whom*
THING	lequel[2]	*which*
INDETERMINATE	quoi	*what, which*
EXPRESSION OF TIME		
OR PLACE	où	*where*

1. **Qui** is ordinarily used to refer to persons. (**Lequel** is also correct, but is much less frequently used.) **Lequel** is used to refer to specified things.

> **Jean est le touriste avec qui (lequel) ma sœur est sortie.**
> John is the tourist my sister has gone out with.

> **Voici la fiche sur laquelle il a écrit son nom.**
> Here's the form he wrote his name on.

The preposition often ends the sentence in English, but almost never does so in French.

2. **Quoi** is used to refer to something indeterminate: something other than persons or specified things (e.g., ideas or unspecified things).

> **Il a appris le français, après quoi il s'est senti plus à l'aise.**
> He learned French, after which he felt more at ease.

> **Je ne comprends pas avec quoi elle compte acheter ces souvenirs!**
> I don't understand what she intends to buy these souvenirs with!

> **Ce à quoi je m'intéresse ne vous regarde pas!**
> What I'm interested in is none of your business!

Note that **ce** + *preposition* + **quoi** is used to begin a sentence.

> **Ce à quoi je pense n'est pas agréable.**
> What I'm thinking about isn't pleasant.

3. The relative **où** is often used after expressions of time and place:

au moment où   le jour où
la semaine où   la maison où
le pays où

> **Sa vie a changé le jour où elle est arrivée en France.**
> Her life changed the day she arrived in France.

---

[2] The form used—**lequel, laquelle, lesquels,** or **lesquelles**—depends on the number and gender of the antecedent. The forms contract normally with the prepositions **à** and **de: auquel, desquelles,** etc.

Le pays où nous allons passer nos vacances est un pays francophone.
The country where we are going to spend our vacation is a French-speaking country.

Note that the conjunction **quand** is not a relative and cannot be used after expressions of time.

EXERCICE

Remplacez les tirets par **qui, lequel (laquelle,** *etc.***), quoi** *ou* **où.**

1. Je me suis sentie libre le jour _____ j'ai quitté ce pays étranger.
2. Ces touristes à _____ je viens de parler ont l'air agréables.
3. Les habitants du village _____ nous avons passé la nuit manquaient d'égards envers nous.
4. Les indigènes à _____ j'ai rendu visite n'ont pas compris mon accent.
5. Les Français avec_____ j'ai dîné ont commandé des escargots formidables!
6. Je ne comprends pas avec _____ il compte ouvrir ses valises!
7. Nous avons senti une odeur délicieuse au moment _____ nous sommes entrés dans ce restaurant français.
8. Elle a passé la douane, après _____ sa famille l'a accueillie.
9. Voici l'autocar (*bus*) dans _____ nous allons faire notre excursion accompagnée.
10. Ce guide n'était pas si hautain à l'époque _____ je l'ai connu!
11. L'étranger vous a-t-il dit à _____ il s'intéresse?
12. Elle a perdu l'appareil avec_____ elle avait pris de si merveilleuses photos!

Relatives **dont** *and* **ce dont**

ANTECEDENT	RELATIVE	
PERSON	dont	*of whom, whom, whose*
THING	dont	*of which, which, that, whose*
INDETERMINATE	ce dont	*of which, what*

The relatives **dont** and **ce dont** are generally used in two cases: with verbs and verbal expressions ending in **de,** and with the possessive construction.

1. Verbs and expressions ending in **de:**

parler de	rêver de
se méfier de	avoir besoin de
avoir envie de	être content de, etc.
il s'agit de	

Dont refers to persons or specified things, and **ce dont** to something indeterminate: something other than persons or specified things (e.g., ideas or unspecified things).

> **Voici l'étranger mystérieux dont elle se méfie.**
> Here is the mysterious foreigner (whom) she mistrusts.
>
> **Avez-vous trouvé la carte dont j'ai besoin?**
> Have you found the map (that) I need?
>
> **C'est ce dont je suis si fier!**
> That's what I'm so proud of!

a. Keep in mind that the preposition **de** in French verbal expressions often has no specific equivalent in English: **avoir besoin de,** to need; **se méfier de,** to distrust.

b. **De quoi** replaces **ce dont** in statements following the verbs **comprendre, demander, dire,** and **savoir.** Such statements are called indirect questions.

> **Il m'a demandé de quoi j'avais besoin à la plage.**
> He asked me what I needed at the beach.
>
> **Dites-moi de quoi l'agent de voyages vous a parlé.**
> Tell me what the travel agent spoke to you about.

c. The relative **dont** must follow its antecedent immediately. If a prepositional phrase follows the antecedent, the expressions **de qui** (for persons) or **de + lequel** (for things) must be used.

> **Tout à coup l'arbre au pied duquel je me reposais est tombé.**
> Suddenly the tree at the foot of which I was resting fell down.
>
> **On a arrêté le touriste dans la malle de qui on a trouvé des drogues.**
> They arrested the tourist in whose trunk they found drugs.

2. The possessive construction: **dont** meaning *whose*

> *Sentence* 1: **La jeune touriste dont les valises étaient lourdes marchait lentement.**
> The young tourist whose suitcases were heavy was walking slowly.
>
> *Sentence* 2: **Mon ami dont le père est douanier est d'origine africaine.**
> My friend whose father is a customs official is of African origin.
>
> *Sentence* 3: **Le guide dont j'ai remarqué la mauvaise humeur gênait tout le monde.**
> The guide whose bad mood I noticed bothered everybody.

Sentence 4:   **L'amie dont j'ai cassé l'appareil s'est fâchée.**
The friend whose camera I broke got angry.

Note the position of **dont** and *whose* in the above sentences. In sentences 1 and 2, **dont** and *whose* are both immediately followed by the subject of the relative clause. In sentences 3 and 4, however, though **dont** is again immediately followed by the subject of the relative clause, *whose* is followed by the direct object.

> **Dont** is always immediately followed by the subject of the relative clause.

As a practical guide, substitute *of whom* or *of which* for *whose*; the resulting word order will always be correct.

The friend whose camera I broke got angry.
The friend of whom I broke the camera got angry.
L'ami dont j'ai cassé l'appareil s'est fâché.

EXERCICES

1. *Traduisez en français les mots entre parenthèses.*

   1. Cet étranger n'a pas compris _____ (*what the guide was talking about*).
   2. Montrez-moi les photos _____ (*that you're so proud of*).
   3. L'indigène _____ (*next to whom*) j'étais assis m'a invité chez lui.
   4. Je me méfie des touristes_____ (*whose attitude is condescending*).
   5. Voici le type _____ (*whose car we are going to take*).
   6. Oui, c'est précisément _____ (*what I'm afraid of*)!
   7. Voici les voyageurs _____ (*in whose suitcases*) le douanier a trouvé de la contrebande.
   8. Cherchez l'étranger _____ (*whose passport we found*).
   9. C'est un voyage _____ (*that I have dreamed of*).
  10. J'ai demandé à l'agent de voyages _____ (*what I needed*) pour mon voyage.

2. *Remplacez les tirets par* **qui, que, lequel, quoi, où, dont, ce dont** *ou* **de quoi.**

   1. Marie travaillait dans un bureau _____ elle s'ennuyait terriblement.
   2. Sa mère lui a suggéré un voyage aux États-Unis _____ habitaient son oncle et sa tante.
   3. Marie a décidé de faire le voyage au cours de _____ elle pourrait peut-être rencontrer son prince charmant!
   4. Elle a demandé tout de suite à un agent de voyages de _____ elle avait besoin.
   5. Ensuite, elle a acheté tout _____ elle avait besoin.

6. Avant son départ elle a acheté un cadeau _____ elle comptait présenter à son oncle et sa tante.
7. Elle s'est beaucoup amusée sur le bateau _____ elle a rencontré Mike _____ elle a apprécié le sens de l'humour, et Jim _____ le sourire l'a charmée.
8. Elle a souri à la Statue de la Liberté _____ semblait lui souhaiter la bienvenue (*to welcome her*).
9. À la douane elle a vu son oncle _____ l'a accueillie chaleureusement.
10. Elle était impressionnée par la ville de New York _____ elle trouvait vivante.
11. Malheureusement, Marie n'a pas trouvé le prince charmant _____ elle cherchait.
12. Elle a commencé à travailler dans un bureau à New York _____ l'ennuyait plus que celui de Paris!
13. Alors elle a dit au revoir à son oncle et sa tante _____ l'avaient traitée comme leur propre fille.
14. Elle est partie pour le Canada _____ elle a continué à chercher son prince charmant.
15. On ne sait pas si Marie a jamais trouvé le prince _____ elle avait rêvé.

Review of interrogative and relative pronouns

This is a brief review for comparison. Students are referred to Chapter 5 for additional information on interrogative pronouns.

Who (subject)

1. Interrogative: **qui?, qui est-ce qui?**

   Qui veut voyager à l'étranger?
   Qui est-ce qui veut voyager à l'étranger?
   Who wants to travel abroad?

2. Relative: **qui**

   Ces gens qui sortent du Louvre sont des touristes.
   These people who are leaving the Louvre are tourists.

Whom (direct object)

1. Interrogative: **qui?**

   Qui avez-vous vu à Rome?
   Whom did you see in Rome?

2. Relative: **que**

> **Delacroix est le peintre que nous préférons.**
> Delacroix is the painter (whom) we prefer.

Of whom, whom (with de)

1. Interrogative: **de qui?**

> **De qui parliez-vous quand je suis entré?**
> Of whom were you speaking when I entered?
> Whom were you talking about when I entered?

2. Relative: **dont**

> **Voici le type dont je me méfie.**
> Here's the fellow (whom) I mistrust.

What (subject and direct object)

1. Interrogative: **qu'est-ce qui?** (subject); **que?, qu'est-ce que?** (direct object)

> **Qu'est-ce qui se passe actuellement en France?**
> What's going on now in France?
>
> **Qu'est-ce que vous avez rapporté d'Afrique?**
> **Qu'avez-vous rapporté d'Afrique?**
> What have you brought back from Africa?

2. Relative: **ce qui** (subject), **ce que** (direct object)

> **Dites-moi ce qui se passe actuellement en France.**
> Tell me what's going on now in France.
>
> **Montrez-moi ce que vous avez rapporté d'Afrique.**
> Show me what you brought back from Africa.

Of what, what (with de)

1. Interrogative: **de quoi?**

> **De quoi a-t-on besoin pour aller à l'étranger?**
> What does one need to go abroad?

2. Relative: **ce dont**

> **Il ne m'envoie jamais ce dont j'ai besoin!**
> He never sends me what I need!

EXERCICE

Traduisez en français les mots anglais.

1. De _____ (*whom*) le guide se moque-t-il, de moi?
2. Comment s'appelle ce Français _____ (*who*) se sent si dépaysé?
3. De _____ (*what*) s'agit-il dans ce roman?
4. Je n'aime pas _____ (*what*) ces touristes ont l'intention de faire!
5. Il est francophile? _____ (*What*) cela signifie?
6. _____ (*What*) m'intéresse le plus, ce sont ses manières cultivées.
7. Mon ami ne sera jamais capable de me donner _____ (*what*) j'ai envie.
8. Voici _____ (*what*) vous avez laissé chez moi.
9. De _____ (*what*) a-t-elle besoin pour s'amuser à Paris?
10. Cette touriste _____ (*of whom*) ils parlent n'était pas très complaisante.
11. _____ (*What*) a-t-on trouvé à la douane?
12. La cuisine dans le restaurant _____ (*which*) nous avons choisi était très bonne.
13. _____ (*Who*) est ce monsieur qui a l'air si hautain?
14. _____ (*What*) vous impressionne le plus dans la cuisine française?
15. _____ (*What*) je me souviens n'est pas amusant.

Related expressions

N'importe + qui, quoi, où, quand

The expression **n'importe** (lit., *no matter*) is used with **qui, quoi, où,** and **quand** to express indiscrimination.

> n'importe qui   *anyone* (*at all*)
> n'importe quoi   *anything* (*at all*)
> n'importe où   *anywhere* (*at all*)
> n'importe quand   *any time* (*at all*)

Chérie, je vous suivrai n'importe où.
Darling, I will follow you anywhere (at all).

Mon frère prend des photos de n'importe quoi!
My brother takes pictures of anything!

EXERCICE

Remplacez les tirets par **n'importe qui, quoi, où** *ou* **quand**.

1. Vous pouvez me téléphoner le matin ou le soir, enfin _____.
2. Elle irait à Paris ou _____ pour apprendre le français.
3. Il ferait _____ pour gagner assez d'argent pour aller à la Martinique.

4. Il croit que _____ pourrait être guide!

5. Puisqu'elle parle si bien français, elle pourra se débrouiller _____ en France.

Demonstratives_____

Demonstrative adjectives and pronouns are used to point something out. The English demonstratives are *this, that, these, those.*

> **Cet étranger se débrouille très bien!**
> This (that) foreigner gets along very well!

> **Ces photos-ci sont meilleures que celles-là.**
> These photos are better than those.

The demonstrative adjective

	MASCULINE	FEMININE	ENGLISH
SINGULAR	ce, cet	cette	*this, that*
PLURAL	ces	ces	*these, those*

Like all adjectives, the demonstrative adjective agrees in number and gender with the noun it modifies. The masculine singular has two forms: **ce** is used before a noun or adjective beginning with a consonant; **cet** is used before a noun or adjective beginning with a vowel or mute h.

> **Cette autoroute est bien dangereuse!**
> This highway is very dangerous!

> **Ces cathédrales sont célèbres.**
> Those cathedrals are famous.

> **Ce Français aime faire des excursions accompagnées.**
> This Frenchman likes to take guided tours.

> **Cet énorme monument tombe en ruine!**
> That enormous monument is falling into ruin!

It is not usually necessary to distinguish between *this* and *that* in French. However, when a contrast is desired, **-ci** (*this*) and **-là** (*that*) are added to the noun with a hyphen.

> **Ce touriste-ci semble exigeant! Que pensez-vous des autres?**
> This tourist seems demanding! What do you think of the others?

> **La plupart des autoroutes sont bonnes, mais évitez celle-là.**
> Most of the highways are good, but avoid that one.

EXERCICE

*Remplacez les tirets par l'**adjectif démonstratif** convenable. Employez **-ci** ou **-là** s'il y a lieu.*

1. Donnez-moi ＿＿＿ appareil et gardez l'autre.
2. Je me méfie du patron de ＿＿＿ restaurant.
3. Je vais me renseigner sur ＿＿＿ hôtel de luxe.
4. ＿＿＿ agent de voyages a fait mille erreurs!
5. Je suis très impressionné par ＿＿＿ touristes bilingues.
6. J'ai visité beaucoup de monuments, mais pas ＿＿＿ monument.
7. Comment peuvent-ils s'habituer à ＿＿＿ coutumes bizarres?
8. Qui osera avouer qu'il a pris ＿＿＿ photo?
9. ＿＿＿ passeport est en règle mais ＿＿＿ passeport ne l'est pas!
10. Heureusement ＿＿＿ douanier n'a pas trop fouillé mes valises.

The definite demonstrative pronoun

	MASCULINE	FEMININE
SINGULAR	celui	celle
PLURAL	ceux	celles

The definite demonstrative pronoun agrees in number and gender with the noun to which it refers. Never used alone, it is always followed by **-ci** or **-là**, a relative pronoun, or a preposition.

Followed by -ci or -là

The English equivalents are *this one, that one, these, those.*

> **Cet appareil-ci est peut-être chic, mais celui-là est plus utile.**
> This camera is perhaps chic, but that one is more useful.

> **J'aime beaucoup ces valises-ci, mais celles-là sont laides!**
> I like these suitcases very much, but those are ugly!

Celui-là can also mean *the former*, and **celui-ci,** *the latter*.

> **On peut visiter ou les cabarets ou les monuments historiques.**
> **Ceux-ci m'intéressent, ceux-là me passionnent.**
> We can visit either the cabarets or the historical monuments. The former fascinate me, the latter interest me.

Note that in French, contrary to English, the sentence begins with **ceux-ci** (*the latter*). This is because the second noun in the first sentence (**monuments**) is closer to the second sentence, and is therefore referred to first (**ceux-ci** = *these*).

Followed by a relative pronoun

The English equivalents are often *he (she) who, the one(s) who, those, who.*

> **Celui qui s'ennuie chez lui va probablement s'ennuyer à l'étranger.**
> He who gets bored at home will probably get bored abroad.

> **Ceux qui ont l'esprit ouvert vont profiter d'un voyage à l'étranger.**
> Those who have an open mind are going to profit from a trip abroad.

Followed by a preposition

The English equivalent is often *the one* or *the ones.*

> **Voyez-vous ces deux femmes? La deuxième est celle derrière qui je me suis assise dans l'avion.**
> Do you see those two women? The second is the one behind whom I sat on the plane.

> **Les jeunes filles qui vous accompagnent cette année sont vraiment gentilles! Comment s'appellent celles avec qui vous avez fait votre dernière excursion?**
> The girls who are accompanying you this year are really nice! What are the names of the ones with whom you made your last tour?

Note that the construction **celui + de** is equivalent to the English possessive expressed by *'s.*

> **Aimez-vous ce souvenir? —Non, je préfère celui de Nancy.**
> Do you like this souvenir? —No, I prefer Nancy's.

> **Nos guides sont bons. Que pensez-vous de ceux de l'autre groupe?**
> Our guides are good. What do you think of the other group's?

The indefinite demonstrative pronouns

ceci	*this*
cela, ça	*that*

Unlike the definite demonstrative pronouns, which refer to a noun that they agree with in number and gender, the indefinite demonstrative pronouns refer to things without number and gender, such as facts or ideas. **Cela** often means both *this* and *that*, except when a contrast is desired. **Ça** is a familiar form of **cela**.

> **Cela (Ça) m'intéresse beaucoup.**
> That interests me very much.
>
> **Je n'aurais jamais pensé à cela!**
> I'd never have thought of that!
>
> **Prenez ceci; laissez cela.**
> Take this; leave that.

Noté that **ceci, cela,** and **ça** are rarely used with the verb **être. Ce** is most often used with **être** (see the section that follows).

EXERCICES

1. *Remplacez les tirets par* **celui, celle, ceux, celles, ceci** *ou* **cela (ça)**. *Employez* **-ci** *ou* **-là** *s'il y a lieu.*

   1. On parle français en Belgique et à la Guadeloupe. _____ est plus éloignée de la France que _____.
   2. Je ne peux pas accepter ce chèque-ci, monsieur, mais je peux accepter _____.
   3. Il ne faut pas s'excuser! _____ ne fait rien!
   4. _____ qui travaille dur va probablement réussir.
   5. Le costume des touristes fait souvent contraste avec _____ des indigènes.
   6. Comment pouvez-vous préférer ces cadeaux à _____ que je vous ai donnés?
   7. Comment puis-je décider entre la cuisine et la mode? _____ coûte trop cher et _____ me fait grossir!
   8. Je comprends mieux vos habitudes que _____ des Dupont.
   9. Vous êtes très gentil d'avoir dit _____ à votre ami.
   10. J'ai trop à faire! Je n'en peux plus! —Alors, terminez _____ et ne terminez pas _____.

2. *Traduisez en français.*

   1. He who adapts himself to the customs of a foreign country will get along very well.
   2. He liked neither the South nor the North. The former seemed too warm and the latter too cold.
   3. Her trip will be more interesting than her father's.
   4. Take this and run!
   5. I distrust those who are inconsiderate of others.
   6. Paul is the one who visited Canada.
   7. If you give me this, I will give you that.

8. This customs officer is less unpleasant than the one who searched us yesterday.

9. Americans welcome warmly those who seem pleasant and accommodating.

10. She likes neither the boat nor the plane. The former is too slow and the latter too fast.

The demonstrative pronoun ce

Ce is most frequently used with the verb **être: c'est, ce sont.** It is rendered in English by *he, she, it, they, that.*

Ce *or* subject pronoun *with* être

Should **ce** or the subject pronouns **il, elle, ils, elles** be used as the subject of **être?** As a general rule, if what follows **être** makes sense grammatically as its subject, **ce** is used. If what follows **être** could not be its subject, a subject pronoun is used.

1. **Ce** is used when **être** is followed by a noun, a pronoun, or a superlative. **C'est** is used for all persons except the third person plural, for which **ce sont** is generally preferred.

> **Qui vient de débarquer? —C'est votre frère Paul.**
> Who just got off the boat? —It's your brother Paul.
>
> **Que fait votre fils actuellement? —C'est une bonne question!**
> What is your son doing presently? —It's a good question!
>
> **Qui est là? —C'est moi.**
> Who's there? —It is I.
>
> **C'est la plus belle île du monde!**
> It's the most beautiful island in the world!
>
> **Qui a volé nos valises? —Ce sont eux!**
> Who stole our suitcases? —They did!

In the above sentences, note that what follows the verb **être** also makes sense grammatically as its subject.

> **Votre frère Paul est . . .**
>
> **Une bonne question est . . .**
>
> **Moi, je suis . . .**
>
> **La plus belle île du monde est . . .**
>
> **Eux sont . . .**

2. The subject pronouns **il, elle, ils, elles** are used when **être** is followed by an adjective, an adverb, or a phrase—none of which could serve as the subject of **être**.

> **Comment trouvez-vous les Français? —Ils sont très fiers.**
> How do you find the French? —They are very proud.

> **Y a-t-il beaucoup d'Américains à l'étranger? —Ils sont partout!**
> Are there a lot of Americans abroad? —They're everywhere!

> **Où est ma malle? —Elle est à côté de vous!**
> Where is my trunk? —It's next to you!

Note that an unmodified noun of profession, nationality, political allegiance, religion, social class, etc., is treated like an adjective.

> **Quel est son métier? —Il est guide.**
> What is his trade? —He's a guide.

> **Et sa religion? —Il est protestant.**
> And his religion? —He's Protestant.

EXERCICE

Remplacez les tirets par **ce, il, elle, ils** *ou* **elles.**

1. De quelle nationalité est notre guide? —_____ est canadien, je crois.
2. Votre appareil marche-t-il bien? —_____ est le pire appareil que j'ai jamais acheté!
3. Qui est sur cette photo? —_____ est une photo d'une belle Tahitienne.
4. _____ n'est pas la première fois qu'on m'insulte ici
5. Pourquoi ne les a-t-il pas accueillis chaleureusement? —Parce que _____ sont trop hautains!
6. Pourquoi votre ami admire-t-il tellement Pasteur? —_____ est médecin!
7. Je voudrais bien poser quelques questions à notre guide. Est- _____ encore ici?
8. Pourquoi ne veulent-elles pas nous accompagner à l'église? —Je crois que _____ sont des protestantes.
9. Il ne parle pas bien, ce monsieur. —Bien sûr que non, _____ est un étranger!
10. Où se trouve votre agence de voyages? —_____ est au coin de la rue, là-bas.

C'est *and* il est + *adjective referring to an idea*

1. **C'est** + *adjective* is used when referring back to a previously mentioned idea.

> **Je vais faire un voyage à la Martinique. —C'est formidable!**
> I'm going to take a trip to Martinique. —That's great!

J'ai commencé à me découvrir à l'étranger. —C'est normal.
I began to get to discover myself abroad. —That's normal.

In sentences beginning with **c'est** + *adjective*, the preposition **à** precedes an infinitive.

J'aimerais être tout à fait bilingue. —C'est facile à faire!
I would like to be totally bilingual. —It's easy to do!

2. **Il est** + *adjective* is used when referring to a new idea not previously mentioned; the **il** is impersonal. **C'est** may replace **il est** in informal conversational French.

Il est important de porter sa carte d'identité sur soi.
It is important to carry your I.D. card on you.

Il est parfois difficile de bien faire tous les préparatifs.
It is sometimes difficult to make all the preparations properly.

C'est intéressant de faire des voyages imaginaires!
It's interesting to take imaginary trips!

In sentences beginning with **il est (c'est)** + *adjective*, the preposition **de** precedes the infinitive.

EXERCICE

Remplacez le premier tiret par **c'est** *ou* **il est** *et le deuxième par* **à** *ou* **de**, *s'il y a lieu.*

1. _____ amusant _____ essayer de comprendre le créole, la langue d'Haïti.
2. Elle a fait un voyage en Afrique et elle ne veut pas rentrer; _____ difficile _____ comprendre.
3. Mon fils sourit constamment à la serveuse!–_____ normal!
4. _____ extraordinaire _____ ne pas se sentir dépaysé après avoir vécu à l'étranger.
5. _____ plus facile _____ imaginer les voyages que de les faire.
6. La cuisine française a-t-elle influencé la cuisine américaine?–_____ possible.
7. Je ne comprends pas pourquoi _____ si nécessaire _____ faire des projets avant de faire un voyage.
8. J'allais passer ma troisième année universitaire à l'étranger, mais _____ impossible maintenant.

9. _____ intéressant _____ comparer deux cultures différentes.
10. _____ presque impossible _____ se sentir tout à fait à l'aise dans un pays étranger.

Related expressions

The demonstrative ce *followed by a temporal expression*

The demonstrative **ce** is often used with temporal expressions that indicate the present or the past.

Ce + *Temporal Expression*			
PRESENT		PAST	
cette année	*this year*	cette année-là	*that year*
cet après-midi	*this afternoon*	cet après-midi-là	*that afternoon*
ce matin	*this morning*	ce matin-là	*that morning*
cette semaine	*this week*	cette semaine-là	*that week*
ce soir	*tonight*	ce soir-là	*that night*
ce mois-ci	*this month*	ce mois-là	*that month*
aujourd'hui	*today*	ce jour-là	*that day*
en ce moment	*at this time, now*	à ce moment-là	*at that time, then*

1. When **ce (cet, cette)** precedes a temporal expression of the present, it usually means *this*. The expression **ce mois-ci** is an exception in that it also adds **-ci** to the noun.

> **Où allez-vous ce matin?**
> Where are you going this morning?
>
> **Elle a passé ce mois-ci à la Guadeloupe.**
> She spent this month in Guadeloupe.

2. When **ce (cet, cette)** precedes a temporal expression of the past, however, **-là** must be added to the expression. The English equivalent is *that*. **En ce moment** changes to **à ce moment-là** in the past.

> **Où êtes-vous allé ce matin-là?**
> Where did you go that morning?
>
> **Pourquoi avez-vous ri à ce moment-là?**
> Why did you laugh then?
>
> **J'ai eu l'intention de visiter le Louvre ce jour-là.**
> I intended to visit the Louvre that day.
>
> **Elle a passé ce mois-là à la Guadeloupe.**
> She spent that month in Guadeloupe.

Demain, hier, le lendemain, la veille

Demain (*tomorrow*) and **hier** (*yesterday*) are used relevant to a point in the present. The equivalent expressions, relevant to a point in the past, are **le lendemain** (*the next day*) and **la veille** (*the day before*).

> **Je fais mes valises demain.**
> I'm packing tomorrow.
>
> **J'ai fait mes valises le lendemain.**
> I packed the next day.
>
> **J'ai retrouvé ma carte d'identité hier.**
> I found my I.D. card yesterday.
>
> **J'avais retrouvé ma carte d'identité la veille.**
> I had found my I.D. card the day before.

EXERCICE

Mettez les phrases au **passé***. Faites attention aux expressions temporelles.*
modèle: Je pars aujourd'hui.   **Je suis parti ce jour-là.**

1. Je téléphone de Paris en ce moment.
2. Je réserve ma chambre aujourd'hui.
3. Cet après-midi nous allons déjeuner dans un restaurant français.
4. Nous passons ce mois-ci à Haïti.
5. Demain nous passons la douane!
6. Ils ont visité[3] Québec hier.
7. Ce matin je vais prendre dix photos.
8. Nous faisons tous les préparatifs cette semaine.
9. Elle se débrouille très bien en ce moment.
10. Nous allons explorer cette petite île aujourd'hui.

Exercices d'ensemble

I. *Traduisez les mots anglais en français et complétez avec imagination.*

1. _____ (*He who*) visite un pays étranger pour la première fois . . .
2. Vous savez que _____ (*it*) est nécessaire de . . . avant de faire un long voyage.
3. Les Français, _____ (*who*) sont fiers de leur passé, ont exercé une influence considérable dans le domaine de . . .
4. Si vous êtes un Français _____ (*who*) parle bien anglais, les Américains vont . . .

---

[3] Use the pluperfect tense.

5. L'étudiant _____ (*who*) a passé sa troisième année universitaire à l'étranger, et _____ (*whose*) la vie en a été transformée, va . . . quand il rentrera aux États-Unis.
6. Ce touriste _____ (*whose*) la langue est impeccable est probablement . . .
7. Un touriste agréable est _____ (*he who*) . . .
8. Pourquoi voudriez-vous visiter _____ (*this*) pays exotique? —J'ai envie de . . .
9. En passant la douane _____ (*it*) est important, me semble-t-il, _____ (*to*) . . .
10. Le genre de touriste _____ (*whom*) je trouve insupportable est _____ (*he who*) . . .

II. *Traduisez en français.*

1. That bilingual foreigner gets along very well with girls!
2. How did she get used to the customs of that country?
3. Is it really important to make preparations if one is going to take a trip?
4. I found that guide condescending, demanding, and totally unpleasant!
5. When I went through customs, one customs officer searched this suitcase and another searched that one.
6. He adapted so well to life in that country that he wanted to stay there.
7. She decided to spend a year in that small African country.
8. It isn't necessary to open your trunk; I trust you.
9. John is the one I was talking about; he has already lost his traveler's checks and his camera!
10. They felt free the day they arrived.

Sujets de discussion ou de composition

1. Racontez un vrai voyage que vous avez déjà fait. Si vous n'avez rien d'intéressant à raconter, inventez un voyage imaginaire à l'étranger. Racontez par exemple:
   a. le voyage le plus culturel
   b. le voyage le plus comique
   c. le voyage le plus désastreux que vous pouvez imaginer.
2. Vous êtes douanier. Racontez vos difficultés avec deux des personnes suivantes:
   a. une dame hautaine
   b. une riche capitaliste désagréable
   c. un jeune «hippy» américain qui cache de la marijuana
   d. un gangster international
   e. un autre voyageur pittoresque de votre choix

3. Arrivé en Europe, vous comptez faire un magnifique voyage en auto-stop (*hitchhiking*). Vous n'avez qu'un seul blue-jean très usé (*worn*), un sac au dos, un beau sourire et peu d'argent. La police vous arrête (*stop*) à la première frontière et vous demande vos intentions. Racontez.

9

The subjunctive

Chapter 9 at a glance

SUBJUNCTIVE

I.   *Mettez les verbes au* **présent du subjonctif.**

1. parler:
    a. que je _____
    b. que tu _____
    c. qu'elle _____
    d. que nous _____
    e. que vous _____
    f. qu'elles _____
2. que je _____ (faire)
3. que tu _____ (réfléchir)
4. qu'il _____ (répondre)
5. que nous _____ (crier)
6. que vous _____ (venir)
7. qu'ils _____ (venir)

II: *Mettez les verbes au* **passé du subjonctif.**

1. causer:
    a. que je _____
    b. que tu _____
    c. qu'elle _____
    d. que nous _____
    e. que vous _____
    f. qu'elles _____
2. partir:
    a. que je _____
    b. que tu _____
    c. qu'elle _____
    d. que nous _____
    e. que vous _____
    f. qu'elles _____

III. *Mettez les verbes entre parenthèses au* **présent** *ou au* **passé du subjonctif.**

1. Faut-il que nous _____ (connaître) le français pour bien comprendre la culture française?
2. Je voudrais que vous _____ (cesser) de parler incorrectement.
3. Je suis contente qu'il _____ (être) plus agréable à l'avenir.
4. Il est désolé que vous _____ (ne pas perfectionner) votre accent à Paris l'année dernière.

IV. *Mettez les verbes entre parenthèses au temps convenable du* **subjonctif** *ou de l'*indicatif, *selon le cas. Indiquez si c'est l'indicatif ou le subjonctif que vous avez employé.*

1. Je suis étonnée que vous ne _____ (comprendre) pas l'argot.
2. Elle sait que nous _____ (se fâcher) quand nous entendrons la rumeur!
3. Je suis triste que vous _____ (dire) du mal de moi hier.

4. Il est vrai qu'on _____ (apprécier) mieux sa propre langue en étudiant une langue étrangère.
5. Il faut que vous _____ (s'exprimer) lentement mais correctement.
6. Bien que nous _____ (se disputer) de temps en temps, nous nous tutoyons toujours.
7. Je suis certain que mon fils _____ (suivre) un cours de langue l'année prochaine.
8. Vous n'apprendrez pas une langue en une semaine, qui que vous _____ (être).
9. Il croit que chaque langue _____ (contenir) sa propre vision du monde.
10. Croyez-vous vraiment que nous _____ (parler) bien français?
11. Y a-t-il un étudiant dans la classe qui _____ (savoir) parfaitement le subjonctif?
12. C'est la meilleure plaisanterie que je _____ (jamais entendre)!

V. *Gardez les* **infinitifs** *ou mettez-les au* **subjonctif,** *selon le cas.*

1. Je voudrais _____ (être) polyglotte un jour.
2. Je voudrais que vous _____ (parler) plus franchement.
3. Faut-il que nous _____ (étudier) le français tous les jours?
4. Il faut _____ (manger) pour vivre et non pas vivre pour manger.
5. Parlez plus fort pour que je _____ (pouvoir) vous entendre.
6. Il est parfois important de _____ (parler) couramment une langue étrangère.

VI. *Traduisez en français les mots entre parenthèses en employant l'expression* **que + subjonctif.**

1. _____ (*Let him come*) demain.
2. _____ (*Let her answer*) en anglais s'il le faut.

Vocabulaire du thème: La Langue

LANGUE ET LANGAGE

la **langue** *language (of a people)*
la **langue maternelle** *native language*
une **langue vivante (morte)** *a living (dead) language*
une **langue étrangère** *a foreign language*

le **langage** *language (of an individual; vocabulary)*
l' **argot** (m) *slang*
le **jargon** *jargon*

le **dialecte** *dialect*
un **langage cultivé, vulgaire, populaire** *a cultivated, vulgar, popular (i.e., common) language*

l' **idiotisme** (m) *idiom*
le **lieu commun** *commonplace*
le **proverbe** *proverb*
le **néologisme** *neologism*
la **plaisanterie** *joke*

s' **exprimer** *to express oneself*
parler français comme une vache espagnole *to murder French (lit., to speak French like a Spanish cow)*
faire un lapsus *to make a slip of the tongue*
faire des progrès *to make progress*
perfectionner son accent (son français, etc.) *to improve one's accent (one's French, etc.)*

parler couramment, nettement *to speak fluently, clearly*
être bilingue *to be bilingual*
être polyglotte *to be a polyglot, to speak many languages*
tutoyer *to say tu to someone*
vouvoyer *to say vous to someone*

BONNES ET MAUVAISES PAROLES

dire du bien de quelqu'un *to speak well of someone*
réfléchir avant de parler *to think before speaking*
garder un secret *to keep a secret*
parler bas *to speak softly*
flatter *to flatter*
tenir sa parole *to keep one's word*

dire du mal de quelqu'un *to speak badly of someone*
dire des bêtises *to speak nonsense*
bavarder *to chat, to gossip*
parler fort *to speak loudly*
insulter *to insult*
manquer à sa parole *to go back on one's word*
se **disputer** *to quarrel*

The subjunctive

The subjunctive is a mood. The term *mood* is used to define the attitude a speaker has toward a fact or action. There are two principal moods in French, the indicative and the subjunctive. A statement in the indicative mood is considered by the speaker to be certain or objective. A statement in the subjunctive mood, on the other hand, is considered by the speaker to be uncertain, hypothetical, or emotional. The subjunctive is sometimes called the affective (emotional) mood.

INDICATIVE

Richelieu a fondé l'Académie Française.
Richelieu founded the French Academy. *(An objective fact.)*

Je suis certain que le mot anglais «petty» dérive du mot français «petit».
I am certain that the English word *petty* is derived from the French word *petit*. *(The speaker is certain.)*

Je sais que vous dites ce que vous pensez.
I know that you say what you think. *(The speaker is certain.)*

Pensez-vous vraiment que mon ami ne réfléchisse pas avant de parler?
Do you really think that my friend doesn't think before he speaks?
(The speaker is uncertain.)

Je suis étonnée que vous disiez toujours ce que vous pensez!
I'm astounded that you always say what you think!
(The speaker is surprised.)

Il est possible qu'il y ait de la vie sur la planète Mars.
It is possible that there is life on the planet Mars.
(A hypothetical statement.)

The verbs **a fondé, dérive,** and **dites** above are in the indicative because the statements are considered certain and objective. The verbs **réfléchisse, disiez,** and **ait** are in the subjunctive because the statements are considered uncertain, emotional, hypothetical. Note that subordinate clauses in the subjunctive are introduced by **que.**

English-speaking students sometimes find the French subjunctive difficult because it differs from modern English. Once a frequently used mood with its own verb endings, the English subjunctive has gradually disappeared, surviving in only a few forms: *Long live the King*; *I wish I were dead*; *wherever he may be*; etc. The French subjunctive, however, is an actively used and carefully preserved mood. It has four tenses, of which only two, the present and the past, are normally used in spoken French. The imperfect and pluperfect, both literary tenses, are explained in the Appendix.

Formation of the present subjunctive

Regular formations

The present subjunctive of most verbs is formed by replacing the third person plural **-ent** ending of the present indicative by the endings **-e, -es, -e, -ions, -iez, -ent.**

1. Group 1: infinitive ending in **-er**

parler: stem, parl-	
que je parle	que nous parlions
que tu parles	que vous parliez
qu'il qu'elle qu'on parle	qu'ils qu'elles parlent

Note that verbs ending in **-ier** (e.g., **crier, étudier**) have a double **i** in first and second person plural forms: **que nous étudiions, que vous étudiiez.**

2. Group 2: infinitive ending in **-ir**
   a. Verbs like **finir**:

finir: stem, finiss-	
que je finisse	que nous finissions
que tu finisses	que vous finissiez
qu'il qu'elle } finisse qu'on	qu'ils qu'elles } finissent

   b. Verbs like **mentir**:

mentir: stem, ment-	
que je mente	que nous mentions
que tu mentes	que vous mentiez
qu'il qu'elle } mente qu'on	qu'ils qu'elles } mentent

   Common verbs like **mentir** are **dormir, partir, sentir, servir,** and **sortir**.

3. Group 3: infinitive ending in **-re**

répondre: stem, répond-	
que je réponde	que nous répondions
que tu répondes	que vous répondiez
qu'il qu'elle } réponde qu'on	qu'ils qu'elles } répondent

Irregular formations

The present subjunctive stem of many of the commonest verbs is irregular. These verbs fall into three groups: **avoir** and **être**; verbs with one stem; and verbs with two stems. With the exception of **avoir** and **être**, the regular present subjunctive endings are added to the stems.

1. **Avoir** and **être**

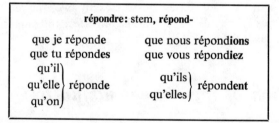

avoir		être	
que j'aie	que nous ayons	que je sois	que nous soyons
que tu aies	que vous ayez	que tu sois	que vous soyez
qu'il qu'elle } ait qu'on	qu'ils qu'elles } aient	qu'il qu'elle } soit qu'on	qu'ils qu'elles } soient

2. Verbs with one stem

faire: stem, fass-		**pouvoir: stem, puiss-**	
que je fasse	que nous fassions	que je puisse	que nous puissions
que tu fasses	que vous fassiez	que tu puisses	que vous puissiez
qu'il qu'elle } fasse qu'on	qu'ils qu'elles } fassent	qu'il qu'elle } puisse qu'on	qu'ils qu'elles } puissent
savoir: stem, sach-		**falloir: stem, faill-**	
que je sache	que nous sachions	qu'il faille	(3ʳᵈ person only)
que tu saches	que vous sachiez	**pleuvoir: stem, pleuv-**	
qu'il qu'elle } sache qu'on	qu'ils qu'elles } sachent	qu'il pleuve	(3ʳᵈ person only)

3. Verbs with two stems

Some verbs have one stem for the singular and the third person plural (stem 1), and another for the first and second person plural (stem 2).

aller	
STEM 1	STEM 2
que j' aille	que nous allions
que tu ailles	que vous alliez
qu'il qu'elle } aille qu'on	
qu'ils qu'elles } aillent	

Other common verbs with two stems:

	STEM 1	STEM 2
boire	que je boive	que nous buvions
croire	que je croie	que nous croyions
devoir	que je doive	que nous devions
envoyer	que j'envoie	que nous envoyions
mourir	que je meure	que nous mourions
prendre	que je prenne	que nous prenions
recevoir	que je reçoive	que nous recevions
tenir	que je tienne	que nous tenions
venir	que je vienne	que nous venions
voir	que je voie	que nous voyions
vouloir	que je veuille	que nous voulions

Formation of the past subjunctive

The past subjunctive is composed of the present subjunctive of **avoir** or **être** and the past participle.

bavarder (conjugated with **avoir**)	
que j' aie bavardé	que nous ayons bavardé
que tu aies bavardé	que vous ayez bavardé
qu'il qu'elle } ait bavardé qu'on	qu'ils qu'elles } aient bavardé

venir (conjugated with **être**)	
que je sois venu(e)	que nous soyons venu(e)s
que tu sois venu(e)	que vous soyez venu(e)(s)
qu'il qu'elle } soit { venu venue qu'on { venu	qu'ils qu'elles } soient { venus venues

EXERCICES

1. *Mettez les verbes au* **présent du subjonctif.**
   modèle: nous (parler)
   que nous parlions

1.	nous (répondre)	**16.**	nous (entendre)
2.	je, vous (prendre)	**17.**	il (savoir)
3.	vous (flatter)	**18.**	nous (partir)
4.	ils (traduire)	**19.**	il (pleuvoir)
5.	il, nous (boire)	**20.**	vous (vouvoyer)
6.	je (parler)	**21.**	vous (s'entendre)
7.	je, vous (tenir)	**22.**	nous (promettre)
8.	nous (s'exprimer)	**23.**	ils (insulter)
9.	vous (comprendre)	**24.**	nous (faire)
10.	je, nous (aller)	**25.**	elle (pouvoir)
11.	ils (faire)	**26.**	je, nous (vouloir)
12.	nous (étudier)	**27.**	il, vous (venir)
13.	elle (dire)	**28.**	nous (mentir)
14.	je (finir)	**29.**	nous (se taire)
15.	tu, nous (devoir)	**30.**	il (falloir)

2. *Mettez les verbes au* **passé du subjonctif.**
   modèle: ils (venir)
   qu'ils soient venus

1.	nous (parler)	**3.**	je (demander)
2.	vous (s'exprimer)	**4.**	ils (mentir)

5. elles (partir)	13. elles (sortir)
6. ils (se taire)	14. elles (se tutoyer)
7. tu (finir)	15. vous (causer)
8. nous (entendre)	16. tu (arriver)
9. elles (chuchoter)	17. nous (étudier)
10. elle (aller)	18. vous (venir)
11. ils (s'entendre)	19. nous (bavarder)
12. je (flatter)	20. ils (consulter)

Use of the present and past subjunctive

The French present and past subjunctive generally correspond to the English present and past indicative.

> **Il est bizarre que Jeanne ne réponde pas au téléphone.**
> It's strange that Jean doesn't answer (isn't answering) the telephone.

> **J'étais heureuse que mon ami m'ait parlé si franchement.**
> I was happy that my friend spoke to me so frankly.

It is important to note that there is no future form.
The present subjunctive is used to express the future.

> **Mes parents regrettent que je ne suive pas ce cours de français l'année prochaine.**
> My parents are sorry that I will not take that French course next year.

> **Il est possible qu'il vous téléphone demain.**
> It is possible that he will call you tomorrow.

EXERCICE

Traduisez les mots entre parenthèses en français en employant le **présent ou le passé du subjonctif.**

1. Je doute que ce politicien menteur _____ (*will keep*) sa parole!
2. Chut! Si vous voulez m'entendre, il faut que vous _____ (*be quiet*).
3. Je suis heureuse que mon fils _____ (*is making*) des progrès.
4. Mes amis étaient étonnés que je _____ (*understood*) ce jargon.
5. L'Académie Française ne veut pas que les Français _____ (*use*) trop d'anglicismes.
6. Il est étrange que vous _____ (*came*) me voir au milieu de la nuit.
7. Mais il est impossible que notre professeur nous _____ (*will give*) encore une composition pour demain!
8. Il est possible que je _____ (*will say*) tout ce que je pense?
9. Je voudrais que vous _____ (*speak*) plus fort, s'il vous plaît.
10. Ils sont ravis que leur frère _____ (*knows*) tout cela.

Expressions that always require the subjunctive

Expressions that by their very nature are uncertain, hypothetical, or emotional always take the subjunctive.

Expressions of wishing, doubting, and emotion

vouloir que
douter que
avoir peur que
craindre que
regretter que
être content, désolé, étonné, heureux, ravi, surpris, triste, etc., que

Je veux que nous sortions ensemble ce soir.
I want us to go out together tonight.

Mon professeur doute que je réfléchisse avant de parler.
My professor doubts that I think before speaking.

J'avais peur que vous ne[1] disiez des bêtises.
I was afraid you'd talk nonsense.

Il est ravi que nous nous soyons enfin mariés!
He's delighted that we got married at last!

1. The verb **espérer** in the affirmative is followed by the indicative and not the subjunctive.

> **J'espère que nous parlerons couramment français avant la fin du semestre.**
> I hope we'll speak French fluently before the end of the semester.

2. The subjunctive is not used if the subject of the main and subordinate clauses is the same; the infinitive is used instead. In such cases, verbs of wishing are followed directly by the infinitive. Expressions of emotion require the preposition **de** before the infinitive.

> **Je veux dire du bien de lui mais je ne peux pas.**
> I want to speak well of him but I can't.
>
> **Je serais heureux de vous tutoyer, mais pas tout de suite.**
> I would be happy to use the *tu* form with you, but not right away.

---

[1] The pleonastic **ne** is optional after expressions of fear in the affirmative. It has no negative value and is not translated.

EXERCICES

1. *Mettez les infinitifs entre parenthèses au* **présent ou au passé du subjonctif,** *s'il y a lieu.*

   1. Je suis surpris que le parti républicain _____ (ne pas gagner) l'élection l'année passée.
   2. Il est étonné que le mot *love* dans l'expression de tennis *love 15, 30, etc.* _____ (dériver) du mot français l'œuf (= *zéro*).
   3. J'espère qu'il _____ (faire) beau demain.
   4. Nous doutons fort que ces gens cultivés _____ (savoir) ces mots d'argot.
   5. Ils sont heureux que vous me _____ (comprendre) quand je parle français!
   6. Je suis désolé, mon vieux, que nous ne _____ (s'entendre) plus.
   7. Je vous prie de vous taire. Je ne veux pas _____ (entendre) le franglais.[2]
   8. Je suis très contente qu'il me _____ (tutoyer) hier!
   9. Comment pouvez-vous douter qu'elle _____ (pouvoir) parler quatre langues?
   10. Nous serions ravies de _____ (recevoir) votre camarade de chambre.

2. *Parlons franglais! Mettez les verbes «franglais» et leurs équivalents «français» au* **subjonctif.**

   1. Les spectateurs veulent que nous _____ (smasher, écraser) la balle de tennis.
   2. Maman, veux-tu que nous _____ (scotcher, coller) les photos dans l'album?
   3. Vite! Je veux que vous _____ (shooter, tirer au but) tout de suite!
   4. Reposez-vous, Jean. Nous voulons que vous _____ (prendre un second souffle, reprendre haleine).

3. *Traduisez en français.*

   1. Please speak more slowly. I want to hear every word.
   2. They're surprised that I told a joke.
   3. Think before speaking! I don't want you to talk nonsense.
   4. She's sorry you know the truth.
   5. I'm afraid they've left.
   6. No, our professor doesn't want us to murder French!
   7. They hope he'll say what he thinks.
   8. He wants you to speak louder, but he doesn't want you to scream!

---

[2] Neologism describing the highly Anglicized French spoken by many Frenchmen today. The term was popularized by the scholar Étiemble's book **Parlez-vous franglais?** (1964), which attacks the use of such jargon.

Impersonal expressions

Impersonal expressions that indicate an uncertain, hypothetical, or emotional point of view are followed by the subjunctive. Impersonal expressions that stress a certain or objective point of view are followed by the indicative. Followed by the subjunctive:

Il est bizarre que	Il est naturel que
Il est bon que	Il est nécessaire que
C'est dommage que	Il est possible que
Il est douteux que	Il est rare que
Il est étonnant que	Il est regrettable que
Il est étrange que	Il semble que
Il faut que	Il est surprenant que
Il est honteux que	Il se peut que
Il est important que	Il vaut mieux que
Il est impossible que	

Il est regrettable que votre père vous ait grondé.
It's too bad your father scolded you.

Il est possible qu'ils soient toujours malades.
It's possible that they're still sick.

Followed by the indicative:

Il est certain que	Il me semble que[4]
Il est clair que	Il est sûr que
Il est évident que	Il est vrai que
Il est probable que[3]	

Il est vrai que l'Académie Française a condamné le franglais.
It is true that the French Academy condemned "franglais."

Il est évident que votre ami tient sa parole.
It is evident that your friend keeps his word.

Note that impersonal expressions introducing general statements are followed by **de** + *infinitive*. **Il faut** and **il vaut mieux,** however, are followed directly by the infinitive.

Est-il possible de communiquer sans se servir de paroles?
Is it possible to communicate without using words?

---

[3] Probability is considered more certain than uncertain and therefore takes the indicative.
[4] Note that **il me semble que** takes the indicative, whereas **il semble que** takes the subjunctive. The first expresses certainty and the second uncertainty on the part of the speaker.

Il faut apprendre les proverbes parce qu'ils expriment souvent la vérité.
One should learn proverbs because they often express the truth.

Il vaut mieux être oiseau de campagne qu'oiseau de cage.
It is better to be a bird in the country than a bird in a cage.

EXERCICES

1. *Complétez les phrases suivantes. Mettez les infinitifs entre parenthèses au* **subjonctif** *ou à* **l'indicatif**, *s'il y a lieu.*

1. Il est regrettable qu'elle _____ (manquer) à sa parole hier!
2. Il est vrai que ce monsieur _____ (être) polyglotte.
3. C'est dommage que beaucoup d'Américains ne _____ (vouloir) pas apprendre les langues étrangères.
4. Il est important de _____ (connaître) une langue étrangère pour bien apprécier et comprendre sa propre langue.
5. Il est probable qu'elle _____ (perfectionner) son accent français pendant son séjour à Paris l'année passée.
6. Chut! Il faut que l'enfant _____ (s'endormir).
7. Il est nécessaire de (consulter) un dictionnaire si on ne sait pas la signification d'un mot.
8. Se peut-il que nous _____ (se tromper) de chemin dimanche dernier?
9. Il est étrange de (entendre) parler une langue sans rien comprendre.
10. Il est impossible que vous _____ (comprendre) ce dialecte.

2. *Récrivez les proverbes en suivant le modèle. Faites tous les changements nécessaires.*
   modèle: If faut vivre à Rome comme à Rome. (vous)
   Il faut que vous viviez à Rome comme à Rome.

1. Il faut commencer par le commencement. (vous)
2. Il ne faut pas réveiller le chat qui dort. (nous)
3. Il ne faut pas dire du mal des absents. (elle)
4. Il faut tourner sept fois la langue dans la bouche avant de parler. (vous)
5. Il ne faut jamais remettre au lendemain ce que l'on peut faire le jour même. (on)
6. Il faut prendre le temps comme il vient. (ils)
7. Il faut manger pour vivre et non pas vivre pour manger. (vous)
8. Il vaut mieux être seul qu'en mauvaise compagnie. (je)
9. Il faut laver son linge sale en famille. (nous)
10. Il faut manger comme un homme en bonne santé et boire comme un malade. (vous)

Conjunctions

Conjunctions introducing hypothetical or restrictive statements are followed by the subjunctive.

> à condition que *on condition that*
> à moins que *unless*
> afin que ⎱
> pour que ⎰ *in order that, so that*
> avant que *before*
> bien que ⎱
> quoique ⎰ *although*
> jusqu'à ce que *until*
> pourvu que *provided that*
> sans que *without*
> que . . . ou non *whether . . . or not*

Notre professeur articule très bien pour que nous puissions le comprendre.
Our professor articulates very well so that we can understand him.

Je compte la tutoyer à moins qu'elle ne⁵ me vouvoie.
I intend to say *tu* to her unless she says *vous* to me.

Qu'il se mette en colère ou non, je vais lui dire la vérité.
Whether he gets angry or not, I'm going to tell him the truth.

If the subject of the main and subordinate clauses is the same, certain conjunctions are replaced by a corresponding preposition and followed by an infinitive. Thus the subjunctive is not used.

CONJUNCTION	PREPOSITION
à condition que	à condition de
à moins que	à moins de
afin que	afin de
avant que	avant de
pour que	pour
sans que	sans

Comment comptez-vous apprendre une langue étrangère sans étudier la grammaire?
How do you intend to learn a foreign language without studying grammar?

Mon amie Jacqueline me téléphone uniquement pour bavarder.
My friend Jacqueline calls me only to gossip.

---

⁵ The pleonastic **ne** is optional after the conjunctions **a moins que** and **avant que**. It has no negative value and is not translated.

The conjunctions **bien que, quoique, jusqu'à ce que,** and **pourvu que** do not have corresponding prepositions. Even when there is no change of subject these conjunctions must be used, repeating the subject of the main clause. As always, they are followed by a verb in the subjunctive.

> **J'aime beaucoup mon cours de français bien que (quoique) je sois toujours en retard!**
> I like my French course a lot, although I'm always late!
>
> **Je vais continuer à étudier le japonais jusqu'à ce que je le connaisse!**
> I am going to keep on studying Japanese until I know it!

EXERCICES

1. *Mettez les infinitifs entre parenthèses au* **subjonctif** *s'il y a lieu.*

    1. L'Académie Française a été établie pour _____ (défendre) la langue française.
    2. Voulez-vous rester ici jusqu'à ce que je _____ (revenir)?
    3. Il faut toujours réfléchir avant de _____ (parler).
    4. Quoique le français _____ (être) sa langue maternelle, il a du mal à prononcer le *u*.
    5. Je vous aiderai avec les mathématiques pourvu que vous me _____ (aider) avec l'espagnol!
    6. Bien qu'il en _____ (comprendre) tous les mots, il ne sait pas la signification de cet idiotisme!
    7. Cet étudiant paresseux essaie d'écrire des compositions sans _____ (consulter) le dictionnaire.
    8. Nancy apprend le français pour _____ (pouvoir) comprendre la civilisation française.
    9. Sa camarade de chambre Gertrude étudie le français afin de mieux _____ (comprendre) l'anglais.
    10. Il continue à employer des mots d'argot bien que son père _____ (se mettre) en colère.

2. *Traduisez en français.*

    1. Speak more slowly so that I can understand you.
    2. We won't quarrel unless he talks nonsense!
    3. Although she has never gone to France, she speaks French fluently.
    4. You will never make progress unless you study.
    5. We will be able to study abroad provided that we improve our French.

Expressions of concession

qui que   *whoever*
où que   *wherever*
si + adjective + que   *however*
quel que   *whatever*
quoi que   *whatever*

Qui que vous soyez, vous avez les mêmes droits que les autres.
Whoever you are (may be), you have the same rights as others.

Si intelligente qu'elle soit, elle n'apprendra pas le français en un mois!
However intelligent she is (may be), she will not learn French in a month!

Note that **quel que** and **quoi que** both mean *whatever*. **Quel que** is used when an adjective is called for, and **quoi que** when a pronoun is called for.

Quelles que soient vos raisons, vous ne devriez pas vous disputer.
Whatever your reasons are (may be), you shouldn't quarrel.

Quoi que je fasse, je ne peux pas plaire à ma petite amie.
Whatever I do, I can't please my girlfriend.

EXERCICE

Traduisez en français.

1. Wherever we go in France, we hear franglais!
2. I'll learn that language, however difficult it is.
3. They will be happy wherever they are.
4. Whatever you tell him, he'll keep his word.
5. Whoever you are, go away!
6. We like to learn the language wherever we travel.
7. Please try to tell the truth, whatever you do!
8. Whatever your intentions are, be prudent.
9. However honest they are, they cannot keep a secret.
10. Whatever he does, he can't please the President.

Expressions that sometimes require the subjunctive

Some expressions that are not inherently uncertain, hypothetical, or emotional become so in certain cases, because of the attitude of the speaker. In these cases they take the subjunctive.

Verbs of thinking and believing

Affirmative verbs of thinking and believing (e.g., **penser, croire, trouver**) are always followed by the indicative. Negative and interrogative verbs of thinking and believing, however are almost always followed by the subjunctive, since they usually introduce uncertain or emotional statements.

Nous trouvons que notre professeur est juste et raisonnable.
We find that our professor is fair and reasonable.

Je crois que cet acteur peut communiquer très bien par gestes.
I think that this actor can communicate very well by gestures.

Je ne pense pas que vous m'ayez compris.
I don't believe you've understood me.

Docteur, croyez-vous vraiment que je sois enceinte?
Doctor, do you really think I'm pregnant?

Trouvez-vous que la vie soit facile ou difficile?
Do you find life is easy or difficult?

The future indicative usually replaces the subjunctive when a future action is expressed.

Croyez-vous que nous apprendrons bientôt quelques mots d'argot?
Do you think we'll soon learn some slang words?

Je ne pense pas que le suspect sera en liberté la semaine prochaine.
I don't think the suspect will be at liberty next week.

EXERCICES

1. *Mettez les verbes entre parenthèses à l'**indicatif** ou au **subjonctif** selon le cas.*

1. Je trouve qu'elle _____ (manquer) à sa parole quand elle m'a parlé hier.
2. Pensez-vous que ce politicien _____ (dire) toujours ce qu'il pense?
3. Je crois que la vie à la campagne _____ (être) plus tranquille que la vie en ville.
4. Pensez-vous que Paul _____ (venir) dîner chez nous la semaine prochaine?
5. Notre professeur trouve que nous _____ (s'exprimer) très bien.
6. Je ne pense pas que mon invité _____ (partir) tout de suite.
7. Je ne crois pas que la musique contemporaine _____ (être) complètement folle!
8. Croyez-vous que je _____ (pouvoir) vous tutoyer?
9. Je ne pense pas du tout que vous _____ (perfectionner) votre accent l'année passée!
10. Pensez-vous que le mariage _____ (rendre) la vie intolérable?

2.

A. *Parlons argot! Étudiez cette liste de mots d'argot.*

avoir l'estomac dans les talons *to be starving (lit., to have one's stomach in one's heels)*

avoir une gueule de bois *to have a hangover (lit., to have a wooden jaw)*

avoir la langue bien pendue   to be very talkative (*lit., to have one's tongue hanging a lot*)

bouffer   to eat like a glutton, to eat (*lit., to puff out*)

être dans la vigne du Seigneur   to be drunk (*lit., to be in the vineyard of the Lord*)

faire dodo   to sleep (*children's language*)

faire l'école buissonnière   to play hooky (*lit., to go to school in the bushes*)

se rincer la dalle   to drink (*lit., to rinse one's slab*; **dalle** = *slab, paving stone*)

mettre les voiles   to take off, to depart (*lit., to set sail*)

perdre les pédales   to be nuts (*lit., to lose one's pedals*)

B. *Voici des réponses. Posez une question en employant* **croyez-vous?** *ou* **pensez-vous?**

 modèle : Oui, votre fils a fait l'école buissonnière hier. Je l'ai vu au cinéma.
    Croyez-vous que mon fils ait fait l'école buissonnière hier?

1. Oui, Jean a perdu les pédales. Il parlait tout seul hier.
2. Non, les enfants ne font pas dodo.
3. Non, Marguerite n'a pas de gueule de bois ce matin. Elle est fatiguée, c'est tout.
4. Oui, nous nous rincerons la dalle ce soir au bar du Dôme.
5. Oui, nos amies ont mis les voiles trop tôt hier soir.
6. Oui, le professeur a fait l'école buissonnière hier!
7. Non, nous n'avons pas bouffé très bien dans ce restaurant hier soir!
8. Oui, il a l'estomac dans les talons. Il mange comme un cochon!
9. Oui, Robert est dans la vigne du Seigneur. Il dit tellement de bêtises!
10. Oui, vous avez la langue bien pendue!

Relative clauses

Verbs in relative clauses are normally in the indicative. The subjunctive is often used, however, if the speaker doubts or denies the existence or attainability of the antecedent.

INDICATIVE

Je connais plusieurs étudiants qui sont complètement bilingues.
I know several students who are completely bilingual.
 (An objective statement of fact.)

Nous avons trouvé un candidat qui n'a pas peur des assassins.
We have found a candidate who isn't afraid of assassins.
 (An objective statement of fact.)

SUBJUNCTIVE

Nous cherchons un candidat qui n'ait pas peur des assassins.
We are looking for a candidate who isn't afraid of assassins.
⎱ (The speaker doubts that he can find one.)

Il n'y a pas de candidat qui soit tout à fait honnête et sincère.
There is no candidate who is totally honest and sincere.
⎱ (The speaker denies the existence of such a candidate.)

The superlative

Superlative expressions and the adjectives **premier, dernier** and **seul** are followed by the indicative when the speaker states a certain or objective fact, and by the indicative *or* the subjunctive when the speaker expresses an uncertain or emotional attitude.

INDICATIVE

Robert est le plus jeune étudiant qui a réussi à l'examen.
Robert is the youngest student who passed the exam. (An objective statement of fact.)

Je suis sûr que le Brésil est le plus grand pays qu'ils ont visité.
I am sure that Brazil is the biggest country they visited. (The speaker is certain.)

INDICATIVE OR SUBJUNCTIVE

Est-ce la meilleure plaisanterie que vous avez (ayez) jamais entendue?
Is this the best joke you've ever heard? (The speaker is uncertain, surprised.)

Est-ce le seul étudiant qui sait (sache) ce que c'est qu'un néologisme?
Is he the only student who knows what a neologism is? (The speaker is surprised.)

EXERCICE

Mettez les verbes entre parenthèses au **subjonctif** *ou à* **l'indicatif.**

1. Je suis sûr que c'est le seul homme qui _____ (entrer) dans votre bureau hier soir.
2. Zut! On nous a donné le seul professeur que nous _____ (détester)!
3. Il n'y a pas beaucoup de gens qui _____ (être) polyglottes.
4. J'ai beaucoup d'amis qui _____ (être) très gentils.
5. Est-ce que Boston est la plus grande ville que vous _____ (visiter) l'année passée?
6. C'est mon meilleur étudiant qui me _____ (insulter) hier.

7. John F. Kennedy est le seul catholique qui _____ (devenir) président des États-Unis.
8. Combien de gens y a-t-il qui _____ (pouvoir) garder un secret pour toujours?
9. C'est la dernière composition que vous _____ (être) obligés d'écrire.
10. Ces étudiants cherchent un professeur qui _____ (être) brillant, original, dynamique, patient, aimable, sensible et enthousiaste!

Related expressions

The third person imperative

French uses **que** + *present subjunctive* to express an order or command in the third person singular or plural. The English equivalent is usually *Let . . .*

> **Qu'elle finisse son travail si elle veut sortir!**
> Let her finish her work if she wants to go out!
> **Qu'il me tutoie s'il le veut.**
> Let him use *tu* to me if he wants to.

Note that the imperative of **laisser** + *infinitive* is frequently used to express *Let . . .*

> **Laisse-le me tutoyer s'il le veut.**
> Let him use *tu* to me if he wants to.

EXERCICE

Traduisez en français.

1. Let her talk nonsense if she wishes.
2. Let them do it if they have the time.
3. Let him leave at once.
4. Let him keep his word.
5. Let her answer in French if she wants to.

Exercices d'ensemble

I. *Mettez les verbes entre parenthèses au* **subjonctif** *ou à* **l'indicatif,** *s'il y a lieu.*

1. Est-il nécessaire de _____ (traduire) ces phrases françaises en anglais?
2. Il ne faut pas que nous _____ (insulter) les autorités.
3. Il est vrai que vous _____ (flatter) des imbéciles.
4. Nous doutons que notre fils _____ (dire) du bien de ses amis.

5. Nous croyons que la langue écrite _____ (être) plus précise que la langue parlée.

6. Il est probable qu'ils _____ (se disputer) entre eux aujourd'hui, demain et après-demain!

7. Je crois que vous _____ (pouvoir) me tutoyer dès maintenant.

8. Qui que vous _____ (être), vous serez obligé de travailler comme les autres!

9. Je cherche un sage qui _____ (savoir) la réponse à toutes les questions!

10. Croyez-vous que je _____ (devoir) punir mon petit frère pour avoir manqué à sa parole?

11. Il a beaucoup étudié les langues étrangères parce qu'il _____ (vouloir) devenir polyglotte.

12. Il est vrai que le mot anglais *too-da-loo* _____ (venir) de l'expression française *tout à l'heure.*

II. *Complétez avec imagination.*

1. Je vais vous insulter jusqu'à ce que . . .
2. Nous espérons que ce criminel violent . . .
3. Pour se libérer véritablement, il faut que les femmes . . .
4. Je doute que le terrorisme . . .
5. Trouvez-vous que l'amour . . .
6. Nous avons peur que la civilisation américaine . . .
7. Je ne crois pas qu'un vrai révolutionnaire . . .
8. Si vous voulez scandaliser le monde, il faut que vous . . .
9. Ils sont contents que ce vieux fou . . .
10. Il voudrait se faire millionnaire sans . . .

Sujets de discussion ou de composition

1. Vous êtes-vous jamais trouvé dans une situation gênante ou même compromettante parce que vous aviez fait un lapsus? Racontez.

2. Formulez quelques proverbes personnels qui commencent par **Il faut que.**

3. Les Français ont dénoncé les emprunts (*borrowings*) à l'anglais qu'ils appellent le franglais. Les Américains, au contraire, n'ont pas dénoncé les nombreux emprunts au français (e.g., **de rigueur, chic, détente, comme il faut**). Voyez-vous des attitudes différentes chez les Américains et chez les Français à l'égard de leur langue?

10

Possessives and prepositions

Chapter 10 at a glance

POSSESSIVES

I. *Traduisez en français les mots entre parenthèses.*

1. (*my*) livre
2. (*her*) place
3. (*his*) imagination
4. (*our*) bibliothèque
5. (*your*) romans
6. (*their*) idées

II. *Traduisez en français les possessifs en employant* **l'adjectif possessif** *ou* **l'article défini.**

1. Cette actrice ne se lave jamais _____ (*her*) cheveux!
2. _____ (*His*) poète favori est Baudelaire.

III. *Traduisez en français* **les pronoms possessifs.**

1. L'imagination de cet écrivain est moins riche que _____ (*yours*).
2. Cet auteur aime bien critiquer les romans des autres, mais il ne veut pas qu'on critique _____ (*his*)!

IV. *Traduisez en français en employant* **être à.**

1. Voyons! Ce roman policier _____ (*is not yours*)!
2. Mais si! Il _____ (*is mine*)!

V. *Traduisez en français en employant une expression avec* **de.**

1. _____ (*Racine's play*) est une tragédie.
2. _____ (*Your friends' ideas*) me scandalisent.

VI. *Traduisez en français en employant* **être malade** *ou* **avoir mal à.**

1. Je crois qu'elle _____ (*has a headache*).
2. L'acteur n'a pas joué parce qu'il _____ (*was sick*).

PREPOSITIONS

VII. *Traduisez en français.*

1. behind the tree
2. against the house
3. between us
4. in the middle of the book
5. near the library

VIII. *Traduisez en français les mots entre parenthèses.*

1. Mon livre est _____ (*on the table next to the window*).
2. Je peux lire ce best-seller _____ (*in one hour*)!
3. Cette actrice charmante _____ (*with brown eyes*) est très gentille _____ (*toward us*).

IX. *Remplacez les tirets par* **à** *ou* **de** *s'il y a lieu.*

1. Nous avons _____ lire trois romans cette semaine.
2. Ce romancier a essayé _____ scandaliser le public mais il n'a pas réussi _____ le faire.
3. Voulez-vous _____ assister au spectacle avec moi?
4. Dans ce roman il s'agit d'un homme qui refuse _____ jouer un rôle.
5. Mon ami m'a conseillé _____ suivre un cours de littérature.

X. *Traduisez en français les mots entre parenthèses.*

1. Je _____ (*am looking for*) un livre de poche intéressant.
2. _____ (*We are interested in*) étudier la littérature surréaliste.
3. Les spectateurs _____ (*laugh at*) vous parce que vous _____ (*resemble*) Charlie Chaplin!

XI. *Remplacez les tirets par* **à** *ou* **de.**

1. Que pensez-vous _____ Balzac?
2. Un acteur pense toujours _____ son public.
3. La littérature pornographique manque souvent _____ valeur artistique.
4. Juliette manque beaucoup _____ Roméo.

XII. *Remplacez les tirets par* **à, en** *ou* **dans.**

1. Ils vont au spectacle _____ bicyclette.
2. Nous allons au festival d'Avignon _____ bateau.

Vocabulaire du thème: La Scène et les Lettres

LA SCÈNE

LA PIÈCE DE THÉÂTRE

l' **auteur** (m) *author*
le **metteur en scène** *director*
l' **acteur** (m) *actor*
l' **actrice** (f) *actress*
 jouer un rôle *to play or act a role*
 savoir (oublier) son texte, son rôle *to know (forget) one's lines*

la **répétition** *rehearsal*
 répéter *to rehearse*

la **scène** *stage, scene*
le **costume** *costume*

le **décor** *decor, scenery*
le **maquillage** *make-up*

la **pièce** *play*
le **spectacle** *show*
la **représentation** *performance*
 représenter *to perform*
le **héros** *hero*
l' **héroïne** (f) *heroine*
le **personnage** *character (in a play, book, etc.)*
l' **intrigue** (f) *plot*

la **critique** *criticism*
le **critique** *critic*
  critiquer *to criticize*
le **public** *audience*
le **spectateur** *spectator*
  assister à *to attend*

applaudir frénétiquement *to applaud wildly*
siffler *to hiss, to boo*
le **succès** *hit*
le **four** *flop* (*theater*)
scandaliser *to scandalize, to shock*

LES LETTRES

ÉCRIVAINS ET LECTEURS

l' **écrivain** (m) *writer*
le **lecteur** *reader*
le **poète** *poet*

le **romancier** *novelist*
raconter une histoire *to tell a story*

LE LIVRE

le **bouquin** (*colloq.*) *book*
l' **ouvrage** (m) *work*
la **nouvelle** *short story*
la **poésie** *poetry*

le **roman** *novel*
le **livre de chevet** *bedside book*
le **manuel** *textbook*
le **best-seller** *best seller*

Possessives

Possessives are used to indicate that something belongs to someone. Four common constructions express possession in French: possessive adjectives, possessive pronouns, **être à,** and **de** + *noun*.

Adjective: **Zut! J'ai perdu mon manuel!**
           Darn it! I lost my textbook!

Pronoun: **Servez-vous du mien pour le moment. Le voici.**
          Use mine for the time being. Here it is.

être à: **Merci. Comment! Ce manuel n'est pas à vous! Il est à moi! Voici mon prénom dans le coin!**
          Thanks. Hey, this text isn't yours! It's mine! Here's my name in the corner!

de + *noun:*   **Idiot! C'est l'ancien manuel de mon frère Jean! Il a le même prénom que vous!**
          Idiot! It's my brother John's old book! He has the same first name as you!

Possessive adjectives

MASCULINE	FEMININE	PLURAL	
mon	ma (mon)	mes	*my*
ton	ta (ton)	tes	*your*
son	sa (son)	ses	*his, her, its*
notre	notre	nos	*our*
votre	votre	vos	*your*
leur	leur	leurs	*their*

Agreement

Like all adjectives, the possessive adjectives agree in number and gender with the noun they modify.

SINGULAR	PLURAL
notre roman	**nos romans**
our novel	our novels
leur place	**leurs places**
their seat	their seats
mon ouvrage	**mes ouvrages**
my work	my works

Note that the feminine singular has two forms. **Ma, ta,** and **sa** are used before feminine singular nouns or adjectives beginning with a consonant or aspirate **h. Mon, ton,** and **son** are used before feminine singular nouns or adjectives beginning with a vowel or mute **h.**

ma bibliothèque	**mes bibliothèques**
my library	my libraries
ma hache	**mes haches**
my ax	my axes
ton autre nouvelle	**tes autres nouvelles**
your other short story	your other short stories
mon héroïne	**mes héroïnes**
my heroine	my heroines
son actrice	**ses actrices**
his (her) actress	his (her) actresses

French possessive adjectives are repeated before each noun; this is usually not the case in English.

Il oublie toujours son manuel et son cahier.
He always forgets his text and notebook.

The definite article expressing possession

The definite article is often used to express possession with parts of the body.

> **Il a les cheveux roux.**
> He has red hair. *or:* His hair is red.
>
> **Elle a levé la tête pour mieux voir la scène.**
> She raised her head to see the stage better.
>
> **Elle se lave les cheveux le matin et le soir.**
> She washes her hair in the morning and at night.

1. The possessive adjective is usually used with parts of the body modified by an adjective. Modified parts of the body used in expressions with **avoir,** however, retain the definite article.

> **Le mime levait ses mains musclés pour faire un geste de menace.**
> The mime lifted his muscular hands to make a threatening gesture.
>
> **Elle a les cheveux blonds en été et noirs en hiver.**
> Her hair is blond in the summer and black in the winter.

2. When the subject performs an action on a part of his or her own body, a reflexive verb is used.

> **Elle se lave les cheveux le matin et le soir.**
> She washes her hair in the morning and at night.

In such constructions, the part of the body is the direct object and the reflexive pronoun is the indirect object. Therefore there is no agreement with the past participle in compound tenses, since the past participle does not agree with preceding indirect objects (see p. 77).

> **Elles se sont lavé les cheveux.**
> They washed their hair.

EXERCICES

1. *Remplacez les mots entre parenthèses par un* **adjectif possessif** *ou l'*article défini.

1. Bien que cet acteur joue bien _____ (*his*) rôles, je n'aime pas le caractère de _____ (*his*) personnages!
2. Ils se promènent le long de la Seine en parlant de _____ (*their*) poètes préférés.
3. Cette actrice sera obligée de se laver soigneusement _____ (*her*) visage pour enlever _____ (*her*) maquillage.

4. Comment! Les spectateurs s'ennuyaient pendant la représentation de
_____ (his) pièce!

5. Je relis souvent _____ (my) pièce et _____ (my) roman favoris.

6. Ils iront au théâtre avec vous pourvu que vous payiez _____ (their) places.

7. Cette danseuse me passionne! Elle lève _____ (her) mains et baisse _____ (her) tête avec tant de grâce!

8. Mademoiselle, voulez-vous bouger _____ (your) petite tête adorable pour que je puisse voir la scène?

9. Ce romancier donne à _____ (his) héros et à _____ (his) héroïne beaucoup de liberté.

10. _____ (Our) professeur et _____ (our) parents trouvent que ce roman érotique n'a pas de valeur littéraire.

2. *Répondez à chaque question en employant une des expressions de la colonne de droite. Répondez par une phrase complète. Que fait-on avec:*

1.	une brosse à dents?	se calmer les nerfs
2.	une petite main en plastique?	se couper les ongles
3.	un onglier?	s'essuyer le front
4.	un shampooing (ʃãpwɛ̃)?	se teindre les cheveux
5.	une barre de savon?	se gratter le dos
6.	un oreiller (*pillow*)?	se brosser les dents
7.	un calmant (*tranquilizer*)?	se laver le visage
8.	un couteau, si on ne fait pas attention?	se reposer la tête
9.	la teinture (*dye*)?	se laver les cheveux
10.	un mouchoir, s'il fait chaud?	se couper le doigt

3. *Refaites l'exercice précédent en répondant à cette question: Qu'avez-vous fait avec cette brosse à dents (cette petite main en plastique, etc.)? Dans vos réponses, employez le passé composé.*

Possessive pronouns and the expression être à

The Possessive Pronoun

SINGULAR		PLURAL		
MASCULINE	FEMININE	MASCULINE	FEMININE	
le mien	la mienne	les miens	les miennes	*mine*
le tien	la tienne	les tiens	les tiennes	*yours*
le sien	la sienne	les siens	les siennes	*his, hers, its*
le nôtre	la nôtre	les nôtres	les nôtres	*ours*
le vôtre	la vôtre	les vôtres	les vôtres	*yours*
le leur	la leur	les leurs	les leurs	*theirs*

Like the possessive adjectives, possessive pronouns agree in number and gender with the object possessed. The definite article contracts normally with **à** and **de**.

> **Sa place est bien plus confortable que la mienne!**
> His (her) seat is much more comfortable than mine!

> **Leurs manuels coûtent moins cher que les nôtres.**
> Their texts cost less than ours.

> **Elle s'intéresse plus à votre problème qu'au sien.**
> She's more interested in your problem than in his (hers).

Être à + *noun or disjunctive pronoun*

The expression **être à** followed by a *noun* or *disjunctive pronoun* is used more frequently than the possessive pronoun to express ownership. It may be translated by a possessive pronoun or by the verb *to belong.*

> **Ce livre de poche est-il à vous ou à votre camarade de chambre?**
> Does this paperback belong to you or your roommate?

> **Ce roman policier est probablement à lui.**
> This mystery is probably his.

Note that **appartenir à** is a synonym of **être à**, and that it takes an indirect object pronoun.

> **Ce bouquin ne m'appartient pas; il lui appartient.**
> This book doesn't belong to me; it belongs to her (him).

EXERCICE

Traduisez en français les mots entre parenthèses en employant un **pronom possessif** *ou l'expression* **être à.**

1. Je viens d'acheter deux billets pour la nouvelle représentation à la Comédie-Française. Celui-ci _____ (*is yours*) et celui-là _____ (*is mine*).
2. Je m'occuperai de mes affaires si vous _____ (*attend to yours*).
3. Leur classe va analyser les poèmes de Baudelaire ce semestre. Quel auteur _____ (*is ours going to analyze*)?
4. Il semble toujours oublier que les livres qu'il sort de la bibliothèque _____ (*don't belong to him*).
5. Je crois que la librairie de votre université vend plus de livres que _____ (*ours*).
6. En allant au théâtre j'ai remarqué les vêtements de mon ami qui étaient beaucoup moins habillés (*formal*) que _____ (*mine*).
7. Dans le roman que je lis actuellement, il s'agit d'une femme rêveuse qui décide de se suicider. De quoi s'agit-il dans _____ (*yours*)?
8. J'ai oublié mon manuel de français. Est-ce que votre amie veut me prêter _____ (*hers*)?

The expression de + noun

The structure **de** + *noun* is equivalent to the English expression *noun* + *'s or s'*. The preposition **de** contracts normally with a definite article.

> **Comment s'appelle la pièce de Sartre qui contient l'expression «l'enfer, c'est les autres»?**
> What's the name of Sartre's play that contains the expression, "Hell is other people"?

> **Marcel Proust est l'auteur préféré de mes parents.**
> Marcel Proust is my parents' favorite author.

Note that **chez** + *noun* or *disjunctive pronoun* means *at the home of* or *at the place of*. When referring to artists, it often means *in the works of*.

> **Avant d'aller au théâtre, nous dînons souvent chez les Dupont.**
> Before going to the theater, we often dine at the Duponts'.

> **Chez Balzac il y a plus de deux mille personnages!**
> In Balzac's works there are more than two thousand characters!

EXERCICE

Traduisez en français.

1. Do you know the title of Proust's famous novel?
2. If there is a reading at the Smiths' tonight, I want to go.
3. Let's rehearse at our place.
4. The audience wildly applauded the performance of Shakespeare's play *Hamlet*.
5. What is the hero's importance in Racine?
6. That young actor's first role was a hit.
7. His plays' characters don't interest me.
8. If an author's imagination is lively (*vif*), he will write interesting works.
9. Flaubert's novel *Madame Bovary* scandalized its readers.
10. Style is very important in Flaubert.

Related expressions

Avoir mal à

The expression **avoir mal à** is used to indicate the precise part of the body that is sick. It is followed by the *definite article + the part of the body*. The preposition **à** contracts normally with the definite article.

> **Après avoir terminé sa lecture, il avait mal aux yeux.**
> After having finished his reading, his eyes hurt.

Si les acteurs continuent à parler trop fort, j'aurai mal à la tête.
If the actors continue to speak too loudly, I'll have a headache.

Some common parts of the body:

la bouche *mouth*	**la jambe** *leg*
le bras *arm*	**le menton** *chin*
les cheveux (m) *hair*	**le nez** *nose*
la dent *tooth*	**l'œil, les yeux** (m) *eye, eyes*
le derrière *behind*	**l'oreille** (f) *ear*
le doigt *finger*	**le pied** *foot*
le dos *back*	**la tête** *head*
l'estomac (m) *stomach*	**le visage** *face*

Être malade

The expression **être malade** means *to be sick*. It does not indicate a precise part of the body.

Elle a manqué la répétition parce qu'elle était malade.
She missed the rehearsal because she was sick.

EXERCICES

1. *Répondez en employant l'expression* **avoir mal à.**
   Où aurez-vous mal?

   1. si vous courez trop loin?
   2. si vous essayez de lever un objet trop lourd?
   3. si vous vous asseyez trop longtemps dans la même position?
   4. si vous entendez un bruit très aigu (*shrill*)?
   5. si vous regardez le soleil en face?
   6. si vous buvez trop de bière?
   7. si vous mangez comme un cochon?
   8. si vous dansez toute la soirée?
   9. si vous vous battez avec un type très fort?
   10. si vous mangez des bonbons tous les jours?

2. *Traduisez en français.*

   1. He has a stomach ache because he drank five cokes (*le coca*) last night.
   2. The actress who forgot her lines was probably sick.
   3. The audience applauded so wildly that I got[1] a headache.
   4. I can't go tonight because I'm very sick.
   5. We rehearsed for (*pendant*) eight hours. My feet, my back, and my legs hurt!

   ---
   [1] Use the *passé composé*.

Prepositions————————————

French prepositions often have exact English equivalents.

> **Qui a caché mon manuel de français sous la table?**
> Who hid my French text under the table?
>
> **Elle est allée avec lui.**
> She went with him.

But the use of many prepositions differs significantly from English. In some cases a preposition is used in French where none is used in English, and vice versa. In other cases, the same verb requires one preposition in French and another one in English.

> **Ce jeune romancier refuse de se critiquer.**
> This young novelist refuses to criticize himself.
>
> **Voulez-vous m'attendre ici?**
> Do you want to wait for me here?
>
> **Comme elle joue bien! Elle tient de sa mère!**
> How well she acts! She takes after her mother!

In French, prepositions may be followed by nouns, pronouns, or verbs. Phrases composed of a preposition + noun or pronoun are called prepositional phrases.

Prepositions followed by nouns or pronouns

Simple prepositions

à	*to, at, in*	malgré	*in spite of*
après	*after*	par	*by*
avant	*before*	parmi	*among*
avec	*with*	pour	*for*
contre	*against*	sans	*without*
chez	*at the home, at the place of*	sauf	*except*
dans	*in, into*	selon	
de	*of, from*	suivant	*according to*
derrière	*behind*	d'après	
dès	*from + temporal expression + on*	sous	*under*
devant	*in front of*	sur	*on*
entre	*between*		

> **Si je m'assois derrière cette colonne, je ne verrai pas la scène.**
> If I sit behind this column, I won't see the stage.

Selon ce critique, la nouvelle pièce à la Comédie-Française est un four.
According to this critic, the new play at the Comédie Française is a flop.

Dès maintenant je vais lire un livre par semaine.
From now on I'm going to read one book a week.

Compound prepositions

à cause de   *because of*
à côté de   *beside*
à l'égard de   *regarding*
à l'insu de   *unknown to, without the knowledge of*
au-delà de   *beyond*
au lieu de   *instead of*
au milieu de   *in the middle of*

autour de   *around*
en dépit de   *despite*
en face de   *opposite*
jusqu'à   *as far as, until*
le long de   *along*
loin de   *far from*
près de   *near*
quant à   *as for*

The end prepositions **de** and **à** contract normally with the definite article.

Est-il possible de trouver une place au milieu du théâtre?
Is it possible to find a seat in the middle of the theater?

Elle va se faire actrice en dépit des protestations de ses parents!
She is going to become an actress despite her parents' protests!

EXERCICE

Traduisez en français les mots entre parenthèses.

1. Il a beaucoup aimé le théâtre d'Ionesco _____ (*because of the language*).
2. Quelle chance! Il s'est assis _____ (*between two beautiful girls*)!
3. J'admire tous les personnages dans ce roman _____ (*except the hero*).
4. _____ (*Unknown to my best friends*), j'étais hypocrite.
5. _____ (*Between us*), je dois avouer que ce roman pornographique est _____(*without*) valeur.
6. Mon professeur est _____ (*against*) la littérature uniquement «artistique.»
7. J'étais assis si _____ (*far from the stage*) que je n'ai entendu que des murmures.
8. Le monsieur _____ (*next to me*) sifflait si souvent que j'ai dû lui demander de se taire.
9. Dans cette farce il y avait des acteurs partout _____ (*on the stage, in front of the stage, behind the stage, and under the stage*)!
10. Les acteurs répètent leurs rôles dans une salle _____ (*opposite the theater*).
11. Mon professeur a des idées profondément personnelles _____ (*regarding the imagination*).

12. Je ne comprends pas pourquoi le metteur en scène a choisi ce mauvais acteur _____ (*instead of you*)!

13. Mon frère, qui se passionne pour le théâtre, compte suivre cette troupe _____ (*as far as Paris*).

14. Dans ce spectacle à Avignon, l'action a lieu _____ (*among the spectators*).

15. _____ (*According to a famous critic*), il est impossible qu'un roman soit tout à fait objectif.

French equivalents of English prepositions

In some cases, two or more French prepositions must be used to render one English preposition.

1. Avec, de, à meaning *with*

a. Avec means *with* in most cases.

> **Pourquoi êtes-vous allé au théâtre avec ma meilleure amie?**
> Why did you go to the theater with my best friend?

b. De means *with* after expressions of satisfaction and dissatisfaction, and after certain past participles.

content de	**chargé de**
satisfied with	*loaded with*
satisfait de	**couvert de**
satisfied with	*covered with*
mécontent de	**entouré de**
dissatisfied with	*surrounded with (by)*
	rempli de
	filled with

Remember that when these indefinite expressions are used with nouns, *de* alone is used (see p. 60).

> **Je crois que le public est satisfait de cette représentation.**
> I think the audience is satisfied with this performance.
>
> **Quel succès! L'actrice est entourée d'admirateurs!**
> What a hit! The actress is surrounded with (by) admirers!

c. à + *definite article* means *with* in expressions denoting distinguishing characteristics.

> **Cette actrice aux longs cheveux noirs a l'air séduisante.**
> This actress with long black hair looks attractive.
>
> **Ce monsieur au chapeau gris est mon père.**
> That gentleman with (in) the gray hat is my father.

2. **En** and **dans** meaning *in* with temporal expressions

   a. **En** stresses the duration of time needed to perform an action.

      Robert compte terminer ce roman en un jour!
      Robert intends to finish that novel in one day!

   b. **Dans** stresses the moment an action is to begin. In this usage it is synonymous with **après.**

      La pièce va commencer dans cinq minutes (après cinq minutes).
      The play is going to begin in five minutes.

3. **Pendant** and **depuis** meaning *for*

   a. **Pendant** means *for* in the sense of *during*. Like *for* in English, **pendant** is often omitted in French.

      J'ai attendu (pendant) dix minutes.
      I waited (for) ten minutes.

      Pour usually replaces **pendant** after verbs of motion.

      Cette troupe est venue pour une semaine seulement.
      This troupe has come for one week only.

   b. **Depuis** means *for* when used with verbs in the present perfect and past perfect: *I have (had) been reading for* . . . (see pp. 23–24, 81).

      Nous sommes dans cette librairie depuis deux heures et vous n'avez rien acheté.
      We've been in this bookstore for two hours and you've bought nothing.

      Je le lisais depuis longtemps.
      I had been reading it for a long time.

4. **Vers** and **envers** meaning *toward*

   a. **Vers** means *toward* in both a physical and a figurative sense

      Quelqu'un a crié «au feu!» et tout le monde s'est précipité vers la sortie.
      Someone shouted "fire!" and everybody ran toward the exit.

      Nous avons eu un rendez-vous vers la fin de la soirée.
      We had a date toward the end of the evening.

   b. **Envers** means *toward* when referring to persons in a figurative sense.

      Cet acteur hautain manque d'égards envers tout le monde.
      This condescending actor lacks respect for everyone.

EXERCICE

Traduisez en français les mots entre parenthèses.

1. Cette jeune actrice charmante _____ (*with blue eyes*) me plaît énormément.
2. Comment! Ne pouvez-vous pas lire ce petit bouquin _____ (*in one hour*)?
3. Le public n'est pas du tout satisfait _____ (*with his performance*).
4. Il est vrai que cet acteur est généralement impossible _____ (*toward the other actors*), mais il est très gentil _____ (*towards his friends*).
5. J'ai assisté à quatre représentations théâtrales _____ (*during my stay*) à Londres.
6. Il devrait être très content _____ (*with his hit*).
7. J'avais mal aux oreilles parce que les spectateurs applaudissaient _____ (*for five minutes*)!
8. J'ai eu peur _____ (*during the reading*) des nouvelles de Poe.
9. Le metteur en scène est bien trop exigeant _____ (*toward the actresses*).
10. La Comédie-Française va venir aux États-Unis _____ (*for two months*).
11. Comment s'appelle le personnage héroïque _____ (*with a long nose*) qui n'ose pas déclarer son amour pour Roxane?
12. Elle a commencé à s'endormir _____ (*toward the end*) de la pièce.
13. On prétend que Balzac a écrit *Le Père Goriot* _____ (*in three weeks*) environ.
14. La salle était tout à fait remplie _____ (*with spectators*).
15. La musique de cette comédie musicale ne va pas du tout _____ (*with the decor*).

Prepositions following verbs

There are two kinds of verbs followed by prepositions in French: verbs that are followed by **à** or **de** before an infinitive (though many verbs take no preposition at all), and verbs that require certain prepositions before a noun or pronoun.

Verbs followed by **à** before an infinitive

aider à   *to help*
s'amuser à   *to amuse oneself, to have fun*
apprendre à   *to learn, to teach*
arriver à   *to succeed*
avoir à   *to have (to do something)*
commencer à   *to begin*
consentir à   *to consent*
continuer à   *to continue*
encourager à   *to encourage*

enseigner à   *to teach*
s'habituer à   *to get used to*
hésiter à   *to hesitate*
inviter à   *to invite*
se mettre à   *to begin*
recommencer à   *to begin again*
réussir à   *to succeed*
songer à   *to think, to dream*
tarder à   *to delay*

Invitons les Mercier à dîner chez nous.
Let's invite the Merciers to dinner at our place.

Elle n'a pas réussi à terminer le nouveau best-seller.
She didn't succeed in finishing the new best seller.

Verbs followed by de before an infinitive

s'agir de *to be a question of*	essayer de *to try*
avoir peur de *to be afraid of*	finir de *to finish*
cesser de *to stop*	oublier de *to forget*
commencer de[2] *to begin*	refuser de *to refuse*
continuer de[2] *to continue*	regretter de *to regret*
craindre de *to fear*	remercier de *to thank*
décider de *to decide*	tâcher de *to try*
se dépêcher de *to hurry*	

Il s'agit de lire très attentivement.
It is a question of reading very closely.

Elle a décidé de sortir deux livres de la bibliothèque.
She decided to take out two books from the library.

Verbs that take no preposition before an infinitive

Many common verbs require neither **à** nor **de** before an infinitive. These verbs are followed directly by the infinitive.

aimer *to like*	falloir *to be necessary*
aimer mieux *to prefer*	laisser *to leave, to let*
aller *to go*	oser *to dare*
compter *to intend*	paraître *to appear*
croire *to believe*	pouvoir *to be able, can*
désirer *to desire, to wish*	préférer *to prefer*
devoir *to have to, ought*	savoir *to know, to know how*
entendre *to hear*	sembler *to seem*
espérer *to hope*	venir *to come*
faire *to do, to make*	voir *to see*
	vouloir *to want, to wish*

Savez-vous critiquer une pièce et un roman?
Do you know how to criticize a play and a novel?

---

[2] The verbs **commencer** and **continuer** may be followed by either **à** or **de.**

Cet auteur préfère vivre dans son imagination.
This author prefers to live in his imagination.

EXERCICES

1. *Examinez-vous les uns les autres! En choisissant parmi les trois groupes de verbes aux pages 210–211, chaque étudiant prépare une liste de dix verbes qu'il apporte en classe. Un étudiant lit ses verbes, un à un, à un autre étudiant qui répond le plus vite possible par «à,» «de» ou «rien.» Tous les livres sont fermés pendant l'exercice.*

2. *Traduisez en français les verbes entre parenthèses. Ajoutez* **à** *ou* **de** *s'il y a lieu.*

   1. Il _____ (*decided*) sortir un roman de Camus de la bibliothèque.
   2. Elle _____ (*hopes*) assister à la nouvelle pièce d'Ionesco.
   3. Cet auteur célèbre _____ (*continues*) scandaliser le public avec ses romans pornographiques.
   4. Il _____ (*prefers*) lire les biographies parce qu'il aime les histoires croyables.
   5. Zut! Je _____ (*forgot*) demander le nom du type que j'ai rencontré au spectacle!
   6. Nous _____ (*will begin*) applaudir dès que le deuxième acte sera terminé.
   7. L'intrigue _____ (*ceased*) m'intéresser au moment où elle est devenue trop compliquée.
   8. La troupe _____ (*will finish*) répéter demain ou après-demain.
   9. Est-ce que la littérature _____ (*should*) plaire ou enseigner?
   10. Cet auteur _____ (*didn't succeed*) créer une illusion de la vie réelle dans son nouveau roman.
   11. À l'université il _____ (*learned*) lire des pièces mais il _____ (*didn't learn*) les critiquer.
   12. Je _____ (*tried*) trouver la pièce *Le Cid* de Corneille à la bibliothèque municipale, mais on l'avait sortie.
   13. Elle _____ (*hesitated*) acheter le nouveau best-seller parce que les critiques ne l'avaient pas recommandé.
   14. Je suis contente que le public _____ (*refused*) applaudir ce four!
   15. Il _____ (*had to*) lire une pièce de Sartre pour son cours de littérature française.
   16. Elle _____ (*dared*) me dire que la pornographie est plus intéressante que la littérature!
   17. _____ (*Hurry*) trouver nos places avant le commencement de la pièce!
   18. Je vous _____ (*will help*) bien critiquer la littérature si vous me promettez de lire plus attentivement.
   19. Notre professeur nous _____ (*encouraged*) lire des pièces et des romans de Samuel Beckett.
   20. _____ (*Would you like*) aller voir cette comédie musicale avec moi la semaine prochaine?

Verbs followed by à + *noun and* de + *infinitive*

Some French verbs that are followed by **de** + *infinitive* also take an indirect object.

conseiller à quelqu'un de   *to advise someone to*
défendre à quelqu'un de   *to forbid someone to*
demander à quelqu'un de   *to ask someone to*
dire à quelqu'un de   *to tell someone to*
écrire à quelqu'un de   *to write someone to*
ordonner à quelqu'un de   *to order someone to*
permettre à quelqu'un de   *to permit someone to*
promettre à quelqu'un de   *to promise someone to*
téléphoner à quelqu'un de   *to telephone someone to*

Son professeur de chimie a conseillé à Jean de suivre au moins un cours de littérature française.
His chemistry professor advised John to take at least one French literature course.

Mon ami m'a demandé d'acheter un billet.
My friend asked me to buy a ticket.

EXERCICE

Traduisez en français.

1. Ask your French professor to recommend a good bedside book.
2. Promise them to listen attentively.
3. I advise you to rehearse every day.
4. My parents forbid me to read the novels of the marquis de Sade.
5. The director ordered the actor to begin again.
6. If you permit me to play the main (*principal*) character in your play, it will be a hit.
7. If I criticize her poetry, she tells me to shut up.
8. I am asking you to write plays that are more believable (*croyable*).

Verbs that require a preposition before a noun or pronoun

1. Some common verbs take a preposition in English but none in French.

attendre   *to wait for*   écouter   *to listen to*
chercher   *to look for*   payer   *to pay for*
demander   *to ask for*   regarder   *to look at*

Allez-vous regarder la pièce de Shakespeare à la télévision ce soir?
Are you going to watch the Shakespeare play on television tonight?

Je vous attends depuis deux heures!
I have been waiting for you for two hours!

EXERCICE

Traduisez en français.

1. I'm asking for a good novel.
2. The police are looking for you.
3. She listens attentively to her professor's ideas.
4. She has been waiting for them for three hours.
5. That girl refuses to pay for her books.
6. Look at that!
7. Listen to your friends.

2. Some common verbs take a preposition in French but none in English.

s'approcher de   *to approach*
assister à   *to attend*
changer de   *to change (one thing for another)*
douter de   *to doubt*
se douter de   *to suspect (the existence of)*
entrer dans   *to enter*
se fier à   *to trust*

se marier avec   *to marry*
se méfier de   *to distrust*
obéir à   *to obey*
plaire à   *to please*
se rendre compte de   *to realize*
répondre à   *to answer*
résister à   *to resist*
ressembler à   *to resemble*
se servir de   *to use*
se souvenir de   *to remember*

The end prepositions **de** and **à** contract normally with the definite article.

Je ne peux pas entrer dans une librairie sans acheter au moins un ouvrage de science fiction.
I can't enter a bookstore without buying at least one work of science fiction.

Elle n'a pas répondu à sa dernière lettre.
She didn't answer his last letter.

Elle ne veut pas assister aux représentations de cette troupe.
She doesn't want to attend the performances of that troupe.

EXERCICE

Traduisez les mots entre parenthèses en français en faisant tous les autres change-ments nécessaires.

1. Cette actrice _____ (*changes*) amis comme elle _____ (*changes*) costumes!
2. Ce mime excellent _____ (*resembles*) le mime français Marcel Marceau.
3. C'est un acteur obstiné qui _____ (*doesn't obey*) son metteur en scène.
4. Quand mon père _____ (*married*) ma mère, c'était une grande erreur.
5. Les comédies de Molière semblent _____ (*to please*) tout le monde.

6. Ils _____ (*will never realize*) l'effort qu'il faut pour écrire quelque chose d'original.
7. C'est un auteur sûr de lui qui _____ (*doesn't doubt*) son talent.
8. _____ (*Don't resist*) la police!
9. Si vous voulez jouer le rôle d'une vieille dame, _____ (*use*) beaucoup de maquillage.
10. Préférez-vous _____ (*to attend*) les représentations ou les regarder à la télévision?
11. J'étais certain que cet éditeur _____ (*distrusted*) les auteurs «inspirés»!
12. Le roman que je viens de lire _____ (*resembles*) beaucoup le roman que nous avons étudié en classe.
13. Quand vous _____ (*approach*) la rivière, tournez à gauche. Vous verrez le théâtre.
14. Mon fils est un jeune homme optimiste qui _____ (*trusts*) tout le monde.
15. Ils voulaient cacher le scandale, mais _____ (*I suspected*) quelque chose.

3. Some common verbs take one preposition in French and another in English.

> dépendre de   *to depend on*
> être en colère contre   *to be angry with*
> s'intéresser à   *to be interested in*
> s'occuper de   *to busy oneself with, to attend to*
> remercier de, remercier pour   *to thank for*
> rire de   *to laugh at*
> tenir de   *to take after (resemble)*

Je m'intéresse beaucoup à la philosophie de Sartre.
I am very interested in Sartre's philosophy.

Je vous remercie du bouquin que vous m'avez donné comme cadeau.
I thank you for the book that you gave me as a gift.

EXERCICE

Traduisez les mots entre parenthèses en faisant tous les autres changements nécessaires.
modèle: Elle _____ (is interested in) les poètes.
          Elle s'intéresse aux poètes.

1. Vous ne devriez pas _____ (*be angry with him*) tout simplement parce qu'il est malade.
2. Ce type à côté de moi _____ (*is laughing at*) toutes les actions sérieuses dans cette tragédie!
3. La qualité de la lecture _____ (*depends on*) la qualité du lecteur.
4. Vous _____ (*don't take after*) votre mère qui dévorait les romans!
5. Il _____ (*will thank you for*) votre avis.
6. On _____ (*is interested in*) le théâtre parce qu'on a l'habitude de jouer des rôles dans la vie.

7. _____ (*Don't be angry with*) moi si je vous dis que vous êtes un mauvais acteur.

8. Moi, je _____ (*busy myself with*) le décor tandis que lui _____ (*attends to*) les costumes.

4. Some common French verbs may be followed by either **à** or **de**.

    a. The verb **jouer à** means *to play a game*; **jouer de** means *to play a musical instrument*.

> **Vous ne devriez pas jouer au bridge pendant la répétition!**
> You shouldn't play bridge during rehearsal!
>
> **C'est mon frère qui joue de la guitare dans la comédie musicale.**
> It's my brother who plays the guitar in the musical.

    b. The verb **manquer à** means *to miss someone, to feel their absence*. When the French sentence is translated into English, subject and object are reversed.

> **Juliette manque à Roméo.**
> Romeo misses Juliet. (lit., Juliet is lacking to Romeo.)
>
> **Il m'a beaucoup manqué.**
> I missed him very much. (lit., he was very much lacking to me.)

Manquer de means *to lack something*.

> **Ce jeune auteur manque d'argent.**
> This young author lacks money.

But when **manquer** is followed directly by a direct object, it means *to miss* in the sense of not *to catch or hit*.

> **J'ai manqué le dernier métro.**
> I missed the last subway.
>
> **Il a lancé une pierre qui m'a manqué.**
> He threw a stone that missed me.

    c. The verb **penser à** means *to think of* in the sense of *to reflect about*.

> **À quoi pensez-vous? —Je pense à mon prochain succès!**
> What are you thinking about? —I'm thinking about my next hit!

But **penser de** means *to think of* in the sense of *to have an opinion about*.

> **Que pensez-vous de cette actrice? —Je la trouve brillante et honnête.**
> What do you think of that actress? —I find her brilliant and honest.

EXERCICES

1. *Traduisez en français les mots entre parenthèses en faisant tous les autres changements nécessaires.*

   1. Cet acteur _____ (*plays the piano and the guitar*[3]).
   2. Que _____ (*do you think of*) la représentation de *Phèdre* à la Comédie-Française?
   3. Voudriez-vous _____ (*to play tennis*) avec moi?
   4. Quand je commence à _____ (*to think about*) ce spectacle, j'ai envie de crier!
   5. Dites-moi franchement ce que _____ (*you think of*) ma poésie.
   6. _____ (*Let's play cards*) ce soir.
   7. Ce critique de théâtre _____ (*lacks*) respect pour nos acteurs.

2. *Traduisez en français en employant* **manquer** *ou* **manquer à.**

   1. Mary misses John.
   2. John misses Mary.
   3. I miss you a lot.
   4. We missed the plane.
   5. Will you miss me tomorrow?
   6. Do you miss your parents this semester?
   7. Fortunately the tomato (*la tomate*) missed me!

Related expressions

Expressions of means of locomotion

As a rule, the preposition **à** is used if one rides *on* the means of locomotion, and **dans** or **en** if one rides *in* it.

à bicyclette *by bicycle*	**en autostop** *by hitchhiking*
à cheval *on horseback*	**en (par) avion** *by plane*
à (en) moto *by motorcycle*	**en bateau** *by boat*
à pied *on foot*	**en métro** *by subway*
à vélo *by bike*	**en taxi** *by taxi*
en autobus *by bus*	**dans le train** *by train*
	en voiture *by car*

EXERCICE

Répondez en français par une phrase complète.

1. Comment voyagez-vous pendant les vacances d'été?
2. Si vous comptiez faire un voyage en France, comment iriez-vous?
3. Comment venez-vous à l'université?

---

[3] Repeat the preposition.

4. Comment pouvait-on aller de New York jusqu'à l'océan Pacifique vers 1800?
5. Comment y va-t-on maintenant?
6. Comment peut-on se déplacer le plus rapidement dans les grandes villes modernes?
7. Comment rendez-vous visite à un ami qui habite à côté de vous?
8. Comment les cow-boys se déplaçaient-ils de préférence?
9. Vous êtes en retard pour une représentation théâtrale à New York. Comment comptez-vous y arriver le plus vite possible?
10. Si on veut faire un long voyage aujourd'hui, quel est le moyen de transport le moins cher? le moyen de transport le plus snob? le plus sain? le moins dangereux? le plus reposant? celui qui fait le moins de pollution? le plus de bruit?

Exercices d'ensemble

I. *Répondez en français par une phrase complète.*

1. Qui est votre acteur favori?
2. Pouvez-vous nommer quelques pièces de Molière?
3. Quand avez-vous mal à la tête?
4. Invitez-vous souvent vos amis chez vous? Pourquoi ou pourquoi pas?
5. Avez-vous été souvent malade ce semestre?
6. Aimez-vous mieux les notes de votre camarade de chambre ou les vôtres?
7. La voiture que vous conduisez actuellement est-elle à vous ou à vos parents?
8. Quel est votre livre de chevet en ce moment?
9. Quelle est votre pièce favorite? votre roman favori?

II. *Répondez en français par une phrase complète.*

1. Combien avez-vous payé vos livres ce semestre?
2. De quel instrument jouez-vous?
3. À quel sport jouez-vous le mieux?
4. À qui ressemblez-vous?
5. Qui ou quoi vous manque le plus ce semestre?
6. De qui tenez-vous?
7. De quoi vous servez-vous pour écrire une composition?
8. En combien de temps pouvez-vous lire un roman de trois cents pages?
9. Pendant combien de temps comptez-vous rester à l'université?
10. De quoi manquez-vous en ce moment?

III. *Remplacez les tirets par* **à** *ou* **de** *s'il y a lieu.*

1. A-t-il essayé _____ jouer?
2. Elle commence _____ critiquer ma conduite.

3. Ose-t-il _____ parler au président?
4. Ils n'ont pas fini _____ applaudir.
5. N'oubliez pas _____ le faire!
6. Elle s'amuse _____ lire son roman.
7. Il a réussi _____ créer un rôle.
8. Ils refusaient _____ partir.
9. Nous aurons peur _____ demander cela.
10. Je dois _____ cesser _____ jouer.

IV. *Traduisez en français.*

1. His last role lacked life, but it wasn't wholly monotonous (*monotone*).
2. The book on the table in your room belongs to me.
3. The actress's face was covered with make-up.
4. My professor permitted me to read one of Voltaire's books instead of another novel.
5. His essays (*essais*) pleased me so much that I decided to ask for them at the bookstore.
6. I go to shows because I can't resist them!
7. I had to read Hugo's novel very attentively because the style was difficult.
8. The play was a flop for many reasons: the plot was not believable, the actors didn't know their lines, and the scenery and costumes lacked style.

Sujets de discussion ou de composition

1. Résumez une pièce ou un roman que vous admirez: le thème, les personnages, l'action, l'intrigue, le décor, les costumes, le style, etc.
2. Vrai ou faux? Ceux qui lisent et écrivent la littérature veulent échapper (*escape*) à la vie réelle.
3. La littérature pornographique est-elle jamais justifiée? Dans quelles circonstances? Discutez.

11

The passive voice, the present participle, the causative construction

Chapter 11 at a glance

THE PASSIVE VOICE

I. *Traduisez en français les verbes entre parenthèses.*

1. Cette chanson folklorique _____ (*is sung by*) un groupe sensationnel.
2. Le morceau de Debussy _____ (*will be played by*) un pianiste américain.
3. Cette farce _____ (*was written*) au moyen âge.

II. *Mettez les phrases à la* **voix passive** *si c'est possible.*

1. Ce documentaire violent a scandalisé le grand public.
2. Robert se passionne pour les films de Truffaut.
3. Cet acteur jouera deux grands rôles l'année prochaine.

III. *Mettez les phrases actives à la* **voix passive** *en employant* **on** *comme sujet.*

1. Les bonbons et le pop-corn ont été mangés en deux minutes.
2. Comment! Le dessin animé de Disney a été censuré?

IV. *Traduisez en français en employant un* **verbe réfléchi.**

1. That is done only in the movies!
2. His books are quickly sold.

THE PRESENT PARTICIPLE

V. *Mettez les verbes au* **participe présent.**

1. écouter
2. se divertir
3. vendre
4. faire
5. avoir

VI. *Traduisez en français les mots entre parenthèses en employant le* **participe présent.** *Employez* **en** *ou* **tout en** *s'il y a lieu.*

1. Comment s'appelle la jeune fille _____ (*singing*) cette mélodie charmante?
2. Ce compositeur buvait de la bière _____ (*while composing*) une chanson à boire!
3. Ce film de guerre est sérieux _____ (*while being at the same time*) très drôle.

VII. *Mettez les infinitifs au* **participe présent** *en faisant l'accord s'il y a lieu.*

1. Les nouveaux films au drive-in sont _____ (divertir).
2. Cette chanteuse n'est ni _____ (amuser) ni _____ (intéresser).

VIII. *Traduisez en français les verbes entre parenthèses.*

1. Il passe plus de temps à _____ (*looking at*) les westerns à la télévision qu'à _____ (*studying*).
2. Comment peut-elle regarder ce film _____ (*without leaving*)?
3. Je l'ai entendu _____ (*singing*) une chanson risquée au cabaret.

THE CAUSATIVE CONSTRUCTION

IX. *Traduisez en français en employant la construction* **faire** + infinitif.

1. He is having his guitar sold.
2. Is he having it done right away?
3. He has his friend leave.

Vocabulaire du thème: Chanson et Cinéma

LA CHANSON
MUSICIENS

le **chanteur**, la **chanteuse**   *singer*
le **compositeur**   *composer*
composer   *to compose*
le **chansonnier**   *chansonnier: a composer and singer of risqué, satirical songs who is somewhat akin to the American folk singer.*

le **musicien**, la **musicienne**   *musician*
jouer (**de la guitare, du piano,** etc.)
   to play (*the guitar, the piano, etc.*)
le **débutant**   *beginner*
le **concert**   *concert*
la **discothèque**   *discothèque*

L'ENREGISTREMENT

l' **enregistrement** (m)   *recording*
enregistrer   *to record*
la **bande**   *tape*

le **magnétophone**   *tape recorder*
le **disque**   *record* (*music*)
le **tourne-disque**   *record player*

L'ART DE LA CHANSON

l' **harmonie** (f)   *harmony*
la **mélodie**   *melody, tune*

les **paroles** (f)   *words, lyrics*
le **rythme**   *rhythm*

LE CINÉMA
LE FILM

le **cinéma**   *movies, cinema; movie theater*
cinématographique   *cinematographic*
le **film**   *film*
filmer   *to film*
la **caméra**   *camera* (*movie*)
tourner un film   *to make a film*
le **plan**   *shot* (*film*)
la **piste sonore**   *sound track*

le **scénario**   *script, scenario*
le **réalisateur**   *director*
la **vedette**   (*movie*) *star*
le **dénouement heureux**   *happy ending*
en version originale   *in the original*
le **sous-titre**   *subtitle*
sous-titrer   *to subtitle* (*a film*)
doubler   *to dub* (*a film*)

le, la **cinéphile**   *movie fan*
  le **grand public**   *the general public*
    apprécier   *to appreciate*
    censurer   *to censor*

faire la queue   *to wait in line*
siffler   *to whistle, to boo*
se **passionner pour**   *to be crazy about*

The passive voice

Like English verbs, French verbs possess an active and a passive voice. A verb is in the active voice if the subject acts, and in the passive voice if the subject is acted upon.

Active voice: **Un débutant a composé cette chanson folklorique.**
A beginner composed this folk song.

Jean analyse les films de Truffaut dans son cours de cinéma.
John analyzes Truffaut's films in his cinema course.

Passive voice: **Le nouveau film d'Altman sera discuté par toute la classe.**
Altman's new film will be discussed by the entire class.

Cette chanson folklorique a été composée par un débutant.
This folk song was composed by a beginner.

Formation of the passive

The passive sentence is composed of:

subject + *passive verb* (+agent)

Le rôle principal sera joué par un acteur inconnu.
The main role will be played by an unknown actor.

Ce film d'épouvante a été beaucoup discuté.
This horror film has been discussed a lot.

Note that, as in the second example, the agent is not always expressed.

The passive verb

A verb in the passive is composed of two parts:

a tense of **être** + *past participle*

The past participle agrees in number and gender with the subject.

> **Ces disques brisés ont été vendus par un vendeur malhonnête!**
> These broken records were sold by a dishonest salesman!

> **Les paroles seront écrites par la chanteuse elle-même.**
> The lyrics will be written by the singer herself.

The agent

The person or thing that performs the action on the subject is called the agent. The preposition **par** is normally used to introduce the agent. **Par** tends to stress specific actions performed by the agent.

> **Le scénario a été écrit par un romancier célèbre.**
> The script was written by a famous novelist.

> **Tout le pop-corn a été mangé par ma camarade de chambre!**
> All the popcorn was eaten by my roommate!

The preposition **de** often replaces **par** with less dynamic verbs such as **accompagner, précéder, suivre, voir,** and verbs that express a state of mind:

aimer	respecter
admirer	accompagner
apprécier	précéder
détester	

> **La musique de Beethoven était admirée de presque tout le monde.**
> Beethoven's music was admired by almost everyone.

> **Ce jeune chanteur était toujours accompagné d'admirateurs.**
> This young singer was always accompanied by admirers.

Note that the imperfect of **être** is often used with verbs of description and state of mind (**admirée** and **accompagné** above), whereas the **passé composé** of **être** is used with verbs expressing specific actions (**écrit** and **mangé** above).

EXERCICE

Traduisez en français les mots entre parenthèses en employant la **voix passive.**

1. Cette chanson sentimentale _____ (*was composed by*) un chansonnier célèbre et _____ (*was sung by*) Édith Piaf.
2. Je suis sûr que ce jeune compositeur _____ (*will be admired by*) tout le monde à l'avenir.
3. Ce film comique français _____ (*was dubbed by*) un type qui ne connaît pas le français!
4. Vous êtes venu trop tard! Tous les disques de Piaf _____ (*have already been sold*).

5. La musique moderne _____ (*was influenced by*) le jazz américain.
6. Ces concerts à la télévision _____ (*will be seen by*) beaucoup de spectateurs.
7. Comment! Est-il possible que ce film documentaire _____ (*will be censored by*) le gouvernement?
8. Cette vedette _____ (*was not respected by*) la majorité des cinéphiles, mais elle _____ (*was admired by*) le grand public.
9. Ce morceau de musique harmonieux _____ (*was composed by*) un débutant.
10. Elle préfère les films d'amour qui _____ (*were made by*) les grands réalisateurs de Hollywood parce qu'elle aime les dénouements heureux.

Use of the passive

The use of the passive voice is limited in French. It is generally used only with a verb that is regularly accompanied by a direct object (a transitive verb). As a rule of thumb, the direct object of an active verb becomes the subject of a passive verb, and the subject of an active verb becomes the agent of a passive verb.

ACTIVE VOICE	PASSIVE VOICE
Jean a tourné le film.	**Le film a été tourné par Jean.**
John made the film.	The film was made by John.
Marie chante la chanson.	**La chanson est chantée par Marie.**
Mary sings the song.	The song is sung by Mary.

Note that reflexive verbs, and verbs that take only indirect objects, cannot usually be made passive.

ACTIVE VOICE	PASSIVE VOICE
Tout le monde s'est amusé à la discothèque.	No passive possible: **s'amuser** is a reflexive verb.
Everyone had a good time at the discothèque.	
A good time was had by all at the discothèque.	
Cette musique plaît à Nancy.	No passive possible: **plaire (à)**
This music pleases Nancy.	takes only an indirect object.
Nancy is pleased by this music.	

EXERCICE

Mettez les phrases actives à la **voix passive** *si c'est possible.*
modèle: Les étudiants ont chanté une chanson à boire dans le bar.
   Une chanson à boire a été chantée par les étudiants dans le bar.
1. Les partisans de l'avant-garde ont employé de nouvelles techniques cinématographiques.
2. Il a composé la musique mais son frère a écrit les paroles.

3. Ce nouveau film classé «x» a scandalisé le grand public.
4. Toute la famille a apprécié le concert de musique folklorique.
5. Dans ce western, le héros ressemble au vilain!
6. À mon avis, ce critique a mal interprété la signification profonde du film d'Antonioni.
7. Mon frère s'intéresse beaucoup au morceau *l'Après-midi d'un faune* de Debussy.
8. Dans ce film d'amour, le héros ment à l'héroïne pour la protéger.
9. Les cinéphiles admirent certains films français à cause de leur valeur artistique.
10. Ils ont analysé le mouvement, le suspens et le rythme des plans.

Avoiding the passive

Whenever possible, the French use the active voice in preference to the passive. The active voice is also used to render English passive constructions that do not have direct French equivalents.

Avoiding the French passive

1. If a passive sentence has an agent expressed, the passive verb may be put into the active voice with the passive agent as subject.

   Passive: **La Marseillaise a été chantée par les spectateurs.**
   The *Marseillaise* was sung by the spectators.

   Active: **Les spectateurs ont chanté la Marseillaise.**
   The spectators sang the *Marseillaise*.

2. If the passive sentence has no agent expressed, the passive verb is put into the active voice with the indefinite pronoun **on** as subject. **On** may be translated in English by *we, they,* or *one,* or more often by the English passive voice.

   Passive: **La glace a été mangée en cinq minutes.**
   The ice cream was eaten in five minutes.

   Active: **On a mangé la glace en cinq minutes.**
   We (they) ate the ice cream in five minutes.

   or: The ice cream was eaten in five minutes.

   Note that **on** is used as a subject only if the unexpressed agent is a person. Otherwise, the sentence remains in the passive voice.

   Le cinéma a été totalement détruit en deux minutes.
   The movie theater was totally destroyed in two minutes.
   (It was destroyed by a natural disaster.)

Avoiding the English passive

English may use the passive voice to state general facts or actions. This English construction is often rendered in French by a reflexive verb.

Tapes are sold everywhere.
Les bandes se vendent partout.
That is not easily understood.
Ça ne se comprend pas facilement.

EXERCICES

1. *Mettez les phrases passives à la* **voix active** *en faisant tous les changements nécessaires.*
   modèles: À mon avis, cette vedette a été exploitée.
   À mon avis, on a exploité cette vedette.

   Le premier prix au festival de Cannes a été gagné par un film policier.
   Un film policier a gagné le premier prix au festival de Cannes.

   1. Beaucoup de chansons tristes et sentimentales ont été chantées par elle.
   2. Ce film d'amour a été tourné en un mois.
   3. Le morceau moderne a été mieux interprété que le morceau classique.
   4. Tous les rôles dans ce film ont été joués par un seul acteur!
   5. Malheureusement, le nouveau film de Bergman a été mal sous-titré.
   6. Un excellent chansonnier a été choisi par le réalisateur pour jouer le rôle principal dans sa comédie musicale.
   7. Beaucoup de romans français célèbres ont été filmés.
   8. Le réalisateur a été interrogé par un reporter qui lui a posé des questions idiotes.
   9. L'atmosphère bizarre et mystérieuse a été bien rendue dans ce film d'épouvante (*horror*).
   10. La caméra a été inventée en 1895 par les frères Lumière.

2. *Traduisez en français.*

   1. Good actors are not easily found.
   2. That is not done here.
   3. Rock-and-roll music (*le rock*) sells better than classical music (*la musique classique*).
   4. Bad movies are quickly forgotten.
   5. Good music is not easily composed.

The present participle_____

The present participle is called a verbal adjective because it can be used as both a verb and an adjective. The present participle in English ends in *-ing:* *acting, singing, interesting.*

Formation of the present participle

The French present participle is formed by dropping the **-ons** ending of verbs in the present tense and adding **-ant.**

> chanter: nous chantons, chantant *singing*
> applaudir: nous applaudissons, applaudissant *applauding*
> mentir: nous mentons, mentant *lying*
> vendre: nous vendons, vendant *selling*

The present participles of **avoir, être,** and **savoir** are irregular.

> avoir: ayant *having*
> être: étant *being*
> savoir: sachant *knowing*

EXERCICE

Changez les infinitifs en **participes présents.**

1.	interpréter	6.	insulter	11.	rire	16.	fouiller
2.	applaudir	7.	apprécier	12.	critiquer	17.	tourner
3.	être	8.	mentir	13.	étudier	18.	finir
4.	choisir	9.	savoir	14.	réfléchir	19.	tutoyer
5.	exploiter	10.	gagner	15.	partir	20.	vendre

Use of the present participle

The participle used as a verb

1. When used as a verb, the present participle is invariable. Like all verbs, it may indicate an action or a state of being.

   > **J'ai rencontré quelques musiciens sifflant une mélodie.**
   > I met some musicians whistling a tune.

   > **Se sentant bien seul, il est allé au cinéma.**
   > Feeling very lonely, he went to the movies.

2. The expression **en** + *present participle* is used to indicate that two actions are somewhat simultaneous. When **en** is so used, its English equivalent is *by, while, on, upon, in,* or *when.* The expression generally refers to the subject of the sentence.

   > **En me promenant dans le parc, j'ai rencontré un vieillard jouant du violon.**
   > While walking in the park, I met an old man playing the violin.

Ce réalisateur est devenu célèbre en scandalisant le grand public.
This director became famous by scandalizing the general public.

En touchant la main de la belle chanteuse, il s'est évanoui.
Upon touching the beautiful singer's hand, he fainted.

Tout is placed before **en** to stress the idea of simultaneity and/or opposition.

Ce réalisateur tournait un film d'amour tout en écrivant le scénario d'un documentaire.
This director was making a romantic film while at the same time writing the script of a documentary.

Ce morceau moderne est harmonieux tout en étant discordant.
This modern piece is harmonious even while being discordant.

EXERCICE

Mettez les verbes entre parenthèses au **participe présent.** *Employez* **en** *ou* **tout en** *s'il y a lieu.*

1. J'ai entendu un bruit derrière moi causé par un jeune homme _____ (jouer) de l'harmonica.
2. Il sifflait _____ (se promener) dans la rue.
3. Qui est ce monsieur distingué _____ (sortir) du cabaret?
4. Mon fils, vous ne composerez des morceaux magnifiques que _____ (travailler) tous les jours!
5. Je ne sais pas comment elle peut danser _____ (chanter)!
6. Dans les westerns, il y a toujours des cow-boys _____ (se battre) dans les saloons.
7. J'ai fait la connaissance chez Maxime de quatre acteurs _____ (jouer) actuellement dans le nouveau film de Godard.
8. Elle a perfectionné son rythme _____ (enregistrer) sa voix.
9. Ce réalisateur aimable m'a offert un petit rôle dans un film de science fiction _____ (savoir) que je n'étais qu'un débutant.
10. Le cinéma joue un rôle social important _____ (montrer) une image fidèle de la société moderne.
11. Ce monsieur qui gesticule comme un fou est un mime _____ (répéter) son rôle.
12. Avez-vous jamais assisté au concert d'un chansonnier _____ (chanter) des chansons risquées et satiriques?
13. _____ (Juger) par la foule qui l'entoure, c'est une vedette _____ (signer) dans les programmes.
14. Ce réalisateur est devenu l'idole des cinéphiles _____ (refuser) de compromettre son art.
15. Cette actrice est un paradoxe! Elle est très admirée _____ (être) très critiquée.

The participle used as an adjective

When used as an adjective, the present participle, like all adjectives, agrees in number and gender with the noun or pronoun it modifies. It is usually placed after the noun. Many present participles have become commonly used adjectives: **amusant, charmant, intéressant,** etc.

Les paroles de cette chanson d'amour sont très touchantes.
The words of this love song are very touching.

Les films expérimentaux sont souvent divertissants.
Experimental movies are often entertaining.

EXERCICE

Mettez les infinitifs au **participe présent** *en faisant, s'il y a lieu, tous les autres changements nécessaires.*

1. Je trouve la musique de Mozart très _____ (vivre).
2. Comment s'appelle le beau jeune homme _____ (bavarder) avec son amie devant le drive-in?
3. J'étais surpris par les idées _____ (frapper) de cette actrice.
4. Ce réalisateur montre son génie _____ (tourner) des films originaux.
5. J'ai pris une photo de Jacques Brel _____ (chanter) ses chansons populaires.
6. Il préfère la musique _____ (amuser) à la musique sérieuse.
7. L'humeur (*mood*) des spectateurs est très _____ (changer) ce soir!
8. Les personnages dans ce film n'étaient pas très _____ (intéresser), mais l'intrigue était _____ (fasciner).
9. Les réalisateurs imaginatifs et passionnés sont presque toujours _____ (étonner).
10. Il a écrit son scénario en un mois, _____ (étonner) tout le monde!

The English present participle and the French infinitive

It is sometimes necessary to render an English present participle by an infinitive in French.

Commencer par *and* finir par + *infinitive*

The verbs **commencer** and **finir** require **par** + *infinitive* instead of **en** + *present participle*. If the verbs are followed by a direct object, however, **en** + *present* *participle* is used. The English equivalents are *to begin by*, and *to finish by* or *to finally* . . .

> **Le réalisateur a commencé par filmer un plan tranquille et il a fini par filmer un plan violent.**
> The director began by filming a quiet shot and finished by filming a violent shot.
>
> **Il a fini par accepter le rôle.**
> He finally accepted the role.

but: **Nous avons commencé la soirée en allant au drive-in.**
We began the evening by going to the drive-in.

Passer à + *infinitive*

When the verb **passer** means *to spend time*, the expression **à** + *infinitive* must be used to render the English present participle.

> **Nous avons passé une heure à chercher un bon film dans le journal.**
> We spent one hour looking for a good film in the newspaper.

Avant de *and* sans + *infinitive*

The prepositions **avant de** and **sans** followed by the infinitive render the English *before* and *without* + *present participle*.

> **Il faut répéter beaucoup avant de chanter devant le public.**
> It is necessary to rehearse a lot before singing before the public.
>
> **Il est allé voir le film sans savoir que c'était un navet!**
> He went to see the film without knowing it was a flop!

Note that the preposition **après** must be followed by the past infinitive (**avoir** or **être** + *past participle*). Its most frequent English equivalent is *after* +*present participle*.

> **Il a décidé d'aller au concert après en avoir lu une critique favorable.**
> He decided to attend the concert after reading a favorable criticism of it.
>
> **Après être rentrés, ils ont bu un coca.**
> After returning home, they drank a coke.

Verbs of perception + *infinitive*

In French, a progressive action is often expressed by an infinitive after a verb of perception like:

apercevoir	regarder
écouter	sentir
entendre	voir

The infinitive is rendered in English by the present participle.

> **Je l'ai vu parler avec elle il y a cinq minutes.**
> I saw him speaking with her five minutes ago.

> **En passant devant le cabaret, j'ai entendu chanter mon chansonnier favori.**
> While passing in front of the cabaret, I heard my favorite chansonnier singing.

> **J'ai vu construire le nouveau cinéma.**
> I saw the new movie theater being built.

This construction may also be used to state a fact, rather than to express a progressive action.

> **Je l'ai entendu chanter beaucoup de fois.**
> I heard him sing many times.

EXERCICE

Traduisez en français les mots entre parenthèses.

1. Le professeur de cinéma a commencé _____ (*by describing*) le film et il a fini _____ (*by discussing*) sa signification profonde.
2. Ils lisent toujours des critiques _____ (*before going to see*) un film.
3. Elle a passé toute la soirée _____ (*listening to*) ses nouveaux disques.
4. Quelle chance! Nous avons vu un grand réalisateur _____ (*making*) un film.
5. Les spectateurs ont commencé _____ (*by applauding*) et ils ont fini _____ (*by booing*).
6. Pendant sa jeunesse, ce musicien américain a passé beaucoup de temps _____ (*composing*) de la musique populaire.
7. Ils étaient plus impressionnés quand ils l'ont vue _____ (*singing*) le blues en personne que quand ils l'ont entendue _____ (*singing*) le blues à la radio.
8. _____ (*After finishing*) son exécution parfaite du morceau de Bach, la violoniste s'est assise.
9. Cet acteur comique a fini sa carrière _____ (*by playing*) un rôle sérieux dans un film de guerre.
10. Comment s'appelle cette jeune fille _____ (*whistling*) dans le parc?
11. Mon frère vient de passer cinq heures _____ (*rehearsing*) pour son concert demain.
12. Elle ne peut pas aller voir un film _____ (*without dreaming*) qu'elle en est la vedette!
13. _____ (*After eating*) tout le pop-corn, mon amie a commencé à manger de la glace!
14. Je pouvais passer des heures _____ (*watching*) cet acteur _____ (*playing*) son rôle favori.

The causative construction_____

The causative construction is used to express the idea of *having someone do something* or *having something done*. It is composed of two parts:

a tense of **faire** + *infinitive*

Je ferai réparer mon tourne-disque.
I will have my record player repaired.

Comme il fait travailler ses acteurs!
How he has (makes) his actors work!

The causative construction may have one or two objects.

The causative with one object

When the causative has only one object, the object is a direct object.

Chut! Le président fait enregistrer votre voix!
Quiet! The President is having your voice taped!

Il fait partir les journalistes.
He has (makes) the reporters leave.

Note that the objects follow the infinitive in French, but come between the two verbs in English.

The causative with two objects

When the causative has two objects, one object is usually a person and the other a thing. The person is the indirect object and the thing the direct object.

Il fait analyser le film aux étudiants.
He has the film analyzed by the students.
or: He has the students analyze the film.

Nous avons fait composer la piste sonore à un musicien de première qualité.
We had the sound track composed by a first-rate musician.
or: We had a first-rate musician compose the sound track.

The preposition **par** replaces **à** in cases where **à** would mean both *by* and *to*.

J'ai fait envoyer le film à mon frère.
I had the film sent to my brother.
or: I had the film sent by my brother.

J'ai fait envoyer le film par mon frère.
I had the film sent by my brother.

Object pronouns with the causative

Position

Direct and indirect objects are placed before **faire.**

> **Je le fais envoyer demain.**
> I am having it sent tomorrow.
>
> **Je la lui fais composer.**
> I am having it composed by him.

Agreement of past participle

The past participle **fait** is invariable in the causative and does not agree with a preceding direct object in a compound tense.

> **Je les ai fait venir.**
> I had them come.
> *or:* I made them come.

EXERCICES

1. *Répondez à chaque question en employant une des expressions de la colonne de droite, ou une autre de votre choix.*
   modèle: Qu'est-ce qu'une comédie vous fait faire? **Elle me fait rire.**

1. Qu'est-ce qu'un film d'épouvante vous fait faire?	sourire
	danser
2. un film de science fiction?	rêver
3. un film policier?	rire
4. un film tragique?	penser à l'avenir
5. un film de guerre?	réfléchir longuement
6. un film de propagande?	pleurer
7. une comédie musicale?	tenir la main de mon ami(e)
8. le rock?	bâiller (*to yawn*)
9. une chanson sentimentale?	crier (*to scream*)
	frissonner (*to shudder*)
	chanter
	sursauter (*to jump*)
	perdre la tête

2. *Traduisez en français.*

1. We are having the movie filmed in France.
2. The director had the chansonnier play the guitar.
3. What! They're having that bad actress play this difficult role?
4. Our professor is having us analyze Truffaut's film *Jules et Jim*.
5. The director had the movie criticized before filming the last shot.

6. He has the fans come in.
7. We will have the sound track composed by a young composer.
8. The director had one of the actors write the scenario.
9. She is having the class listen to the tape.
10. The government had the movie censored.

Exercices d'ensemble

I. *Répondez en employant une ou deux phrases complètes.*

1. Avez-vous jamais été scandalisé par un film?
2. Avez-vous jamais passé des heures dans une file (*line*)?
3. Allez-vous voir des films avant d'en lire les critiques dans le journal?
4. Avez-vous jamais vu tourner un film?
5. Avez-vous jamais vu jouer votre musicien favori (vos musiciens favoris) en personne?
6. Qu'est-ce qui ou qui est-ce qui vous fait rire?
7. Avez-vous jamais rencontré un acteur ou une actrice célèbre en faisant une promenade?
8. Pouvez-vous bien étudier en écoutant la musique à la radio ou en regardant la télévision?
9. Est-ce que la musique vous fait changer d'humeur?
10. Qu'est-ce que vous aimez faire après avoir vu un film le samedi soir?
11. Avez-vous jamais été gêné ou amusé par un film doublé ou sous-titré?
12. Préférez-vous la musique moderne ou la musique classique?
13. Avez-vous jamais quitté un cinéma sans voir le film jusqu'au bout?
14. Que préférez-vous écouter dans une discothèque, des disques ou des musiciens chantant en personne?
15. Avez-vous une collection intéressante de disques ou de bandes?

II. *Traduisez en français.*

1. The composer spent only one hour composing this song.
2. The movie *Les Enfants du paradis* will always be appreciated by movie fans.
3. She likes to hear the audience applaud.
4. We entertained ourselves by singing old sentimental songs.
5. Instead of jazz (*le jazz*), rock-and-roll was being played in that discothèque.
6. While waiting in line, I saw the director of the film go in.
7. The new cinematographic techniques in that film will certainly be admired by movie fans.
8. The musicians spent the evening recording the song.
9. Our professor had us analyze the meaning (*la signification*) of the film.
10. He began to appreciate music after studying harmony and rhythm.

Sujets de discussion ou de composition

1. Décrivez un film que vous avez vu (genre, réalisateur, acteurs, personnages, intrigue, atmosphère, etc.). Faites deviner (guess) le titre du film aux autres étudiants.

2. Quel rôle la musique joue-t-elle dans votre vie? Quel genre préférez-vous— le rock, le blues, le jazz, la musique classique, folklorique, populaire, etc.? Qui sont vos musiciens et vos compositeurs préférés? Où et quand aimez-vous écouter la musique? etc.

3. Remarquez-vous une différence entre les films américains et les films étrangers? Expliquez.

Appendix

Useful Expressions

Cardinal Numbers

1	un/une	22	vingt-deux	71	soixante et onze
2	deux	23	vingt-trois	72	soixante-douze
3	trois	24	vingt-quatre	80	quatre-vingts
4	quatre	25	vingt-cinq	81	quatre-vingt-un
5	cinq	26	vingt-six	82	quatre-vingt-deux
6	six	27	vingt-sept	90	quatre-vingt-dix
7	sept	28	vingt-huit	91	quatre-vingt-onze
8	huit	29	vingt-neuf	92	quatre-vingt-douze
9	neuf	30	trente	100	cent
10	dix	31	trente et un	101	cent un
11	onze	32	trente-deux	200	deux cents
12	douze	40	quarante	201	deux cent un
13	treize	41	quarante et un	1000	mille
14	quatorze	42	quarante-deux	1001	mille un
15	quinze	50	cinquante	1700	dix-sept cents, mille sept cents
16	seize	51	cinquante et un	1720	dix-sept cent vingt, mille sept cent vingt
17	dix-sept	52	cinquante-deux	5000	cinq mille
18	dix-huit	60	soixante	10,000	dix mille
19	dix-neuf	61	soixante et un	100,000	cent mille
20	vingt	62	soixante-deux	1,000,000	un million
21	vingt et un	70	soixante-dix	1,000,000,000	un milliard

1. The numbers *81* and *91* do not take **et**.
2. **Quatre-vingts** and multiples of **cent** require **s** except when followed by another number: **quatre-vingts, quatre-vingt-un; deux cents, deux cent un. Mille** never takes **s: cinq mille.**
3. The decimal point and comma are reversed in English and French: *10,000* in English = **10.000** in French; *1.5* in English = **1,5** in French.

Ordinal Numbers

Ordinal numbers are formed by adding the suffix **-ième** to cardinal numbers. If a cardinal number ends in mute **e**, the **e** is dropped before adding the suffix. The ordinal numbers **premier (première), cinquième** and **neuvième** are exceptions.

premier/première	*first*
deuxième	*second*

troisième	*third*
quatrième	*fourth*
cinquième	*fifth*
sixième	*sixth*
septième	*seventh*
huitième	*eighth*
neuvième	*ninth*
dixième	*tenth*
vingtième	*twentieth*
vingt et unième	*twenty-first*
centième	*one hundredth*

Collective Numbers

Collective numbers indicate approximate value. They are equivalent to the expression *about, around* + number in English. Collective numbers are formed by adding the suffix **-aine** to cardinal numbers (the number **dizaine** is an exception). If a cardinal number ends in mute **e,** the **e** is dropped before adding the suffix. Collective numbers are feminine with the exception of **un millier** (about, around a thousand).

une dizaine	*about, around 10*
une vingtaine	*about, around 20*
une cinquantaine	*about, around 50*
une centaine	*about, around 100*
un millier	*about, around 1,000*

Fractions

$^1/_2$	la moitié, demi(e)	$^1/_5$	un cinquième
$^1/_3$	un tiers	$^1/_6$	un sixième
$^1/_4$	un quart	$^7/_8$	sept huitièmes
$^3/_4$	trois quarts	$^3/_{10}$	trois dixièmes

Note that ½ used as a noun is expressed by **la moitié** and as an adjective by **demi(e): la moitié de la classe, une demi-heure.**

DATES

Days		Months			
lundi	*Monday*	janvier	*January*	juillet	*July*
mardi	*Tuesday*	février	*February*	août	*August*
mercredi	*Wednesday*	mars	*March*	septembre	*September*
jeudi	*Thursday*	avril	*April*	octobre	*October*
vendredi	*Friday*	mai	*May*	novembre	*November*
samedi	*Saturday*	juin	*June*	décembre	*December*
dimanche	*Sunday*				

Quel jour sommes-nous aujourd'hui?
What is the day today?

C'est aujourd'hui $\begin{cases} \textbf{lundi, le 15 septembre.} \\ \textbf{le lundi 15 septembre.} \end{cases}$

Today is Monday, September 15.

Quand êtes-vous né?
When were you born?

Je suis né le 2 août 1958.

Je suis né le deux août, $\begin{cases} \textbf{dix-neuf cent cinquante-huit.} \\ \textbf{mil neuf cent cinquante-huit.} \end{cases}$

I was born on August 2, 1958.

1. Days and months are masculine in gender and are written in small letters in French.
2. In dates the form **mil** (not **mille**) is used: **en mil soixante-six.**
3. Dates of the month are expressed by cardinal numbers except *first* which requires the ordinal number: **le premier janvier, le deux janvier.**

WEATHER EXPRESSIONS

Weather expressions with *faire*

Il fait beau.	*The weather is fine.*
Il fait mauvais.	*The weather is bad.*
Il fait chaud.	*It is warm.*
Il fait frais.	*It is cool.*
Il fait doux.	*It is mild.*
Il fait sec.	*It is dry.*
Il fait humide.	*It is humid.*
Il fait bon.	*It is nice.*
Il fait du vent.	*It is windy.*
Il fait du soleil.	*It is sunny.*
Il fait jour.	*It is daylight.*
Il fait nuit.	*It is dark.*
Il fait clair.	*It is clear.*
Il se fait tard.	*It is getting late.*
Il fait glissant.	*It is slippery.*
Il fait de l'orage.	*It is stormy.*
Il fait du tonnère.	*It is thundering.*
Il fait brumeux.	*It is misty.*

Weather expressions with other verbs

Il neige.	*It is snowing.*
Il pleut.	*It is raining.*
Il tonne.	*It is thundering.*
Il gèle.	*It is freezing.*
Il grêle.	*It is hailing.*

SEASONS

été *summer*	en été	*in the summer*
automne *fall*	en automne	*in the fall*
hiver *winter*	en hiver	*in the winter*
printemps *spring*	au printemps	*in the spring*

Note that the seasons are masculine in gender and are written in small letters in French.

TIME

Quelle heure est-il?
What time is it?

1 h.

Il est une heure.

1h.05

Il est une heure cinq.

1h.15

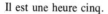

Il est une heure et quart

1h.20

Il est une heure vingt.

1h.30

Il est une heure et demie.

1h.35

Il est deux heures moins vingt-cinq.

1h.45

Il est deux heures moins le quart

1h.53

Il est deux heures moins sept

2h.

Il est deux heures.

12h.

Il est midi (minuit).

Note that A.M. and P.M. are expressed by **du matin** *(in the morning),* **de l'après-midi** *(in the afternoon),* and **du soir** *(in the evening).*

Verbs

In addition to the **passé simple** (p. 11), French possesses three other literary tenses: the *past anterior,* the *imperfect subjunctive,* and the *pluperfect subjunctive.* These literary tenses, which almost never appear in the spoken language, are presented here so that students will be able to recognize them in the literature they read.

Past Anterior

FORMATION OF THE PAST ANTERIOR

passé simple of the auxiliary + past participle	
parler	**venir**
j'eus parlé	je fus venu(e)
tu eus parlé	tu fus venu(e)
il ⎫	il ⎫ venu
elle ⎬ eut parlé	elle ⎬ fut venue
on ⎭	on ⎭ venu
nous eûmes parlé	nous fûmes venu(e)s
vous eûtes parlé	vous fûtes venu(e)(s)
ils ⎫	ils ⎫ venus
elles ⎬ eurent parlé	elles ⎬ furent
	venues

USE OF THE PAST ANTERIOR

The *pluperfect tense* (p. 141) is usually used to express a past action that precedes another past action. The past anterior, however, is used to express a past action that immediately precedes another past action which is expressed by the **passé simple.** It usually appears after the conjunctions **quand, lorsque, dès que, aussitôt que** and **après que.**

Dès que le criminel eut commis le crime, on l'arrêta.
As soon as the criminal had committed the crime, he was arrested.
Nous commençâmes à bavarder après que le professeur fut sorti.
We began to chat after the professor had gone out.

Note that the past anterior and the pluperfect have the same English translation.

Imperfect Subjunctive

FORMATION OF THE IMPERFECT SUBJUNCTIVE

The *imperfect subjunctive* is formed by dropping the endings of the **passé simple** and adding the imperfect subjunctive endings. Like the **passé simple,** the imperfect subjunctive has three sets of endings. The pairings below show the corresponding **passé simple** and imperfect subjunctive endings.

PASSÉ SIMPLE ENDINGS	IMPERFECT SUBJUNCTIVE ENDINGS

parler

je parl*ai*	que je parl*asse*
tu parl*as*	que tu parl*asses*
il	qu'il
elle } parl*a*	elle } parl*ât*
on	on
nous parl*âmes*	que nous parl*assions*
vous parl*âtes*	que vous parl*assiez*
ils	qu'ils
} parl*èrent*	} parl*assent*
elles	elles

finir

je fin*is*	que je fin*isse*
tu fin*is*	que tu fin*isses*
il	qu'il
elle } fin*it*	elle } fin*ît*
on	on
nous fin*îmes*	que nous fin*issions*
vous fin*îtes*	que vous fin*issiez*
ils	qu'ils
} fin*irent*	} fin*issent*
elles	elles

connaître

je conn*us*	que je conn*usse*
tu conn*us*	que tu conn*usses*
il	qu'il
elle } conn*ut*	elle } conn*ût*
on	on
nous conn*ûmes*	que nous conn*ussions*
vous conn*ûtes*	que vous conn*ussiez*
ils	qu'ils
} conn*urent*	} conn*ussent*
elles	elles

USE OF THE IMPERFECT SUBJUNCTIVE

The *imperfect subjunctive* corresponds to the *imperfect indicative* and the *present conditional*.

Indicative:	**Je savais qu'elle venait me rendre visite.**
	I knew she was coming to visit me.
Subjunctive:	**Je doutais qu'elle vînt me rendre visite.**
	I doubted that she was coming to visit me.
Indicative:	**Nous savions qu'il se sentirait à l'aise en France.**
	We knew that he would feel at ease in France.
Subjunctive:	**Nous ne croyions pas qu'il se sentît à l'aise en France.**
	We didn't think that he would feel at ease in France.

In the spoken language, the *imperfect subjunctive* is usually replaced by the *present subjunctive* (p. 179).

Pluperfect Subjunctive

imperfect subjunctive of the auxiliary + past participle

finir	aller
que j'eusse fini	que je fusse allé(e)
que tu eusses fini	que tu fusses allé(e)
qu'il ⎫	qu'il ⎫ allé
elle ⎬ eût fini	elle ⎬ fût allée
on ⎭	on ⎭ allé
que nous eussions fini	que nous fussions allé(e)s
que vous eussiez fini	que vous fussiez allé(e)(s)
qu'ils ⎫	qu'ils ⎫ allés
⎬ eussent fini	⎬ fussent
elles ⎭	elles ⎭ allées

USE OF THE PLUPERFECT SUBJUNCTIVE

The pluperfect subjunctive corresponds to the *pluperfect indicative* and the *past conditional.*

Indicative: **Je savais qu'ils s'étaient mariés!**
I knew they had got married!

Subjunctive: **Je craignais qu'ils ne se fussent mariés!**
I was afraid that they had got married!

Indicative: **J'étais sûr qu'on l'aurait condamné sans votre témoignage.**
I was sure that he would have been convicted without your testimony.

Subjunctive: **J'étais étonné qu'on l'eût condamné sans votre témoignage.**
I was astounded that he would have been convicted without your testimony.

The *pluperfect subjunctive* may replace the *pluperfect indicative* or the *past conditional,* or both, in conditional sentences.

Si ·elle avait suivi un régime, elle aurait été plus séduisante.
Si elle eût suivi un régime, elle aurait été plus séduisante.
Si elle avait suivi un régime, elle eût été plus séduisante.
Si elle eût suivi un régime, elle eût été plus séduisante.
If she had gone on a diet, she would have been more attractive.

In the spoken language, the *pluperfect subjunctive* is usually replaced by the *past subjunctive* (p. 182).

244

REGULAR *-er, -ir, -re* VERBS

INFINITIVE PARTICIPLES	INDICATIVE			
	Present	**Imperfect**	**Passé Composé**	**Future**
parler (*to speak*) parlant parlé	parle parles parle parlons parlez parlent	parlais parlais parlait parlions parliez parlaient	ai parlé as parlé a parlé avons parlé avez parlé ont parlé	parlerai parleras parlera parlerons parlerez parleront
finir (*to finish*) finissant fini	finis finis finit finissons finissez finissent	finissais finissais finissait finissions finissiez finissaient	ai fini as fini a fini avons fini avez fini ont fini	finirai finiras finira finirons finirez finiront
dormir (*to sleep*) dormant dormi	dors dors dort dormons dormez dorment	dormais dormais dormait dormions dormiez dormaient	ai dormi as dormi a dormi avons dormi avez dormi ont dormi	dormirai dormiras dormira dormirons dormirez dormiront
perdre (*to lose*) perdant perdu	perds perds perd perdons perdez perdent	perdais perdais perdait perdions perdiez perdaient	ai perdu as perdu a perdu avons perdu avez perdu ont perdu	perdrai perdras perdra perdrons perdrez perdront

COMMON IRREGULAR VERBS

acquérir (*to acquire*) acquérant acquis	acquiers acquiers acquiert acquérons acquérez acquièrent	acquérais acquérais acquérait acquérions acquériez acquéraient	ai acquis as acquis a acquis avons acquis avez acquis ont acquis	acquerrai acquerras acquerra acquerrons acquerrez acquerront

CONDITIONAL	IMPERATIVE	SUBJUNCTIVE	LITERARY TENSES	
Present		**Present**	**Passé Simple**	**Imperfect Subjunctive**
parlerais		parle	parlai	parlasse
parlerais	parle	parles	parlas	parlasses
parlerait		parle	parla	parlât
parlerions	parlons	parlions	parlâmes	parlassions
parleriez	parlez	parliez	parlâtes	parlassiez
parleraient		parlent	parlèrent	parlassent
finirais		finisse	finis	finisse
finirais	finis	finisses	finis	finisses
finirait		finisse	finit	finît
finirions	finissons	finissions	finîmes	finissions
finiriez	finissez	finissiez	finîtes	finissiez
finiraient		finissent	finirent	finissent
dormirais		dorme	dormis	dormisse
dormirais	dors	dormes	dormis	dormisses
dormirait		dorme	dormit	dormît
dormirions	dormons	dormions	dormîmes	dormissions
dormiriez	dormez	dormiez	dormîtes	dormissiez
dormiraient		dorment	dormirent	dormissent
perdrais		perde	perdis	perdisse
perdrais	perds	perdes	perdis	perdisses
perdrait		perde	perdit	perdît
perdrions	perdons	perdions	perdîmes	perdissions
perdriez	perdez	perdiez	perdîtes	perdissiez
perdraient		perdent	perdirent	perdissent

acquerrais		acquière	acquis	acquisse
acquerrais	acquiers	acquières	acquis	acquisses
acquerrait		acquière	acquit	acquît
acquerrions	acquérons	acquérions	acquîmes	acquissions
acquerriez	acquérez	acquériez	acquîtes	acquissiez
acquerraient		acquièrent	acquirent	acquissent

INFINITIVE PARTICIPLES	INDICATIVE			
	Present	Imperfect	Passé Composé	Future
aller *(to go)* allant allé	vais vas va allons allez vont	allais allais allait allions alliez allaient	suis allé(e) es allé(e) est allé(e) sommes allé(e)s êtes allé(e)(s) sont allé(e)s	irai iras ira irons irez iront
s'asseoir[1] *(to seat)* asseyant assis	assieds assieds assied asseyons asseyez asseyent	asseyais asseyais asseyait asseyions asseyiez asseyaient	suis assis(e) es assis(e) est assis(e) sommes assis(es) êtes assis(e/s) sont assis(es)	assiérai assiéras assiéra assiérons assiérez assiéront
assoyant	assois assois assoit assoyons assoyez assoient	assoyais assoyais assoyait assoyions assoyiez assoyaient		assoirai assoiras assoira assoirons assoirez assoiront
avoir *(to have)* ayant eu	ai as a avons avez ont	avais avais avait avions aviez avaient	ai eu as eu a eu avons eu avez eu ont eu	aurai auras aura aurons aurez auront
battre *(to beat)* battant battu	bats bats bat battons battez battent	battais battais battait battions battiez battaient	ai battu as battu a battu avons battu avez battu ont battu	battrai battras battra battrons battrez battront
boire *(to drink)* buvant bu	bois bois boit buvons buvez boivent	buvais buvais buvait buvions buviez buvaient	ai bu as bu a bu avons bu avez bu ont bu	boirai boiras boira boirons boirez boiront

[1]The verb **s'asseoir** takes a subject and a reflexive pronoun: **je m'assieds.** (Certain tenses of **s'asseoir** have two forms.)

CONDITIONAL	IMPERATIVE	SUBJUNCTIVE	LITERARY TENSES	
Present		**Present**	**Passé Simple**	**Imperfect Subjunctive**
irais		aille	allai	allasse
irais	va	ailles	allas	allasses
irait		aille	alla	allât
irions	allons	allions	allâmes	allassions
iriez	allez	alliez	allâtes	allassiez
iraient		aillent	allèrent	allassent
assiérais		asseye	assis	assisse
assiérais	assieds-toi	asseyes	assis	assisses
assiérait		asseye	assit	assît
assiérions	asseyons-nous	asseyions	assîmes	assissions
assiériez	asseyez-vous	asseyiez	assîtes	assissiez
assiéraient		asseyent	assirent	assissent
assoirais		assoie		
assoirais	assois-toi	assoies		
assoirait		assoie		
assoirions	assoyons-nous	assoyions		
assoiriez	assoyez-vous	assoyiez		
assoiraient		assoient		
aurais	aie	aie	eus	eusse
aurais		aies	eus	eusses
aurait	ayons	ait	eut	eût
aurions	ayez	ayons	eûmes	eussions
auriez		ayez	eûtes	eussiez
auraient		aient	eurent	eussent
battrais		batte	battis	battisse
battrais	bats	battes	battis	battisses
battrait		batte	battit	battît
battrions	battons	battions	battîmes	battissions
battriez	battez	battiez	battîtes	battissiez
battraient		battent	battirent	battissent
boirais		boive	bus	busse
boirais	bois	boives	bus	busses
boirait		boive	but	bût
boirions	buvons	buvions	bûmes	bussions
boiriez	buvez	buviez	bûtes	bussiez
boiraient		boivent	burent	bussent

INFINITIVE PARTICIPLES	INDICATIVE			
	Present	**Imperfect**	**Passé Composé**	**Future**
conduire (*to lead*) conduisant conduit	conduis conduis conduit conduisons conduisez conduisent	conduisais conduisais conduisait conduisions conduisiez conduisaient	ai conduit as conduit a conduit avons conduit avez conduit ont conduit	conduirai conduiras conduira conduirons conduirez conduiront
connaître (*to be acquainted*) connaissant connu	connais connais connaît connaissons connaissez connaissent	connaissais connaissais connaissait connaissions connaissiez connaissaient	ai connu as connu a connu avons connu avez connu ont connu	connaîtrai connaîtras connaîtra connaîtrons connaîtrez connaîtront
courir (*to run*) courant couru	cours cours court courons courez courent	courais courais courait courions couriez couraient	ai couru as couru a couru avons couru avez couru ont couru	courrai courras courra courrons courrez courront
craindre (*to fear*) craignant craint	crains crains craint craignons craignez craignent	craignais craignais craignait craignions craigniez craignaient	ai craint as craint a craint avons craint avez craint ont craint	craindrai craindras craindra craindrons craindrez craindront
croire (*to believe*) croyant cru	crois crois croit croyons croyez croient	croyais croyais croyait croyions croyiez croyaient	ai cru as cru a cru avons cru avez cru ont cru	croirai croiras croira croirons croirez croiront
devoir (*to have to, to owe*) devant dû, due[2]	dois dois doit devons devez doivent	devais devais devait devions deviez devaient	ai dû as dû a dû avons dû avez dû ont dû	devrai devras devra devrons devrez devront

[2]Note that only the masculine singular form of the past participle takes a circumflex accent.

CONDITIONAL	IMPERATIVE	SUBJUNCTIVE	LITERARY TENSES	
Present		**Present**	**Passé Simple**	**Imperfect Subjunctive**
conduirais		conduise	conduisis	conduisisse
conduirais	conduis	conduises	conduisis	conduisisses
conduirait		conduise	conduisit	conduisît
conduirions	conduisons	conduisions	conduisîmes	conduisissions
conduiriez	conduisez	conduisiez	conduisîtes	conduisissiez
conduiraient		conduisent	conduisirent	conduisissent
connaîtrais		connaisse	connus	connusse
connaîtrais	connais	connaisses	connus	connusses
connaîtrait		connaisse	connut	connût
connaîtrions	connaissons	connaissions	connûmes	connussions
connaîtriez	connaissez	connaissiez	connûtes	connussiez
connaîtraient		connaissent	connurent	connussent
courrais		coure	courus	courusse
courrais	cours	coures	courus	courusses
courrait		coure	courut	courût
courrions	courons	courions	courûmes	courussions
courriez	courez	couriez	courûtes	courussiez
courraient		courent	coururent	courussent
craindrais		craigne	craignis	craignisse
craindrais	crains	craignes	craignis	craignisses
craindrait		craigne	craignit	craignît
craindrions	craignons	craignions	craignîmes	craignissions
craindriez	craignez	craigniez	craignîtes	craignissiez
craindraient		craignent	craignirent	craignissent
croirais		croie	crus	crusse
croirais	crois	croies	crus	crusses
croirait		croie	crut	crût
croirions	croyons	croyions	crûmes	crussions
croiriez	croyez	croyiez	crûtes	crussiez
croiraient		croient	crurent	crussent
devrais		doive	dus	dusse
devrais	dois	doives	dus	dusses
devrait		doive	dut	dût
devrions	devons	devions	dûmes	dussions
devriez	devez	deviez	dûtes	dussiez
devraient		doivent	durent	dussent

INFINITIVE PARTICIPLES	INDICATIVE			
	Present	Imperfect	Passé Composé	Future
dire *(to say, tell)* disant dit	dis dis dit disons dites disent	disais disais disait disions disiez disaient	ai dit as dit a dit avons dit avez dit ont dit	dirai diras dira dirons direz diront
écrire *(to write)* écrivant écrit	écris écris écrit écrivons écrivez écrivent	écrivais écrivais écrivait écrivions écriviez écrivaient	ai écrit as écrit a écrit avons écrit avez écrit ont écrit	écrirai écriras écrira écrirons écrirez écriront
envoyer *(to send)* envoyant envoyé	envoie envoies envoie envoyons envoyez envoient	envoyais envoyais envoyait envoyions envoyiez envoyaient	ai envoyé as envoyé a envoyé avons envoyé avez envoyé ont envoyé	enverrai enverras enverra enverrons enverrez enverront
être *(to be)* étant été	suis es est sommes êtes sont	étais étais était étions étiez étaient	ai été as été a été avons été avez été ont été	serai seras sera serons serez seront
faire *(to do, make)* faisant fait	fais fais fait faisons faites font	faisais faisais faisait faisions faisiez faisaient	ai fait as fait a fait avons fait avez fait ont fait	ferai feras fera ferons ferez feront
falloir *(to be necessary)* fallu	il faut	il fallait	il a fallu	il faudra

CONDITIONAL	IMPERATIVE	SUBJUNCTIVE	LITERARY TENSES	
Present		**Present**	**Passé Simple**	**Imperfect Subjunctive**
dirais		dise	dis	disse
dirais	dis	dises	dis	disses
dirait		dise	dit	dît
dirions	disons	disions	dîmes	dissions
diriez	dites	disiez	dîtes	dissiez
diraient		disent	dirent	dissent
écrirais		écrive	écrivis	écrivisse
écrirais	écris	écrives	écrivis	écrivisses
écrirait		écrive	écrivit	écrivît
écririons	écrivons	écrivions	écrivîmes	écrivissions
écririez	écrivez	écriviez	écrivîtes	écrivissiez
écriraient		écrivent	écrivirent	écrivissent
enverrais		envoie	envoyai	envoyasse
enverrais	envoie	envoies	envoyas	envoyasses
enverrait		envoie	envoya	envoyât
enverrions	envoyons	envoyions	envoyâmes	envoyassions
enverriez	envoyez	envoyiez	envoyâtes	envoyassiez
enverraient		envoient	envoyèrent	envoyassent
serais		sois	fus	fusse
serais	sois	sois	fus	fusses
serait		soit	fut	fût
serions	soyons	soyons	fûmes	fussions
seriez	soyez	soyez	fûtes	fussiez
seraient		soient	furent	fussent
ferais		fasse	fis	fisse
ferais	fais	fasses	fis	fisses
ferait		fasse	fit	fît
ferions	faisons	fassions	fîmes	fissions
feriez	faites	fassiez	fîtes	fissiez
feraient		fassent	firent	fissent
il faudrait		il faille	il fallut	il fallût

INFINITIVE PARTICIPLES	INDICATIVE			
	Present	**Imperfect**	**Passé Composé**	**Future**
fuir *(to flee)* fuyant fui	fuis fuis fuit fuyons fuyez fuient	fuyais fuyais fuyait fuyions fuyiez fuyaient	ai fui as fui a fui avons fui avez fui ont fui	fuirai fuiras fuira fuirons fuirez fuiront
joindre *(to join)* joignant joint	joins joins joint joignons joignez joignent	joignais joignais joignait joignions joigniez joignaient	ai joint as joint a joint avons joint avez joint ont joint	joindrai joindras joindra joindrons joindrez joindront
lire *(to read)* lisant lu	lis lis lit lisons lisez lisent	lisais lisais lisait lisions lisiez lisaient	ai lu as lu a lu avons lu avez lu ont lu	lirai liras lira lirons lirez liront
mettre *(to put)* mettant mis	mets mets met mettons mettez mettent	mettais mettais mettait mettions mettiez mettaient	ai mis as mis a mis avons mis avez mis ont mis	mettrai mettras mettra mettrons mettrez mettront
mourir *(to die)* mourant mort	meurs meurs meurt mourons mourez meurent	mourais mourais mourait mourions mouriez mouraient	suis mort(e) es mort(e) est mort(e) sommes mort(e)s êtes mort(e)(s) sont mort(e)s	mourrai mourras mourra mourrons mourrez mourront
naître *(to be born)* naissant né	nais nais naît naissons naissez naissent	naissais naissais naissait naissions naissiez naissaient	suis né(e) es né(e) est né(e) sommes né(e)s êtes né(e)(s) sont né(e)s	naîtrai naîtras naîtra naîtrons naîtrez naîtront

CONDITIONAL	IMPERATIVE	SUBJUNCTIVE	LITERARY TENSES	
Present		**Present**	**Passé Simple**	**Imperfect Subjunctive**
fuirais		fuie	fuis	fuisse
fuirais	fuis	fuies	fuis	fuisses
fuirait		fuie	fuit	fuît
fuirions	fuyons	fuyions	fuîmes	fuissions
fuiriez	fuyez	fuyiez	fuîtes	fuissiez
fuiraient		fuient	fuirent	fuissent
joindrais		joigne	joignis	joignisse
joindrais	joins	joignes	joignis	joignisses
joindrait		joigne	joignit	joignît
joindrions	joignons	joignions	joignîmes	joignissions
joindriez	joignez	joigniez	joignîtes	joignissiez
joindraient		joignent	joignirent	joignissent
lirais		lise	lus	lusse
lirais	lis	lises	lus	lusses
lirait		lise	lut	lût
lirions	lisons	lisions	lûmes	lussions
liriez	lisez	lisiez	lûtes	lussiez
liraient		lisent	lurent	lussent
mettrais		mette	mis	misse
mettrais	mets	mettes	mis	misses
mettrait		mette	mit	mît
mettrions	mettons	mettions	mîmes	missions
mettriez	mettez	mettiez	mîtes	missiez
mettraient		mettent	mirent	missent
mourrais		meure	mourus	mourusse
mourrais	meurs	meures	mourus	mourusses
mourrait		meure	mourut	mourût
mourrions	mourons	mourions	mourûmes	mourussions
mourriez	mourez	mouriez	mourûtes	mourussiez
mourraient		meurent	moururent	mourussent
naîtrais		naisse	naquis	naquisse
naîtrais	nais	naisses	naquis	naquisses
naîtrait		naisse	naquit	naquît
naîtrions	naissons	naissions	naquîmes	naquissions
naîtriez	naissez	naissiez	naquîtes	naquissiez
naîtraient		naissent	naquirent	naquissent

INFINITIVE PARTICIPLES	INDICATIVE			
	Present	Imperfect	Passé Composé	Future
offrir *(to offer)* offrant offert	offre offres offre offrons offrez offrent	offrais offrais offrait offrions offriez offraient	ai offert as offert a offert avons offert avez offert ont offert	offrirai offriras offrira offrirons offrirez offriront
ouvrir *(to open)* ouvrant ouvert	ouvre ouvres ouvre ouvrons ouvrez ouvrent	ouvrais ouvrais ouvrait ouvrions ouvriez ouvraient	ai ouvert as ouvert a ouvert avons ouvert avez ouvert ont ouvert	ouvrirai ouvriras ouvrira ouvrirons ouvrirez ouvriront
paraître *(to appear)* paraissant paru	parais parais paraît paraissons paraissez paraissent	paraissais paraissais paraissait paraissions paraissiez paraissaient	ai paru as paru a paru avons paru avez paru ont paru	paraîtrai paraîtras paraîtra paraîtrons paraîtrez paraîtront
peindre *(to paint)* peignant peint	peins peins peint peignons peignez peignent	peignais peignais peignait peignions peigniez peignaient	ai peint as peint a peint avons peint avez peint ont peint	peindrai peindras peindra peindrons peindrez peindront
plaire *(to please)* plaisant plu	plais plais plaît plaisons plaisez plaisent	plaisais plaisais plaisait plaisions plaisiez plaisaient	ai plu as plu a plu avons plu avez plu ont plu	plairai plairas plaira plairons plairez plairont
pleuvoir *(to rain)* pleuvant plu	il pleut	il pleuvait	il a plu	il pleuvra

CONDITIONAL	IMPERATIVE	SUBJUNCTIVE	LITERARY TENSES	
Present		Present	Passé Simple	Imperfect Subjunctive
offrirais		offre	offris	offrisse
offrirais	offre	offres	offris	offrisses
offrirait		offre	offrit	offrît
offririons	offrons	offrions	offrîmes	offrissions
offririez	offrez	offriez	offrîtes	offrissiez
offriraient		offrent	offrirent	offrissent
ouvrirais		ouvre	ouvris	ouvrisse
ouvrirais	ouvre	ouvres	ouvris	ouvrisses
ouvrirait		ouvre	ouvrit	ouvrît
ouvririons	ouvrons	ouvrions	ouvrîmes	ouvrissions
ouvririez	ouvrez	ouvriez	ouvrîtes	ouvrissiez
ouvriraient		ouvrent	ouvrirent	ouvrissent
paraîtrais		paraisse	parus	parusse
paraîtrais	parais	paraisses	parus	parusses
paraîtrait		paraisse	parut	parût
paraîtrions	paraissons	paraissions	parûmes	parussions
paraîtriez	paraissez	paraissiez	parûtes	parussiez
paraîtraient		paraissent	parurent	parussent
peindrais		peigne	peignis	peignisse
peindrais	peins	peignes	peignis	peignisses
peindrait		peigne	peignit	peignît
peindrions	peignons	peignions	peignîmes	peignissions
peindriez	peignez	peigniez	peignîtes	peignissiez
peindraient		peignent	peignirent	peignissent
plairais		plaise	plus	plusse
plairais	plais	plaises	plus	plusses
plairait		plaise	plut	plût
plairions	plaisons	plaisions	plûmes	plussions
plairiez	plaisez	plaisiez	plûtes	plussiez
plairaient		plaisent	plurent	plussent
il pleuvrait		il pleuve	il plut	il plût

INFINITIVE PARTICIPLES	INDICATIVE			
	Present	Imperfect	Passé Composé	Future
pouvoir *(to be able)* pouvant pu	peux, puis peux peut pouvons pouvez peuvent	pouvais pouvais pouvait pouvions pouviez pouvaient	ai pu as pu a pu avons pu avez pu ont pu	pourrai pourras pourra pourrons pourrez pourront
prendre *(to take)* prenant pris	prends prends prend prenons prenez prennent	prenais prenais prenait prenions preniez prenaient	ai pris as pris a pris avons pris avez pris ont pris	prendrai prendras prendra prendrons prendrez prendront
recevoir *(to receive)* recevant reçu	reçois reçois reçoit recevons recevez reçoivent	recevais recevais recevait recevions receviez recevaient	ai reçu as reçu a reçu avons reçu avez reçu ont reçu	recevrai recevras recevra recevrons recevrez recevront
rire *(to laugh)* riant ri	ris ris rit rions riez rient	riais riais riait riions riiez riaient	ai ri as ri a ri avons ri avez ri ont ri	rirai riras rira rirons rirez riront
savoir *(to know)* sachant su	sais sais sait savons savez savent	savais savais savait savions saviez savaient	ai su as su a su avons su avez su ont su	saurai sauras saura saurons saurez sauront
suivre *(to follow)* suivant suivi	suis suis suit suivons suivez suivent	suivais suivais suivait suivions suiviez suivaient	ai suivi as suivi a suivi avons suivi avez suivi ont suivi	suivrai suivras suivra suivrons suivrez suivront

CONDITIONAL	IMPERATIVE	SUBJUNCTIVE	LITERARY TENSES	
Present		**Present**	**Passé Simple**	**Imperfect Subjunctive**
pourrais		puisse	pus	pusse
pourrais		puisses	pus	pusses
pourrait		puisse	put	pût
pourrions		puissions	pûmes	pussions
pourriez		puissiez	pûtes	pussiez
pourraient		puissent	purent	pussent
prendrais		prenne	pris	prisse
prendrais	prends	prennes	pris	prisses
prendrait		prenne	prit	prît
prendrions	prenons	prenions	prîmes	prissions
prendriez	prenez	preniez	prîtes	prissiez
prendraient		prennent	prirent	prissent
recevrais		reçoive	reçus	reçusse
recevrais	reçois	reçoives	reçus	reçusses
recevrait		reçoive	reçut	reçût
recevrions	recevons	recevions	reçûmes	reçussions
recevriez	recevez	receviez	reçûtes	reçussiez
recevraient		reçoivent	reçurent	reçussent
rirais		rie	ris	risse
rirais	ris	ries	ris	risses
rirait		rie	rit	rît
ririons	rions	riions	rîmes	rissions
ririez	riez	riiez	rîtes	rissiez
riraient		rient	rirent	rissent
saurais		sache	sus	susse
saurais	sache	saches	sus	susses
saurait		sache	sut	sût
saurions	sachons	sachions	sûmes	sussions
sauriez	sachez	sachiez	sûtes	sussiez
sauraient		sachent	surent	sussent
suivrais		suive	suivis	suivisse
suivrais	suis	suives	suivis	suivisses
suivrait		suive	suivit	suivît
suivrions	suivons	suivions	suivîmes	suivissions
suivriez	suivez	suiviez	suivîtes	suivissiez
suivraient		suivent	suivirent	suivissent

INFINITIVE PARTICIPLES	INDICATIVE			
	Present	**Imperfect**	**Passé Composé**	**Future**
tenir *(to hold,* *keep)* tenant tenu	tiens tiens tient tenons tenez tiennent	tenais tenais tenait tenions teniez tenaient	ai tenu as tenu a tenu avons tenu avez tenu ont tenu	tiendrai tiendras tiendra tiendrons tiendrez tiendront
vaincre *(to conquer)* vainquant vaincu	vaincs vaincs vainc vainquons vainquez vainquent	vainquais vainquais vainquait vainquions vainquiez vainquaient	ai vaincu as vaincu a vaincu avons vaincu avez vaincu ont vaincu	vaincrai vaincras vaincra vaincrons vaincrez vaincront
valoir *(to be worth)* valant valu	vaux vaux vaut valons valez valent	valais valais valait valions valiez valaient	ai valu as valu a valu avons valu avez valu ont valu	vaudrai vaudras vaudra vaudrons vaudrez vaudront
venir *(to come)* venant venu	viens viens vient venons venez viennent	venais venais venait venions veniez venaient	suis venu(e) es venu(e) est venu(e) sommes venu(e)s êtes venu(e)(s) sont venu(e)s	viendrai viendras viendra viendrons viendrez viendront
vivre *(to live)* vivant vécu	vis vis vit vivons vivez vivent	vivais vivais vivait vivions viviez vivaient	ai vécu as vécu a vécu avons vécu avez vécu ont vécu	vivrai vivras vivra vivrons vivrez vivront
voir *(to see)* voyant vu	vois vois voit voyons voyez voient	voyais voyais voyait voyions voyiez voyaient	ai vu as vu a vu avons vu avez vu ont vu	verrai verras verra verrons verrez verront

CONDITIONAL	IMPERATIVE	SUBJUNCTIVE	LITERARY TENSES	
Present		**Present**	**Passé Simple**	**Imperfect Subjunctive**
tiendrais		tienne	tins	tinsse
tiendrais	tiens	tiennes	tins	tinsses
tiendrait		tienne	tint	tînt
tiendrions	tenons	tenions	tînmes	tinssions
tiendriez	tenez	teniez	tîntes	tinssiez
tiendraient		tiennent	tinrent	tinssent
vaincrais		vainque	vainquis	vainquisse
vaincrais	vaincs	vainques	vainquis	vainquisses
vaincrait		vainque	vainquit	vainquît
vaincrions	vainquons	vainquions	vainquîmes	vainquissions
vaincriez	vainquez	vainquiez	vainquîtes	vainquissiez
vaincraient		vainquent	vainquirent	vainquissent
vaudrais		vaille	valus	valusse
vaudrais	vaux	vailles	valus	valusses
vaudrait		vaille	valut	valût
vaudrions	valons	valions	valûmes	valussions
vaudriez	valez	valiez	valûtes	valussiez
vaudraient		vaillent	valurent	valussent
viendrais		vienne	vins	vinsse
viendrais	viens	viennes	vins	vinsses
viendrait		vienne	vint	vînt
viendrions	venons	venions	vînmes	vinssions
viendriez	venez	veniez	vîntes	vinssiez
viendraient		viennent	vinrent	vinssent
vivrais		vive	vécus	vécusse
vivrais	vis	vives	vécus	vécusses
vivrait		vive	vécut	vécût
vivrions	vivons	vivions	vécûmes	vécussions
vivriez	vivez	viviez	vécûtes	vécussiez
vivraient		vivent	vécurent	vécussent
verrais		voie	vis	visse
verrais	vois	voies	vis	visses
verrait		voie	vit	vît
verrions	voyons	voyions	vîmes	vissions
verriez	voyez	voyiez	vîtes	vissiez
verraient		voient	virent	vissent

INFINITIVE PARTICIPLES	INDICATIVE			
	Present	**Imperfect**	**Passé Composé**	**Future**
vouloir *(to wish, want)* voulant voulu	veux veux veut voulons voulez veulent	voulais voulais voulait voulions vouliez voulaient	ai voulu as voulu a voulu avons voulu avez voulu ont voulu	voudrai voudras voudra voudrons voudrez voudront

CONDITIONAL	IMPERATIVE	SUBJUNCTIVE	LITERARY TENSES	
Present		**Present**	**Passé Simple**	**Imperfect Subjunctive**
voudrais		veuille	voulus	voulusse
voudrais	veuille	veuilles	voulus	voulusses
voudrait		veuille	voulut	voulût
voudrions	veuillons	voulions	voulûmes	voulussions
voudriez	veuillez	vouliez	voulûtes	voulussiez
voudraient		veuillent	voulurent	voulussent

Answers to Chapter at a Glance Sections

CHAPTER 2

I.

1.	vous flirtez	5.	je bois	9.	vous apprenez
2.	nous finissons	6.	ils vont	10.	nous divorçons
3.	vous mentez	7.	ils craignent	11.	tu achètes
4.	ils répondent	8.	nous mettons	12.	elles emploient

II.

1. b.
2. a.
3. b.

III.

1. *Depuis quand* Jeannine flirte-t-elle avec mon petit ami?
2. *Depuis combien de temps* sortez-vous avec Robert?

IV.

1. Brigitte vient de trouver une maison.
2. Ils viennent d'aller à Paris.

V.

1. *Choisis (choisissons, choisissez)* un mari.
2. *Réponds (répondons, répondez)* tout de suite.
3. *Fais (faisons, faites)* la cuisine.
4. *Sois (soyons, soyez)* indépendante(s)!

VI.

1. *N'*allons *pas* au cinéma!
2. *Ne* faites *pas* le lit!

VII.

1. *Tiens!* J'ai une bonne idée!
2. *Voyons!* Vous n'êtes pas vraiment sérieuse!

VIII.

1. Jeannine *le* déteste.
2. Elle n'*en* parle jamais.
3. Elles veulent *y* habiter.
4. Ne *lui* parlez pas!

IX.

1. Robert *lui en* donne.
2. Laure *le leur* a annoncé.

X.

1. Je suis sûr que Madeleine est amoureuse de *lui*.
2. *Vous et moi* (or *Toi et moi*), nous sommes toujours en retard.

XI.

1. Votre sœur est-elle libérée?—Oui, *elle l'est*.
2. Hélène et Barbara sont-elles traditionnelles?—Non, *elles ne le sont pas*.

CHAPTER 3

I.

1. communication/*féminin*
2. biologie/*féminin*
3. latin/*masculin*
4. Californie/*féminin*
5. promesse/*féminin*
6. travail/*masculin*
7. moment/*masculin*
8. symbolisme/*masculin*

II.

1. l'ami   l'*amie*
2. l'oncle   la *tante*
3. l'écrivain   l'*écrivain femme* (or la *femme écrivain*)
4. l'acteur   l'*actrice*
5. le chat   la *chatte*

III.

1. Avez-vous vu *la* Tour Eiffel?
2. Je vais faire *le* tour du monde.

IV.

1. la mère/*les mères*
2. l'œil/*les yeux*
3. le fils/*les fils*
4. le bijou/*les bijoux*
5. le journal/*les journaux*
6. le grand-père/*les grands-pères*
7. le feu/*les feux*
8. le pique-nique/*les pique-niques*

V.

1. *Le peuple* américain respecte la famille.
2. Il y avait vingt *personnes* à notre réunion de famille.
3. *On* dit qu'il ressemble à sa mère.

VI.

1. *Les parents* devraient-ils jouer avec leurs enfants?
2. *Le petit Robert* est impossible *le matin*.

VII.

1. Paris se trouve en France.
2. New York se trouve aux États-Unis.
3. Les Champs-Élysées se trouvent à Paris.
4. La Nouvelle-Orléans se trouve en Louisiane.
5. Londres se trouve en Angleterre.
6. Tokyo se trouve au Japon.

VIII.

1. *Les* enfants ont-ils *des* obligations envers leurs parents?
2. J'ai *des* tantes qui me donnent toujours *des* cadeaux.

IX.

1. Il a deux sœurs mais il n'a pas *de* frères.
2. Les Mercier font beaucoup *de* sacrifices pour leurs enfants.
3. Je connais *des* filles qui n'obéissent pas à leurs parents.
4. Ma camarade de chambre a *d*'excellents rapports avec sa famille.
5. Avez-vous souvent *des* disputes avec vos parents?

X.

1. Quand votre famille va-t-elle revenir *de* France?
2. Mon avion part *des* États-Unis la semaine prochaine.
3. Mon camarade de chambre vient *du* Canada.

CHAPTER 4

I.

1. je me lave
2. tu te couches
3. elle s'habille
4. nous nous parlons
5. vous vous endormez
6. ils se téléphonent

II.

1. *Ne* vous asseyez *pas.*
2. *Ne* te dépêche *pas!*
3. *Ne* nous marions *pas!*

III.

1. Ils s'embrassent l'un l'autre.
2. Nous nous regardons l'un l'autre. *or* Nous nous regardons les un(e)s les autres.

IV.

1. *Nous nous rappelons* or *nous nous souvenons de* la pollution à Los Angeles.
2. Oui, *je me souviens de* (or *je me rappelle*) Geneviève!

V.

1. nous avons visité
2. ils ont entendu
3. j'ai fini
4. nous avons dit
5. j'ai fait
6. tu as pris
7. elle est allée
8. elles se sont promenées
9. ils se sont parlé
10. nous avons visitées

VI.

1. je dansais
2. tu allais
3. elle choisissait
4. nous étions
5. vous aviez
6. elles nageaient

VII.

1. Elle *a entendu* un oiseau chanter dans les arbres.
2. Ils *parlaient* de l'atmosphère poétique de Paris.
3. Quand il *était* jeune, il *regardait* ce lac pendant des heures!
4. Hier le ciel *était* bleu et l'air *était* frais.
5. Oui, nous *avons vu* un artiste célèbre à Montmartre.
6. Ils *attendaient* depuis une heure quand ils ont vu le train.

VIII.

L'été dernier ma famille et moi, nous *sommes allés* à la campagne. Il *faisait* beau et le ciel *était* bleu. Alors nous *avons décidé* de faire un pique-nique dans le bois. Pendant que nous *étions* assis, nous *avons entendu* un bruit étrange derrière nous. Nous *nous sommes retournés* et nous *avons vu* un ours qui s'*approchait* de nous! Il *avait* l'air méchant! Nous *nous sommes levés* tout de suite et nous *avons couru* jusqu'à la voiture. L'ours *a mangé* les sandwiches et la limonade!

IX.

1. Nous *sommes sorti(e)s* du bar à trois heures du matin.
2. Où *avez-vous laissé* (or *as-tu*) votre chapeau?
3. Nous *avons quitté* la ville à cause de la pollution.

X.

1. Ils *venaient de finir* (or *venaient de terminer*) l'examen quand le professeur a demandé les copies.
2. Nous *venions de voir* New York.

CHAPTER 5

I.

1. *Sort-il* du ghetto?
2. Une société sans classes *est-elle* possible?
3. Cette jeune fille *a-t-elle* de la classe?
4. Son père *a-t-il* gagné beaucoup d'argent?

II.

1. *Est-ce qu'il sort* du ghetto? Il sort du ghetto, *n'est-ce pas?*
2. *Est-ce qu'une société* sans classes *est* possible? Une société sans classes possible, *n'est-ce pas?*
3. *Est-ce que cette jeune fille a* de la classe? Cette jeune fille a de la classe, *n'* pas?
4. *Est-ce que son père a gagné* beaucoup d'argent? Son père a gagné b d'argent, *n'est-ce pas?*

III.

1. *Pourquoi ira-t-il* loin?
2. *Comment est* ce millionnaire? *Comment* ce millionnaire *est-il?*

IV.

1. *Qu'est-ce qu'il est devenu* après ses études? or: *Qu'est-il devenu* après ses études?
2. *Qu'est-ce qui l'intéresse* beaucoup?
3. *Qui a* (or *Qui-est ce qui*) une grande fortune?

V.

1. *Quelle* mauvaise odeur!
2. *Laquelle* de ces jeunes filles a de si bonnes manières?

VI.

1. *Qu'est-ce que* (or *Qu'est-ce que c'est que*) la bourgeoisie?
2. *Quelle est* la date aujourd'hui?

VII.

1. Elle *n'*est *pas* vendeuse.
2. *Ne* jouent-ils *pas* au bridge ce soir?
3. Je *n'*aime *pas* stéréotyper les gens.
4. Pourquoi *ne* suis-*je* pas né riche?
5. Il est important de *ne pas* être snob.

VIII.

1. Je *ne* suis *jamais* allé à l'opéra.
2. Je *n'*ai *plus* de bière.

IX.

1. Ce millionnaire *n'*a *rien* fait pour aider les pauvres.
2. *Personne ne* veut vivre dans la misère.

X.

1. Elle *n'*est vulgaire *qu'*avec ses amies.
2. Elle *n'*aime *que* les gens cultivés.

XI.

1. Ils *n'*ont *aucune* intention de partir.
2. *Aucune* classe sociale *n'*est parfaite.
   Il *ne* veut devenir *ni* médecin *ni* avocat.

que non.
n d'intéressant ici!
en. or: Merci.— Il n'y a pas de quoi.

CHAPTER 6

4. subjectif/*subjective*
5. long/*longue*
6. blanc/*blanche*

7. gros/*grosse*
8. doux/*douce*
9. gentil/*gentille*
10. beau/*belle*

II.

1. les avocats dangereux
2. les crimes prémédités
3. les nouveaux juges
4. les témoins principaux

III.

1. un crime *prémédité*
2. un *bon* avocat
3. l'*ancien* prisonnier
4. une *vieille* femme *algérienne*

IV.

1. des institutions *sociales*
2. un juge et une sentence *justes*
3. une robe *bleu foncé*
4. une *demi*-heure

V.

1. Le juge a l'air raisonnable.
2. L'argent la rend contente. *or* L'argent la rend heureuse.

VI.

1. arbitraire/*arbitrairement*
2. sérieux/*sérieusement*
3. innocent/*innocemment*
4. meilleur/*mieux*
5. bon/*bien*

VII.

1. On parle beaucoup du crime passionnel.
2. On l'a déjà déclarée innocente.
3. On est moralement responsable de ses actions.

VIII.

1. Peut-être l'accusé est-il coupable. or: Peut-être que l'accusé est coupable.
2. A peine le criminel a-t-il compris son crime.

IX.

1. J'ai l'impression que *tous* les suspects sont innocents.
2. Pourquoi *toutes* les sentences de ce juge sont-elles si indulgentes?
3. Ce pauvre homme a *tout* perdu à cause de cette indiscrétion.
4. L'avocat était *tout* triste parce que le jury avait condamné son client.

X.

1. Un professeur est *plus (moins, aussi)* sérieux qu'un étudiant.
2. Une prison est *moins (plus, aussi)* confortable que ma maison.

XI.

1. le plus jeune père
2. le livre le plus difficile

XII.

1. Mon avocat plaide *mieux que* le vôtre.
2. Bien sûr, c'est le *meilleur* avocat de la ville!

CHAPTER 7

I.

le FUTUR	le CONDITIONNEL
1. je voterai	je voterais
2. tu applaudiras	tu applaudirais
3. elle perdra	elle perdrait
4. nous ferons	nous ferions
5. vous serez	vous seriez
6. elles auront	elles auraient

II.

le FUTUR ANTÉRIEUR	le CONDITIONNEL PASSÉ	le PLUS-QUE-PARFAIT
1. j'aurai gagné	j'aurais gagné	j'avais gagné
2. tu auras menti	tu aurais menti	tu avais menti
3. il aura attendu	il aurait attendu	il avait attendu
4. nous aurons promis	nous aurions promis	nous avions promis
5. vous serez venu(e)(s)	vous seriez venu(e)(s)	vous étiez venu(e)(s)
6. ils seront partis	ils seraient partis	ils étaient partis

III.

1. Je suis sûr que notre candidat *gagnera!*
2. Quand j'*aurai* dix-huit ans, je *pourrai* voter aux élections présidentielles.
3. Il *aura perdu* l'éléction avant la fin de la campagne!

IV.

1. Si j'étais à votre place, je n'*irais* pas.
2. Le public ne savait pas que le président *avait déjà menti* mille fois.
3. Si nous *avions fait* cela, nous *aurions gagné*.

V.

1. Quand le sénateur était jeune, il *pensait* toujours à la politique.
2. Tous les candidats ont dit qu'ils *feraient* des réformes.

VI.

1. Non, elle n'est pas obligée de voter, mais elle *devrait* le faire!
2. Ce politicien *devait* faire beaucoup de voyages à Washington.
3. Il *a dû* déclarer la guerre à cause de la crise politique.
4. Un politicien honnête *ne devrait pas* accepter de l'argent.
5. Ce journaliste *n'aurait pas dû* écrire cet éditorial injuste.
6. Tiens! Il a refusé cette sinécure! Il *doit* être honnête!
7. Le gangster *devait* assassiner le président, mais on l'a arrêté.

VII.

1. Il *a été obligé* (or *était obligé*) de voter pour son frère.
2. Un politicien dynamique *n'est pas censé* dire cela.

CHAPTER 8

I.

1. Comment! Nous avons perdu les chèques de voyage *qui* étaient dans vos valises?
2. Voilà la belle étrangère *que* nous avons déjà vue à Versailles.

II.

1. Expliquez-nous *ce que* vous avez vu à Haïti.
2. Quel gourmand! La cuisine française est tout *ce qui* l'intéresse!

III.

1. Je vous présente Babette, la femme *avec qui* (or *avec laquelle*) je compte visiter le Sénégal.
2. Il est sorti de la banque à côté de *laquelle* se trouvait l'agence de voyages.

IV.

1. Je suis fatiguée et il n'y a rien sur *quoi* je puisse m'asseoir!
2. Elle m'a dit ⟨⟨Bonjour⟩⟩ au moment *où* elle m'a vu.

V.

1. Voici le touriste désagréable *dont* je parlais.
2. C'est *ce dont* il est si fier!

VI.

1. Il est francophone? *Qu'est-ce que* cela signifie?
2. Voici *ce qu'* on a trouvé dans sa chambre!
3. Voilà cette femme bizarre *que* j'ai rencontrée au Louvre.
4. *Qui* avez-vous vu pendant les vacances?

VII.

1. Idiot! *N'importe qui* pourrait lire cette carte!
2. Ce francophile ferait *n'importe quoi* pour visiter la Martinique.

VIII.

1. *cette* dame   3. *ce* livre
2. *cet* étranger   4. *ces* maisons
5. *Ces coutumes-ci* nous sont familières tandis que *ces coutumes-là* nous sont étrangères.

IX.

1. *Celui* qui a l'esprit ouvert n'aura pas de problèmes.
2. Geneviève et Marguerite sont des touristes opposées; *celle-ci* est gentille tandis que *celle-là* est insolente!
3. Quelles photos préférez-vous, *celles* sur la carte postale ou *celles* de Marc?

X.

1. *Ça* (or *Cela*) m'est égal.
2. Faisons un échange! Si vous me donnez *ceci* (or *cela*) je vous donne *cela* (or *ceci*).

XI.

1. Sont-*elles* Françaises ou Canadiennes?
2. *C'*est une excursion qu'il faut faire!
3. *Ce* sont les pays exotiques dont nous avons parlé.

XII.

1. *Il est* (or *C'est*) intéressant *de* comparer deux cultures différentes.
2. Vous êtes-vous jamais senti tout seul?—Oui, et *c'est* difficile *à* supporter!

XIII.

1. Nous avons rendu visite à nos parents *ce matin-là*.
2. Nous passons *ce mois-ci* à la Guadeloupe.
3. Il est parti *le lendemain*.
4. Moi, je pars *demain*.

CHAPTER 9

I.

1. parler
   a. que je parle
   b. que tu parles
   c. qu'elle parle
   d. que nous parlions
   e. que vous parliez
   f. qu'elles parlent
2. que je fasse
3. que tu réfléchisse
4. qu'il réponde
5. que nous criions
6. que vous veniez
7. qu'ils viennent

II.

1. causer
   a. que j'aie causé
   b. que tu aies causé
   c. qu'elle ait causé
   d. que nous ayons causé
   e. que vous ayez causé
   f. qu'elles aient causé
2. partir
   a. que je sois parti(e)
   b. que tu sois parti(e)
   c. qu'elle soit partie
   d. que nous soyons parti(e)s
   e. que vous soyez parti(e)(s)
   f. qu'elles soient parties.

III.

1. Faut-il que nous *connaissions* le français pour bien comprendre la culture française?
2. Je voudrais que vous *cessiez* de parler incorrectement.
3. Je suis contente qu'il *soit* plus agréable à l'avenir.
4. Il est désolé que vous *n'ayez pas perfectionné* votre accent à Paris l'année dernière.

IV.

1. Je suis étonnée que vous ne *compreniez* pas l'argot. (subj.)
2. Elle sait que nous nous *fâcherons* quand nous entendrons la rumeur! (ind.)
3. Je suis triste que vous *ayez dit* du mal de moi hier. (subj.)
4. Il est vrai qu'on *apprécie* mieux sa propre langue en étudiant une langue étrangère. (ind.)
5. Il faut que vous vous *exprimiez* lentement mais correctement. (subj.)
6. Bien que nous nous *disputions* de temps en temps, nous nous tutoyons toujours. (subj.)
7. Je suis certain que mon fils *suivra* un cours de langue étrangère l'année prochaine. (ind.)
8. Vous n'apprendrez pas une langue en une semaine, qui que vous *soyez*. (subj.)
9. Il croit que chaque langue *contient* sa propre vision du monde. (ind.)

10. Croyez-vous vraiment que nous *parlions* bien français? (subj.)
11. Y a-t-il un étudiant dans la classe qui *sache* parfaitement le subjonctif? (subj.)
12. C'est la meilleure plaisanterie que j'*ai jamais entendue*. (ind.) or: C'est la meilleure plaisanterie que j'*aie jamais entendue*. (subj.)

V.

1. Je voudrais *être* polyglotte un jour.
2. Je voudrais que vous *parliez* plus franchement.
3. Faut-il que nous *étudiions* le français tous les jours?
4. Il faut *manger* pour vivre et non pas vivre pour manger.
5. Parlez plus fort pour que je *puisse* vous entendre.
6. Il est parfois important de *parler* couramment une langue étrangère.

VI.

1. Qu'il *vienne* demain.
2. Qu'elle *réponde* en anglais s'il le faut.

CHAPTER 10

I.

1. *mon* livre   3. *son* imagination   5. *vos* (or *tes*) romans
2. *sa* place   4. *notre* bibliothèque   6. *leurs* idées

II.

1. Cette actrice ne se lave jamais *les* cheveux!
2. *Son* poète favori est Baudelaire.

III.

1. L'imagination de cet écrivain est moins riche que *la vôtre* (or *la tienne*).
2. Cet auteur aime bien critiquer les romans des autres, mais il ne veut pas qu'on critique *les siens!*

IV.

1. Voyons! Ce roman policier *n'est pas à vous* (or *à toi*)!
2. Mais si! Il *est à moi!*

V.

1. *La pièce de Racine* est une tragédie.
2. *Les idées de vos amis* me scandalisent.

VI.

1. Je crois qu'elle *a mal à la tête.*
2. L'acteur n'a pas joué parce qu'il *était malade.*

VII.

1. derrière l'arbre   4. au milieu du livre
2. contre la maison   5. près de la bibliothèque
3. entre nous

VIII.

1. Mon livre est *sur la table près de la fenêtre.*

2. Je peux lire ce best-seller *en une heure!*

3. Cette actrice charmante *aux yeux bruns* est très gentille *envers nous.*

IX.

1. Nous avons *à* lire trois romans cette semaine.

2. Ce romancier a essayé *de* scandaliser le public mais il n'a pas réussi *à* le faire.

3. Voulez-vous assister au spectacle avec moi? (no preposition)

4. Dans ce roman il s'agit d'un homme qui refuse *de* jouer un rôle.

5. Mon ami m'a conseillé *de* suivre un cours de littérature.

X.

1. Je *cherche* un livre de poche intéressant.

2. *Nous nous intéressons à* étudier la littérature surréaliste.

3. Les spectateurs *rient de* vous parce que vous *ressemblez à* Charlie Chaplin!

XI.

1. Que pensez-vous *de* Balzac?

2. Un acteur pense toujours *à* son public.

3. La littérature pornographique manque souvent *de* valeur artistique.

4. Juliette manque beaucoup *à* Roméo.

XII.

1. Ils vont au spectacle *à* bicyclette.

2. Nous allons au festival d'Avignon *en* bateau.

CHAPTER 11

I.

1. Cette chanson folklorique *est chantée par* un groupe sensationnel.

2. Le morceau de Debussy *sera joué par* un pianiste américain.

3. Cette farce *a été écrite* au moyen age.

II.

1. Le grand public a été scandalisé par ce documentaire violent.

2. The sentence cannot be made passive—reflexive verbs cannot be made passive.

3. Deux grands rôles seront joués par cet acteur l'année prochaine.

III.

1. On a mangé les bonbons et le pop-corn en deux minutes.

2. Comment! On a censuré le dessin animé de Disney?

IV.

1. Cela (Ça) ne se fait qu'au cinéma! or: Cela (ça) se fait seulement au cinéma!

2. Ses livres se vendent vite.

V.

1. écouter/*écoutant*

2. se divertir/*se divertissant*

3. vendre/*vendant*

4. faire/*faisant*

5. avoir/*ayant*

VI.

1. Comment s'appelle la jeune fille *chantant* cette mélodie charmante?
2. Ce compositeur buvait de la bière *en composant* une chanson à boire!
3. Ce film de guerre est sérieux *tout en étant* très drôle.

VII.

1. Les nouveaux films au drive-in sont *divertissants*.
2. Cette chanteuse n'est ni *amusante* ni *intéressante*.

VIII.

1. Il passe plus de temps à *regarder* les westerns à la télévision qu'à *étudier*.
2. Comment peut-elle regarder ce film *sans sortir (partir)?*
3. Je l'ai entendu *chanter* une chanson risquée au cabaret.

IX.

1. Il fait vendre sa guitare.
2. Le fait-il faire tout de suite?
3. Il fait partir (sortir) son ami.

Vocabularies

This vocabulary contains French words and expressions found in the exercises and the *Vocabulaire du thème*. Cognates and other easily recognizable words have not been included.

Abbreviations

adj	adjective	*p*	page
adv	adverb	*pl*	plural
conj	conjunction	*pp*	past participle
f	feminine	*prep*	preposition
fam	familiar	*pron*	pronoun
inf	infinitive	*subj*	subjunctive
m	masculine	*v*	verb
n	noun		

An asterisk (*) indicates a word beginning with an aspirate *h*.

A

l'**abeille** *f* bee
abolir to abolish
abuser to abuse
accueillir to welcome
accusé accused
l'**accusé** *m* defendant
acheter to buy
acquitter to acquit
l'**acteur** *m* actor
l'**actrice** *f* actress
actuel, actuelle present
actuellement presently, now
s'**adapter à** to adapt to
l'**adversaire** *m* opponent
afin: — de (+ *inf*) in order to, to; **— que** (+ *subj*) in order that, so that
l'**agence de voyages** *f* travel bureau
l'**agent de police** *m* policeman
l'**agent de voyages** *m* travel agent
agir to act; **il s'agit de** it is a question of
agréable pleasant
l'**aîné** *m* the elder, the eldest

l'**aise** *f* ease; **se sentir à l'—** to feel at ease
aisé well-to-do
allemand German
aller to go; **s'en —** to leave
améliorer to improve
l'**ami** *m* friend, boyfriend; **le petit — ** boyfriend
l'**amie** *f* friend, girlfriend; **la petite — ** girlfriend
l'**amitié** *f* friendship; **lier — avec** to make friends with
l'**amour** *m* love
amoureux, amoureuse loving; **être — de** to be in love with; **tomber — de** to fall in love with
amusant amusing
amuser to amuse; **s'—** to amuse, enjoy oneself; **s'— bien** to have a good time
angoissé anguished
l'**anniversaire** *m* anniversary, birthday
anonyme anonymous
l'**annonce** *f* announcement; **l'— publicitaire** advertisement

l'appareil (appareil-photo)
m camera
appeler to call; s'— to be called,
named
applaudir to applaud
apprécier to appreciate
apprendre to learn
s'approcher de to approach
l'après-midi *m, f* afternoon
arbitraire arbitrary
l'argent *m* money
l'argot *m* slang
arrêter to stop, arrest
l'arriviste *m, f* social climber
assassiner to assassinate
asseoir to sit, seat; s'— to sit
down
assez enough
l'assiette *f* dish, plate
assister à to attend
assuré assured
assurer to strengthen
attendre to wait for
l'attention *f* attention, care; faire —
à to pay attention to, be careful
aucun any; ne . . . — no, not any
l'augmentation de salaire *f* raise
aussi also; — . . . que as . . . as;
— (+ *inverted verb*) therefore
(p. 125)
aussitôt que as soon as
l'auteur *m* author
l'autorité *f* authority
avant before
avare greedy
avaricieux, avaricieuse greedy
l'avenir *m* future
l'avion *m* plane
l'avis *m* opinion; à mon — in my
opinion
l'avocat *m* lawyer
avoir to have; — besoin de to need;
— du mal à (+ *inf*) to have
trouble; — envie de to feel like;
— l'air to seem
l'avortement *m* abortion

B

la bande tape
la banlieue suburbs
le banquier banker
la barbe beard
la barre bar
bâtir to build

battre to beat, hit; se — to fight
beau (bel), belle beautiful
le beau-frère brother-in-law
le bénéfice du doute benefit of the
doubt
le besoin need; avoir — de to need
le best-seller best seller
bête stupid
la bêtise stupidity; dire des — to
speak nonsense
la bicyclette bicycle; faire de la
— to go bicycle riding
bien well; — que (+ *subj*)
although; — sûr certainly;
— sûr que non certainly not
bientôt soon
le bijou jewel
bilingue bilingual
blâmer to blame
blanc, blanche white
boire to drink
le bois woods
la boîte box, can; la — de nuit night
club
bon, bonne good
le bonbon candy
le bonheur happiness
le bord edge, shore
bouger to move
le bouquin *fam* book
la bourgeoisie middle class
la boutique shop
le bouton button
bref, brève short
la Bretagne Brittany
brillamment brilliantly
la brosse à dents toothbrush
le bruit noise
la brusquerie abruptness
bruyant noisy
bûcher *fam* to cram
le bureau office

C

le cadeau gift
le cadet, la cadette the younger, the
youngest
le calmant tranquilizer
le, la camarade de chambre roommate
la caméra movie camera
le campagnard country dweller
la campagne country
le camping camping: faire du — to
go camping

le **cancre**   bad student, dunce
la **carte**   card, map; **jouer aux —**   to
  play cards
la **carte postale**   post card
la **cause**   cause; **à — de**   because of
  causer   to chat, talk
  ceci   this
la **ceinture**   belt
  cela (ça)   that
  célèbre   famous
  censé   supposed; **être —** (+ *inf*)   to
  be supposed to
  censurer   to censor
  cependant   however
  cesser (de + *inf*)   to stop, cease
  ceux   these, those
  chacun   each (person)
  chaleureusement   warmly
la **chambre**   room
le **champ**   field
la **chance**   luck; **avoir de la —**   to be
  lucky
la **chanson**   song; **la —à**
  boire   drinking song
le **chansonnier**   song-writer,
  song-book
le **chant**   song
le **chanteur**   singer
la **chanteuse**   singer
  charmant   charming
  châtain   brown-haired; **—**
  clair   light brown
le **chèque de voyage**   traveler's check
  cher, chère   dear, expensive (*p.* 117)
  chercher   to look for
le **cheval**   horse; **le — de bois**   flying
  horse
les **cheveux** *m*   hair
  chez   at the home, place of
le **choix**   choice
le **chômage**   unemployment
le **chômeur**   unemployed person
  choquant   shocking
la **chose**   thing
  chuchoter   to whisper
le **ciel** (*pl* **cieux**)   sky
le **cinéma**   movies, cinema
  cinématographique   cinematographic
le, la **cinéphile**   movie fan
la **circonstance**   cicumstance; **la —**
  atténuante   extenuating
  circumstance
la **circulation**   traffic
le **citadin**   city dweller
le **citoyen**   citizen

la **classe**   class; **avoir de la —**   to
  have class
la **clef**   key
le **clochard**   bum
le **cochon**   pig
la **colère**   anger; **se mettre en —**   to
  become angry
le **collègue**   colleague
  coller   to glue, stick
  combien   how much, how many
  comme   like, as; **— il faut**   proper
  comment   how, what; **— + être**
  what is someone or something like
  commettre   to commit
le **communisme**   communism
le **communiste**   communist
  compatissant   compassionate
  complaisant   accommodating
  composer   to compose
le **compositeur**   composer
  comprendre   to understand
  compromettant   compromising
  compromettre   to compromise
le **compromis**   compromise
  compter   to count on, intend
le **concert**   concert
le **condamné**   convict
  condamner   to condemn
  condition *f*   condition; **à — que**
  (+ *subj*)   on condition that
  conduire   to drive
la **confiance**   confidence; **avoir —**
  en   to have confidence in
  confus   confused
  connaître   to know, be acquainted
  with
le **conseiller**   adviser
le **conseil**   advice
  conseiller (à + *n* **de** + *inf*)   to
  advise
le **conservateur**   conservative
  constamment   constantly
  consulter   to consult
le **conte**   short story
le **contraire**   contrary; **au —**   on the
  contrary
le **contraste**   contrast; **faire —**
  avec   to contrast with
  convaincre   to convince
  convenable   proper
le **copain** *fam*   friend, buddy
la **copine** *fam*   friend, buddy
  coquet, coquette   coquettish
  corriger   to correct
le **côté**   side; **à — de**   beside, next to

se **coucher** to go to bed
coupable guilty
couper to cut
couramment fluently
le **courant** current; **être au —** to be
in the know, be up on
courir to run
le **cours** course; **au — de** in the
course of, during; le **—**
facultatif elective; le **—**
obligatoire required course
la **course** run, race, outing; **faire des**
—s to go shopping
le **couteau** knife
coûter to cost; **— cher** to be
expensive
la **coutume** custom
couvrir to cover
craindre to fear, be afraid of
la **crèche** day-care center
créer to create
le **crime** crime; le **— passionnel**
crime of passion; le **—**
prémédité premeditated crime
le **criminel** criminal
la **crise** crisis
la **critique** criticism
le **critique** critic
critiquer to criticize
la **croix** cross
la **cuisine** kitchen; **faire la —** to do
the cooking, cook

D

d'ailleurs besides
la **dame** lady
d'après according to
se **débrouiller** to get along, manage
le **débutant** beginner
le **décor** decor, scenery
décrire to describe
déjà already
déjeuner to have lunch
démissionner to resign
la **démocratie** democracy
dénoncer to denounce
le **dénouement** ending; le **—**
heureux happy ending
le **départ** departure
dépaysé lost, homesick
se **dépêcher** to hurry up
dépenser to spend
se **déplacer** to move about, travel

dériver to derive
dernier, dernière last
le **derrière** behind
dès from. . . on; **—**
maintenant from now on; **—**
que as soon as
désagréable unpleasant
désobéir à to disobey
désolé very sorry, grieved
le **dessin animé** cartoon
détacher: se — de to break away
from
détruire to destroy
devenir to become
deviner to guess
le **devoir** duty; les **—s** homework
le **dialecte** dialect
le **dictateur** dictator
la **dictature** dictatorship
le **dimanche** Sunday
dire to say, tell; **— des bêtises** to
speak nonsense; **— du bien, du**
mal de to speak well, badly of
la **discothèque** discothèque
le **discours** speech; **faire un —** to
make a speech
discret, discrète discreet
disparaître to disappear
la **dispute** quarrel
se **disputer** to quarrel
le **disque** record
distingué distinguished
la **distraction** entertainment
divertir to entertain, amuse; **se**
— to amuse, enjoy oneself
le **documentaire** documentary
le **domaine** domaine; **dans le —**
de in the area, sphere of
le **dommage** damage, injury; **il est,**
c'est — it's a pity
donc therefore
la **douane** customs; **passer la —** to
pass through customs
le **douanier** customs officer
doubler to dub
le **doute** doubt; **mettre en —** to
question
douteux, douteuse doubtful
doux, douce sweet
le **droit** law (the profession, the
study); right (moral, legal); **avoir le**
— de + *inf* to have the right to
droite: de — rightist
d'une part . . . d'autre part on
one hand . . . on the other hand

E

l'**eau** *f* ´ water
l'**échange** *m* exchange
 échouer à to fail
l'**écolier** *m* schoolboy
 écraser to smash
l'**écrivain** *m* writer
l'**éducation** *f* upbringing
 égal equal; **cela m'est —** I don't
 mind, it's all the same to me
l'**égalité** *f* equality
l'**égard** *m* consideration, respect; **à**
 l'— de regarding; **manquer**
 d'—s envers to lack
 consideration, respect for
l'**élève** *m, f* student
 élevé brought up; **bien —** well
 brought up; **mal —** badly brought
 up
 élever to raise, bring up
 éloigné distant, remote
 élu (*pp of* **élire**) elected
 embrasser to kiss
l'**emprisonnement** *m* imprisonment;
 l'**— perpétuel** life imprisonment
l'**emprunt** *m* borrowing
 enceinte pregnant
 encore again, still, yet
s'**endormir** to fall asleep
l'**enfant** *m, f* child; l'**—**
 unique only child
 enlever to take off
l'**ennui** *m* trouble, problem
 ennuyer to bore, trouble; **s'—** to
 be bored
 ennuyeux, ennuyeuse boring
 énorme enormous
l'**enregistrement** *m* recording
 enregistrer to record
l'**enseignement** *m* teaching; l'**—**
 supérieur higher education
 enseigner to teach
 ensemble together
 entendre to hear; **s'— avec** to
 get along with
 entourer to surround
 envers toward (*p.* 209)
l'**envie** *f* wish, desire; **avoir —**
 de to feel like
l'**époque** *f* age, era, time
 épouser to marry
l'**époux,** l'**épouse** spouse
 érotique erotic
l'**escargot** *m* snail

 espagnol Spanish
l'**espagnol** *m* Spanish language
 espérer to hope
l'**espion** *m* spy
 espionner to spy
l'**esprit** *m* mind, spirit; **avoir l'—**
 ouvert to have an open mind
 essayer (de + *inf*) to try (to)
 essuyer to wipe
 établir to establish
l'**étoile** *f* star; **coucher à la belle**
 — to sleep outdoors
 étonné astonished, amazed,
 surprised
 étonner to astonish, amaze, surprise
 étrange strange
 étranger, étrangère foreign
l'**étranger,** l'**étrangère** foreigner
 être to be; **— au courant de** to be
 in the know about; **— en train**
 de to be in the process of
 étroit close, narrow
l'**étude** *f* study
 exceptionnel, exceptionnelle
 exceptional
l'**excursion** *f* tour, trip; l'**—**
 accompagnée guided tour
l'**exemple** *m* example; **par —** for
 example
 exigeant demanding
 exploiter to exploit
 exprimer to express
l'**externe** *m, f* off-campus student
 extirper to extirpate, eradicate

F

la **face** face; **en — de** opposite; **faire**
 — à to face
 fâché angry
se **fâcher** to get angry
 facile easy
 faire to make; **il fait beau** it is a
 beautiful day
 falloir to be necessary
 fauché *fam* broke
 faut: il — it is necessary
la **faute** error
 faux, fausse false
la **femme** woman, wife
la **ferme** farm
 fermé closed
le **fermier** farmer

la **fessée** spanking
la **fête** feast, festival
le **feu** fire
  fidèle faithful
  fier, fière proud
se **fier à** to trust
le **film** film
  filmer to film
  finir (de + *inf*) to finish
  flâner to stroll
  flatter to flatter
  flirter to flirt
la **foi** faith
la **fois** time
  folklorique folk
  formidable *fam* great
  fort strong
le **fossé** ditch, trench; le **— entre les
  générations** generation gap
  fou (fol), folle crazy
  fouiller to search (a person, a
  suitcase, etc.)
la **foule** crowd
le **four** flop (theater)
le **foyer** (the) home
  frais, fraîche fresh, cool
le **franc** franc
  franc, franche frank
  franchement frankly
le, la **francophile** francophile (person
  who is extremely fond of France)
le, la **francophone** francophone (person
  whose native language is French)
  frapper to hit
  frénétiquement wildly
  fréquenter to frequent
le **frère** brother

G

  gagner to earn
  gai gay, lively
  garder to keep
  garer to park
  gaspiller to waste
  gâté spoiled
  gauche: de — leftist
  geler to freeze
  gênant embarrassing, awkward
  gêné bothered
le **génie** genius
le **genou** knee
le **genre** type

les **gens** *m, f* people
  gentil, gentille nice
la **gentillesse** graciousness
  gesticuler to gesticulate
  gifler to slap
le, la **gosse** *fam* kid
le **gourmand** gourmand, glutton
le **goût** taste
  goûter to taste
  grandir to grow
  gras, grasse fat; **faire la grasse
  matinée** to sleep late
la **grève** strike; **faire la —** to go on
  strike, strike
  gris gray, drunk
  gronder to scold
  gros, grosse big, fat
  grossier, grossière gross, coarse
  grossir to get fat
  guère hardly, scarcely
la **guerre** war
le **guide** guide, guidebook

H

s'**habiller** to get dressed
s'**habituer à** to get used to
l'**haleine** *f* breath
***hardi** hardy, daring
l'**harmonie** *f* harmony
***haut** high, tall
***hautain** condescending
la ***haute société** high society
l'**héroïne** *f* heroine
le ***héros** hero
l'**heure** *f* hour, time; **à l'—** on time
  heureusement happily, luckily,
  fortunately
  hier yesterday; **— soir** last night
l'**histoire** *f* history, story
l'**hiver** *m* winter
l'**homme** man; l'**— d'affaires**
  businessman; l'**—
  politique** politician
***honteux, honteuse** shameful
l'**horreur** *f* horror; **faire — à** to
  horrify
***huer** to boo
l'**humeur** *f* mood; **être de bonne
  —** to be in a good mood; **être de
  mauvaise —** to be in a bad mood
l'**humour** *m* humor

I

idiot stupid
l'**idiotisme** *m* idiom
l'**île** *f* island
importer to be important;
   n'importe où anywhere (at all);
   n'importe quand anytime (at
   all); **n'importe qui** anyone (at
   all); **n'importe quoi** anything (at
   all)
impressionné impressed
impressionner to impress
indépendant independent
l'**indigène** *m, f* native
indulgent indulgent, lenient
l'**ingénieur** *m* engineer
ingrat ungrateful
injuste unjust, unfair; **être —
   envers** to be unfair to
inquiet, inquiète worried
l'**instituteur** *m* teacher (elementary
   school)
insulter to insult
insupportable unbearable,
   intolerable
l'**intention** *f* intention; **avoir l'—
   de** to intend to
s'**intéresser à** to be interested in
l'**interne** *m, f* on-campus student
interpréter to interpret
interroger to question
intrépide intrepid, fearless
l'**intrigue** *f* plot
isolé isolated

J

jaloux, jalouse jealous
jamais ever, never;
   ne . . . — never
la **jambe** leg
le **jardin** garden
le **jargon** jargon
jeter to throw; **se — dans la
   politique** to go into politics
le **jeu** game
la **jeune fille** girl
joindre to join; **se — à** to join (an
   organization, club, etc.)
joli pretty
le **journal** newspaper
la **journée** day
le **juge** judge

juif, juive Jewish
le **jumeau**, la **jumelle** twin
le **juré** jury member, juror
le **jury** jury
   jusqu'à until, as far as; **— ce que**
   (+ *subj*) until
   juste just, fair; **être — envers** to
   be fair to

L

là-bas there, over there
le **lac** lake
   lâche loose, cowardly
   laid ugly
   lancer to throw
le **langage** language (of an individual;
   vocabulary)
la **langue** language (of a people); **la —
   étrangère** foreign language; **la —
   maternelle** native language; **la —
   vivante, morte** living, dead
   language
le **lapsus** slip, mistake; **faire un
   —** to make a slip of the tongue
se **laver** to wash up
le **lecteur** reader
le **lendemain** the next day; **le —
   matin** (the) next morning
   lent slow
   lentement slowly
   lever to lift, raise; **se —** to get up
le **libéral** libéral
   libéré liberated
la **liberté** freedom
   libre free
le **lien** tie
le **lieu** place; **au — de** instead of;
   avoir — to take place; **le —
   commun** commonplace; **s'il y a
   —** if necessary
le **linge** linen
le **lit** bed
le **livre** book; **le — de
   chevet** bedside book; **le — de
   poche** paperback
le **logement** lodging, housing
la **loi** law (rule, statute)
   loin far; **de —** by far
   long, longue long
   longuement for a long time
   louche shady, suspicious
   lourd heavy

la **lutte** fight, struggle; la — **des classes** class struggle
le **luxe** luxury

M

le **magasin** store; le **grand** — department store
le **magnétophone** tape recorder
maigrir to lose weight, slim down
maintenant now
maintenir to maintain, uphold
la **mairie** city hall
mais but
la **maison d'étudiants** dormitory
la **maîtresse de maison** housewife
le **mal** evil
malgré in spite of
malheureusement unhappily, unluckily, unfortunately
malin, maligne evil, wicked
la **malle** trunk; **faire la** — to pack the trunk
malsain sick, unhealthy
manger to eat
les **manières** f manners; **faire des** — to put on airs
la **manifestation** demonstration
le **manque** lack
manquer to miss, lack; — **à sa parole** to go back on one's word; — **d'égards envers** to be inconsiderate of
le **manteau** coat
le **manuel** textbook
le **maquillage** make-up
le **marbre** marble
marcher to walk
le **mari** husband
marié married
marier: se — to get married; **se** — **avec** to marry
mauvais bad
méchant mean
le **médecin** doctor
la **médecine** medicine
le **médicament** medicine
méditer to meditate
se **méfier de** to mistrust
meilleur adj better; **le** — the best
la **mélodie** melody, tune
le **melon** melon
même even

le **ménage** housework
mener to lead
le **mensonge** lie
menteur, menteuse lying
le **menteur, la menteuse** liar
mentir to lie
mériter to deserve, earn
le **métier** trade
le **métro** subway
le **metteur en scène** director
mettre to put, place; **se** — **à** to begin; **se** — **en colère** to get angry
le **meurtre** murder
mieux adv better; **le** — the best
le **milieu** milieu, environment
le **ministre** minister
la **mode** fashion
moindre lesser; **le** — the least
moins less, fewer; **à** — **que** (+ subj) unless
le **moment** moment; **au** — **où** at the moment when
la **monarchie** monarchy
le **monde** (p. 49) world, people; **tout le** — everybody
montrer to show
se **moquer de** to make fun of
moralement morally
le **morceau** piece
mou (mol), molle soft
le **mouchoir** handkerchief
mourir to die
le **moustique** mosquito
le **musée** museum
le **musicien, la musicienne** musician
le **mythe** myth

N

nager to swim
naïf, naïve naive
la **naissance** birth; **la limitation des** — birth control
naître to be born
né (pp of **naître**) born
négligé neglected
le **néologisme** neologism (a new word or meaning for an established word)
nerveux, nerveuse nervous
nettement clearly
nettoyer to clean
le **neveu** nephew
le **nez** nose

ni neither; **ne . . . — . . .**
— neither . . . nor
la **nièce** niece
le **nom** name; **au — de** in the name of
la **note** grade
la **nourriture** food
nouveau (nouvel), nouvelle new
la **nouvelle** short story

O

obéir à to obey
objectif, objective objective
obligé obligated; **être — de**
(+ *inf*) to be obligated to, to have to
l'**occasion** *f* opportunity, chance;
avoir l'— de to have the opportunity, chance to
l'**œil** *m* (*pl* **yeux**) eye
l'**œuf** *m* egg
l'**oiseau** *m* bird
l'**oncle** *m* uncle
l'**onglier** *m* manicure set
opprimer to oppress
l'**oreiller** *m* pillow
l'**orphelin** *m* orphan
oublier (de + *inf*) to forget
l'**ours** *m* bear
l'**ouvrage** *m* work
l'**ouvrier** *m* worker
ouvrir to open

P

le **pain** bread
paisible peaceful
la **paix** peace
par by; **— exemple** for example;
— terre on the ground
paraître to appear
pareil, pareille such a
le **parent** parent, relative
paresseux, paresseuse lazy
parfait perfect
parfois sometimes
parmi among
la **parole** word (spoken); **manquer à sa —** to go back on one's word
partager to share
le **parti** party
la **partie** party; la **— de**

billard game of billiards
partir to leave
passé last
le **passeport** passport
le **passe-temps** pastime
passionner to excite; **se — pour** to be crazy about
le **patron** boss
pauvre poor
le, la **pauvre** poor (person)
la **pauvreté** poverty
le **pays** country
le **paysan** peasant, hick
la **pêche** fishing; **aller à la —** to go fishing
peindre to paint
peine: à — hardly, scarcely
la **peine de mort** death penalty
le **peintre** painter
pendant during, for (*p.* 209)
pénible hard, painful
penser to think; **— de, à** to think of (*p* 216)
perceptif, perceptive perceptive
perdre to lose; **se —** to get lost
perfectionner to improve
le **personnage** character (in a play, book, etc.)
la **personne** person
personne no one, nobody; **ne . . . —, — ne** no one, nobody
peser to weigh
petit small
peu little, a few
le **peuple** (the) people
la **peur** fear; **avoir — de** to be afraid of
peut-être perhaps
la **photo** photograph
la **phrase** sentence
la **pièce** play, room
la **pilule** pill
le **pique-nique** picnic; **faire un —** to have a picnic
piquer to sting
pire worse; **le —** the worst
la **piste sonore** sound track
la **pitié** pity; **avoir — de** to have pity for
pittoresque picturesque
la **place** square, seat; **à la —** in its place
plaider to plead
plaire to please
la **plaisanterie** joke

le **plaisir** pleasure
le **plan** shot (film)
plein full
pleuvoir to rain
plus more, most; **de —** furthermore;
en — de in addition to; **moi non
—** neither do I; **ne . . . —** no
more, no longer
la **poésie** poetry
le **poète** poet
le **point** point, period; **ne . . . —**
not
le **poisson** fish
poli polite
la **politesse** politeness, good manners
le **politicien** politician
polyglotte polyglot (speaking or
writing several languages)
la **pomme de terre** potato
poser to put, place; **— sa
candidature** to run for office
le **poste** job
le **pot de vin** bribe
pour in order to, to; **— que**
(+ *subj*) in order that, so that
pourtant however
pourvu provided; **— que**
(+ *subj*) provided that
pouvoir to be able; **il se peut** it is
possible
précis precise
le **préjugé** prejudice
prématuré premature
premier, première first
prendre to take
les **préparatifs** *m* preparations
le **président** president
presque almost
pressé pressed, hurried
prétendre to claim, maintain
prêter to lend
la **prison** prison
le **prisonnier** prisoner
le **prix** price
le **procès** trial; **faire le — de** to
take action against
profond deep
le **programme** program, platform
le **projet** plan, project
la **promenade** walk; **faire une —** to
take a walk
se **promener** to walk; **se — en
voiture** to ride around in a car
la **promesse** promise
promettre to promise

prononcer to pronounce
propre *(after n)* clean; *(before n)*
own
protégé protected
protéger to protect
prouver to prove
le **proverbe** proverb
prudent prudent
le **public** audience, public; **le grand
—** the general public
puisque since
puissant powerful
punir to punish
la **punition** punishment

Q

quand when; **— même** anyway
quant à as for
le **quartier** district, neighborhood
que that, which, who, whom; **—
. . . ou non** whether . . . or not;
— (+ *subj*) let . . .
ne . . . — only
quelquefois sometimes
la **queue** line; **faire la —** to wait in
line
quitter to leave (*p 84*)
quoique (+ *subj*) although

R

raffiné refined
la **raison** reason
raisonnable reasonable
ramasser to gather, pick up
le **rang** rank, station
le **rapport** rapport, relationship
se **raser** to shave
rater to flunk (an exam)
ravi delighted, overjoyed
le **réactionnaire** reactionary
le **réalisateur** director
réaliser to carry out
réaliste realistic
récemment recently
recevoir to receive
reçu (*pp of* **recevoir**) received;
bien, mal — well, badly received
réduit reduced
le **réfectoire** dining hall
réfléchir to think, reflect
la **réforme** reform
refuser (de + *inf*) to refuse

le **régime** diet; **suivre un —** to be (go) on a diet
la **règle** rule
regretter to regret, be sorry
rejeter to reject
remarquer to remark, notice
remercier (de + *inf*) to thank (for)
remettre to put back, put off
rempli filled
rencontrer to meet
le **rendez-vous** date, appointment; **avoir — avec** to have a date with
rendre to return (something); **—** (+ *adj*) to make; **se — compte de** to realize; **— visite à** to visit (a person)
se **renseigner** to inform oneself
répéter to repeat, rehearse
la **répétition** rehearsal
répondre to answer
reposant restful
se **reposer** to rest, relax
la **représentation** performance
représenter to represent, perform
réserver to reserve
respirer to breathe
responsable responsible
ressembler à to resemble
rester to remain, stay
rétablir to re-establish
le **retard** delay; **avoir du —** to be late, not on time; **être en —** to be late
se **retourner** to turn around
la **retraite** retirement; **prendre sa —** to go into retirement
réussir (à + *inf*) to succeed; **— à un examen** to pass an exam
le **réveille-matin** alarm clock
réveiller to awaken; **se —** to wake up
rêver to dream; **— de** to dream about, of
rêveur, rêveuse dreamy
révoltant revolting
se **révolter** to revolt
rien nothing; **ne . . . —, —** ne nothing
rire to laugh
la **rivière** small river
le **roi** king
le **rôle** role
le **roman** novel; le **— policier** mystery
le **romancier** novelist
rompre to break

rusé sly
russe Russian
le **rythme** rhythm

S

sage well-behaved, wise
sain healthy
le **salaire** salary
sale dirty
sans without; **— que** (+ *subj*) without
la **santé** health
sauf except
se **sauver** *fam* to leave
savoir to know (a fact), know how
le **savon** soap
le **scandale** scandal
scandaliser to scandalize, shock
le **scénario** script, scenario
la **scène** stage, scene
sec, sèche dry
le **secret** secret
séduire to seduce
séduisant attractive, sexy
le **séjour** stay
selon according to
sensible sensitive
la **sentence** sentence
sentir to smell, feel; **se —** to feel
sérieux, sérieuse serious; **prendre au —** to take seriously
le **serpent** snake
la **serveuse** waitress
sévère stern
siffler to hiss, boo, whistle
la **signification** meaning
signifier to mean
le **socialisme** socialism
le **socialiste** socialist
la **sœur** sister
soigner to care for, take care of
soigneusement carefully
le **soin** care
le **soir** evening
la **soirée** evening, party
le **soleil** sun
solitaire lonely
le **sommeil** sleep; **avoir —** to be sleepy
somptueux, somptueuse luxurious
la **sonate** sonata
sonner to sound, go off
la **sortie** outing; la **— en famille** family outing

sortir to go out, leave; **— à deux** to go out as a couple; **— en groupe** to go out in a group; **— seul** to go out alone
le **souffle** breath
souffrir to suffer
sourier to smile
le **sourire** smile
sous under
le **sous-titre** subtitle
sous-titrer to subtitle
le **souvenir** souvenir
se **souvenir de** to remember
souvent often
se **spécialiser en** to major in
le **spectacle** show
stimulant stimulating
le **succès** hit
suffisant sufficient
suivant according to
suivre to follow; **— un cours** to take a course
supporter to bear, stand
sur on
surprenant surprising
surprendre to surprise
surpris surprised
le **suspect** suspect
le **suspens** suspense
sympathique nice

T

le **tableau** blackboard, painting
se **taire** to be quiet
tandis que whereas
la **tante** aunt
le **tapis** rug
tard late
les **taudis** *m* slums
teindre to dye
la **teinture** dye
tellement so, so much
le **témoignage** testimony
le **témoin** witness
le **temps** time, weather; **de — en — ** from time to time; **quel — fait-il?** what is the weather?
la **tendance** tendency; **avoir — à** to have a tendency to
tenir to hold
tenter to tempt
terminer to finish
la **terre** earth; **par —** on the ground
terrestre earthly

le **terroriste** terrorist
le **texte** text, lines
tirer to pull; **— au but** to shoot
le **tiret** dash
tôt early
toujours always, still
la **tour** tower
le **tour** tour
le, la **touriste** tourist
le **tourne-disque** record player
tourner to turn; **— un film** to make a film
tout (*p* 126): **tout, tous, toute, toutes** *adj* all, every, any; **tout, toute** *adv* all, quite; *pron* all, everything; **— à fait** totally; **— de suite** right away; **pas du —** not at all
traduire to translate
traiter to treat
le **transport** transportation; le **moyen de —** means of transportation
le **travail** work; les **travaux ménagers** household chores
travailler to work; **— à mi-temps** to work part-time
travailleur, travailleuse hard-working
le **tribunal** court
triste sad
tromper to cheat on, deceive; **se —** to make a mistake
la **trompette** trumpet
le **trompeur,** la **trompeuse** cheater, deceiver
trop too much, too many
trouver to find; **se —** to be located
tutoyer to say *tu* to someone
le **type** guy, fellow

U

l'**union libre** *f* living together out of wedlock, common-law marriage
l'**usine** *f* factory
utile useful

V

les **vacances** *f* vacation
la **vache** cow
le **va-et-vient** coming-and-going

la **vaisselle** dishes; **faire la —** to do the dishes

la **valise** suitcase; **faire la —** to pack the suitcase

valoir to be worth; **il vaut mieux** it is better

la **vedette** movie star

la **vendeuse** saleslady

vendre to sell

venir to come; **— de** to have just, just

le **verdict** verdict

véritablement truly

la **version** version; **en — originale** in the original

le **vêtement** garment; **les —s** clothing, clothes

vieux (vieil), vieille old; **mon vieux** *fam* old man

vilain *adj* nasty, bad; **le —** bad person, guy

le **viol** rape

visiter to visit (a place)

vivant lively

vivre to live

voir to see

le **voisin** neighbor

la **voiture** car

le **vol** theft

le **vôtre** *pron* yours

vouvoyer to say *vous* to someone

le **voyage** trip

le **voyou** hoodlum

vulgaire vulgar

Z

zut darn it

ENGLISH-FRENCH VOCABULARY

This vocabulary contains English words and expressions found in the exercises and the *Vocabulaire du thème.*

Abbreviations

adj	adjective		*p*	page
adv	adverb		*pl*	plural
conj	conjunction		*pp*	past participle
f	feminine		*prep*	preposition
fam	familiar		*pron*	pronoun
inf	infinitive		*subj*	subjunctive
m	masculine		*v*	verb
n	noun			

An asterisk (*) indicates a word beginning with an aspirate *h.*

A

abortion l'avortement *m*
abuse abuser de
accept accepter
accommodating complaisant
according to selon, suivant, d'après
accuse accuser
accused accusé
acquit acquitter
act agir; — **a role** jouer un rôle
action l'action *f*
actor l'acteur *m*
actress l'actrice *f*
adapt oneself to s'adapter à
addition l'addition *f;* **in** — de plus; **in** — **to** en plus de
admire admirer
adopt adopter
advertise faire de la publicité
advise conseiller (à + *n* de + *inf*)
adviser le conseiller
afraid: to be — **of** avoir peur de
African *n* l'Africain *m,* l'Africaine *f;* africain, africaine *adj*
after après
again encore
against contre
air l'air *m;* **to put on** —**s** faire des manières
all (*p* 126) tout, tous, toute, toutes *adj;* tout, toute *adv;* tout, tous, toute, toutes *pron*

already déjà
always toujours
ambition l'ambition *f*
ambitious ambitieux, ambitieuse
American *n* l'Américain *m,* l'Américaine *f;* américain, américaine *adj*
among parmi
analyze analyser
angry fâché *adj;* **to be** — être en colère contre; **to get** — se fâcher
announce annoncer
anonymous anonyme
another un autre
applaud applaudir
appreciate apprécier
approach s'approcher de
April avril *m*
arbitrary arbitraire
arrest arrêter
arrive arriver
as comme; — **for** quant à
ask demander (à + *n* de + *inf*); — **for** demander
assassin l'assassin *m*
assassinate assassiner
attack attaquer
attend assister à; — **to** s'occuper de
attentively soigneusement
attitude l'attitude *f*
attractive séduisant
audience le public
author l'auteur *m*
avoid éviter

B

back le dos
be être; **— in the know about** être au
    courant de; **— in the process of** être
    en train de; **— sick** être malade, avoir
    mal à (*p 204*)
bear l'ours *m*
beautiful beau (bel), belle
because parce que; **— of** à cause de
become devenir
bee l'abeille *f*
before avant (de + *inf*)
begin commencer (à *or* de + *inf*)
beginner le débutant
beginning le commencement, le début
behind le derrière; *prep* derrière
believable croyable
belong être à, appartenir à
benefit le bénéfice
besides d'ailleurs
best le meilleur *adj*; le mieux *adv*
best seller le best-seller
better meilleur *adj*; mieux *adv*; **it is**
    — il vaut mieux
between entre
bicycle la bicyclette; **to go —**
    riding faire de la bicyclette
bilingual bilingue
birth control la limitation des naissances
boat le bateau
boo huer, siffler
book le livre; le bouquin *fam*; **bedside**
    — le livre de chevet; **paperback**
    — le livre de poche; **text —** le
    manuel
bore ennuyer; **to be —d** s'ennuyer
boss le patron
boyfriend le petit ami, l'ami
break away se détacher de
bribe le pot de vin
brilliant brillant
brother le frère
brown brun
buddy le copain, la copine
bum le clochard
businessman l'homme d'affaires *m*
busy occupé; **to be — doing**
    something être en train de + *inf*; **to —**
    oneself with s'occuper de
but mais

C

camera l'appareil (appareil-photo) *m; la*
    caméra (*movie*)

camping le camping; **to go —** faire du
    camping
candidate le candidat
car la voiture, l'auto *f*
care for soigner
career la carrière
cease cesser (de + *inf*)
censor censurer
certainly certainement
change changer de
character le caractère; le personnage (*in
    a play, book, etc.*)
chat bavarder, causer
cheat on tromper
child l'enfant *m, f*; **only —** l'enfant
    unique
chore: household —s les travaux
    ménagers *m*
cinematographic cinématographique
circumstance la circonstance
citizen le citoyen
city la ville
city dweller le citadin
class la classe; **high —** la haute société;
    middle — la bourgeoisie; **working**
    — la classe ouvrière; **to have**
    — avoir de la classe
clean propre
clearly nettement
coarse grossier, grossière
cold froid; **it is —** il fait froid
come venir
commit commettre
commonplace le lieu commun
communism le communisme
communist communiste *adj*; le, la
    communiste *n*
compose composer
composer le compositeur
concerning en ce qui concerne
concert le concert
conclusion la conclusion; **in —** en
    conclusion
condemn condamner
condescending hautain
confused confus
consequently par conséquent
conservative conservateur, conservatrice
    adj; le conservateur *n*
continue continuer (à *or* de + *inf*)
contrary le contraire; **on the —** au
    contraire
convict le condamné
cooking: to do the — faire la cuisine
correct corriger

costume   le costume
country   le pays
country dweller   le campagnard
courageous   courageux, courageuse
courir   to run
course   le cours; **elective** —   le cours
   facultatif; **required** —   le cours
   obligatoire
court   le tribunal
cousin   le cousin, la cousine
cram   bûcher
crazy   fou (fol), folle; **to be** — **about**   se
   passionner pour
create   créer
criminal   le criminel
crime   le crime; — **of passion**   le crime
   passionnel
crisis   la crise
critic   le critique
criticism   la critique
criticize   critiquer
cultural   culturel, culturelle
custom   la coutume
customs   la douane; **customs officer**   le
   douanier, la douanière; **to pass through**
   —   passer la douane

D

dangerous   dangereux, dangereuse
dare   oser
date   la date, le rendez-vous; **to have a**
   — **with**   avoir rendez-vous avec
day   le jour, la journée; **all** —
   long   toute la journée; **the next** —   le
   lendemain
day-care center   la crèche
death penalty   la peine de mort
deceive   tromper
decide   décider (de + *inf*)
declare   déclarer
decor   le décor
defendant   l'accusé *m*
demanding   exigeant
democracy   la démocratie
democratic   démocrate
demonstration   la manifestation
denounce   dénoncer
depend   dépendre; — **on**   dépendre de
describe   décrire
deserve   mériter
detective   l'inspecteur *m*, le détective
dialect   le dialecte
dictator   le dictateur

dictatorship   la dictature
diet   le régime; **to be on a** —   suivre un
   régime
difficult   difficile
dining hall   le réfectoire
director   le réalisateur, le metteur en
   scène
dirty   sale
discothèque   la discothèque
discrimination   la discrimination
dishes: to do the —   faire la vaisselle
disobey   désobéir à
distress   la misère
dollar   le dollar
dormitory   la maison d'étudiants
doubt   le doute *n;* douter de *v*
dream   le rêve *n;* rêver *v*
dub   doubler
dunce   le cancre
during   pendant
dynamic   dynamique

E

earn   mériter, gagner
ease   l'aise *f;* **to feel at** —   se sentir à
   l'aise
easily   facilement
elder   l'aîné *m,* l'aînée *f*
elected   élu (*pp of* élire)
election   l'élection *f*
encourage   encourager (à + *inf*)
end   la fin
ending   le dénouement *(play, film);* **happy**
   —   le dénouement heureux
entertain   divertir; **to** — **oneself**   se
   divertir
entertainment   la distraction
environment   le milieu
equal   égal *adj;* l'égal *m,* l'égale *f*
equality   l'égalité *f*
evening   la soirée
every   tout (toute, *etc.*), chaque
exam   l'examen; **to fail, flunk an**
   —   échouer à, rater un examen; **to pass**
   an —   réussir à un examen; **to take an**
   exam   passer un examen
example   l'exemple *m;* **for** —   par
   exemple
except   sauf
express   exprimer
extenuating   atténuant

F

fact le fait; **in —** en effet
factory l'usine *f*
fair juste
faithful fidèle
family la famille *n*; familial *adj*; **— outing** la sortie en famille
famous célèbre
fan le, la cinéphile *(movie)*
far loin; **as — as** jusqu'à; **— from** loin de
farm la ferme
farmer le fermier, la fermière
fat gras, grasse; gros, grosse; **to become —** grossir
father le père
February février *m*
feel se sentir (mal à l'aise, dépaysé, etc.)
feminine féminin
feminist le, la féministe
field le champ
film le film *n*; filmer *v*; **to make a —** tourner un film
finally enfin, finalement
find trouver
finish finir
first premier, première
fish le poisson
fishing: to go — aller à la pêche
five cinq
flirt flirter *v*
flop le four *(theater)*
fluently couramment
follow suivre
foot le pied
for pour; *(p 209)* pendant, depuis, pour
forbid défendre (à + *n* de + *inf*)
foreign étranger, étrangère
foreigner l'étranger *m*, l'étrangère *f*
forget oublier (de + *inf*)
fortunately heureusement
free libre
frequent fréquenter
friend l'ami *m*, l'amie *f*; **to make —s with** lier amitié avec
frustrated frustré
furthermore de plus

G

generation gap le fossé entre les générations

get

get obtenir; **— along** se débrouiller; **— angry** se fâcher, se mettre en colère; **— lost** se perdre; **— married** se marier; **— sick** tomber malade; **— used to** s'habituer à
ghetto le ghetto
girl la jeune fille
girlfriend la petite amie, l'amie
give donner; **to — a speech** faire un discours
go aller; **— away** s'en aller; **— in** entrer dans; **— out** sortir
grade la note
gross grossier, grossière
guide le, la guide
guidebook le guide
guilty coupable

H

hand la main; **on one — . . . on the other —** d'une part . . . d'autre part
happy heureux, heureuse; content
hard difficile, dur, pénible *(work)*
harmony l'harmonie *f*
hat le chapeau
headache le mal de tête *n*; **to have a —** avoir mal à la tête
hear entendre
help aider (à + *inf*)
hero le *héros
heroine l'héroïne
hesitate hésiter (à + *inf*)
hick le paysan
high society la *haute société
his son, sa, ses
hiss siffler
hit frapper *v*; le coup, le succès *(play, show, etc.)* *n*
hitchhike faire de l'auto-stop
home la maison; **the —** le foyer
homesick dépaysé
homework les devoirs *m*
honest honnête
hoodlum le voyou
hope l'espoir *m*; espérer *v*
hour l'heure *f*
housework: to do the — faire le ménage
however cependant, pourtant; **— + *adj*** si + *adj* + que (+ *subj*)
humanly humainement
hurry se dépêcher (de + *inf*)
husband le mari

I

idiom l'idiotisme *m*
if si
image l'image *f*
imagination l'imagination *f*
importance l'importance *f*
important important
impress impressionner
imprisonment l'emprisonnement *m;* **life**
    — l'emprisonnement perpétuel
improve améliorer, perfectionner
in dans, en, à; — + *temporal*
    expression dans, en (*p* 209)
inconsiderate: to be — of manquer
    d'égards envers
independent indépendant
indulgent indulgent
influence l'influence *f;* influencer *v*
in front of devant
injustice l'injustice *f*
innocent innocent
insect l'insecte *m*
instead of au lieu de
insult l'insulte *f;* insulter *v*
intelligent intelligent
intention l'intention *f*
interest l'intérêt *m;* s'intéresser à *v*
interested intéressé; **to be —**
    in s'intéresser à
interesting intéressant
irresponsible irresponsable
isolated isolé

J

jargon le jargon
jealous jaloux, jalouse
job le poste, la situation
joke la plaisanterie
judge le juge
juror le juré
jury le jury
just juste; **to have — done**
    something venir de + *inf*

K

keep tenir, garder; **— one's word** tenir,
    garder sa parole
kid le, la gosse *fam*
king le roi
kiss embrasser *v*

L

lack le manque *n;* manquer de *v*
lake le lac
language la langue (*of a people*); le
    langage (*of an individual, vocabulary*);
    foreign — la langue étrangère; **native**
    — la langue maternelle; **living, dead**
    — la langue vivante, morte
last dernier, dernière; **— night** hier soir
late en retard
Latin Quarter le Quartier Latin
laugh le rire *n;* rire *v;* **— at** rire de
law le droit (*the profession, the study*); la
    loi (*rule, statute*)
lawyer l'avocat *m*
lazy paresseux, paresseuse
learn apprendre (à + *inf*)
leave (*p* 83) partir, sortir, quitter, s'en
    aller, laisser
leftist de gauche
leg la jambe
lenient indulgent
less moins
let que (+ *subj*); laisser (+ *inf*)
liberal libéral *adj;* le libéral *n*
liberated libéré
lie mentir *v;* le mensonge *n*
life la vie
like aimer *v;* **to feel —** avoir envie de;
    comme *prep*
likeable aimable
line la queue, la file; **to wait in —** faire
    la queue
lines le texte
listen to écouter
live habiter
long long, longue; **as — as** tant que
look regarder
look at regarder
look for chercher
loose lâche
lose perdre; **to — weight** maigrir
lost perdu, dépaysé
lot: a — of beaucoup de
luxurious somptueux, somptueuse
luxury le luxe
lyrics les paroles *f*

M

maintain maintenir
major la spécialisation *n;* se spécialiser
    en *v*

make   faire; — + *adj*   rendre + *adj*; **to
— a film**   tourner un film
make-up   le maquillage *n*; maquiller *v*
male chauvinism   le chauvinisme du mâle
man   l'homme *m*
manners   les manières *f*
many   beaucoup
map   la carte
marriage   le mariage
married   marié
marry   se marier avec; **to get
married**   se marier
mean   méchant
meditate   méditer; — **about**   méditer sur
melody   la mélodie
menu   la carte
Mexico   le Mexique
middle   le milieu; **in the — of**   au milieu
de
millionaire   le, la millionnaire
mind   l'esprit *m*; **to have an open
—**   avoir l'esprit ouvert
minister   le ministre
minute   la minute
miserable   misérable
misery   la misère
mistrust   se méfier de
modest   modeste
monarchy   la monarchie
Monday   lundi *m*; **on —s**   le lundi
money   l'argent *m*
month   le mois
morally   moralement
more   plus
moreover   de plus
morning   matin *m*; **in the —**   le matin
mosquito   le moustique
movies   le cinéma
mug   attaquer
murder   le meurtre *n*; commettre un
meurtre *v*; **to — French**   parler français
comme une vache espagnole *(lit, to
speak French like a Spanish cow)*
musician   le musicien, la musicienne

N

name   le nom; **my — is . . .**   je
m'appelle . . .
native   l'indigène *m, f*
near   près de
necessary   nécessaire; **to be —**   falloir,
être nécessaire
need   avoir besoin de *v*

neglect   négliger *v*
neither   ni; — **. . . nor**   ne . . . ni . . . ni
neologism   le néologisme
never   jamais; ne . . . jamais
next   prochain; — **to**   à côté de
nice   gentil, gentille; sympathique
night club   la boîte de nuit
no   non; — **more, longer**   ne . . . plus;
— + *n*   aucun; — **one**   personne ne,
ne . . . personne
nobody   personne; ne . . . personne,
personne ne
noise   le bruit
North   le Nord
nose   le nez
not   pas, ne . . . pas; — **at all**   pas du
tout
nothing   rien, ne . . . rien, rien ne
nouveau riche   le nouveau riche
novel   le roman *n*
novelist   le romancier

O

obey   obéir a
objective   objectif, objective
offer   offrir
office   le bureau
often   souvent
on   sur; — **the ground**   par terre
only   seulement, ne . . . que
open   ouvrir *v*; ouvert *adj*; **to have an —
mind**   avoir l'esprit ouvert
opinion   l'opinion *f*, l'avis *m; **in my
—**   à mon avis
opponent   l'adversaire *m*
opposite   en face de
oppress   opprimer
order   ordonner (à + *n* de + *inf*)
original   original; **in the —**   en version
originale
others   les autres, autrui
outing   la sortie; **family —**   la sortie en
famille
owe   devoir

P

painful   pénible
pal   le copain, la copine
parent   le parent
park   garer
party   la partie, la soirée; le parti
(political)

passport le passeport
pay for payer
peaceful paisible
peasant le paysan
people (*p* 49) les personnes *f,* les gens *m,* le monde, le peuple, on
perfect parfait
perform représenter
performance la représentation
permit permettre (à + *n* de + *inf*) *v*
person la personne
pessimistic pessimiste
phone le téléphone
picnic le pique-nique; **to have a —** faire un pique-nique
picture la photo
pill la pilule
place l'endroit *m,* le lieu; **at the — of** chez
plan le projet
plane l'avion *m*
platform le programme
play la pièce *n*; jouer *v*; **— an instrument** jouer de + *instrument;* **— a game or sport** jouer à + *game or sport*
plead plaider
pleasant agréable
please s'il vous plaît, veuillez *(formal)*; plaire à *v*
plot l'intrigue *f*
poet le poète
poetry la poésie
police la police
policeman l'agent de police *m*
polite poli
politician le politicien
politics la politique; **to go into —** se jeter dans la politique
pollution la pollution
polyglot polyglotte
pound la livre
prefer préférer
pregnant enceinte
prejudice le préjugé
premeditated prémédité
preparations les préparatifs *m*; **to make —** faire les préparatifs
president le président
press la presse
prison la prison
prisoner le prisonnier
probably probablement, sans doute
profession la profession
professor le professeur

program le programme
progress le progrès; **to make —** faire des progrès
promise promettre (à + *n* de + *inf*) *v*
pronounce prononcer
proper comme il faut
proud fier, fière
prove prouver
proverb le proverbe
public le public; **the general —** le grand public
punish punir
punishment la punition
pursue poursuivre; **to — a career** poursuivre une carrière

Q

quarrel la dispute *n*; se disputer *v*
question la question *n*; interroger, poser une question *v*
quickly vite, rapidement
quiet tranquille *adj*; **to be —** se taire

R

rape le viol
reactionary réactionnaire *adj*; le, la réactionnaire *n*
reader le lecteur
reading la lecture
really vraiment, réellement
reasonable raisonnable
reasonably raisonnablement
received reçu (*pp of* recevoir)
record le disque *n*; enregistrer *v*
record player le tourne-disque
recording l'enregistrement *m*
refined raffiné
reform la réforme
refuse refuser (de + *inf*)
regarding à l'égard de
rehearsal la répétition
rehearse répéter
relationship le rapport
remember se souvenir de, se rappeler
republican le républicain *n*; républicain *adj*
resemble ressembler à
resign démissionner
resist résister à
respect respecter *v*
responsible responsable

return revenir, retourner; —
   home rentrer
revolt la révolte *n*; se révolter *v*
rhythm le rythme
rich riche
right le droit; **to be —** avoir raison; **to
   have the — to** avoir le droit de
right away tout de suite
rightist de droite
river la rivière *(small)*, le fleuve
rock-and-roll le rock
role le rôle
room la chambre, la pièce
roommate le, la camarade de chambre
run courir; **— for office** poser sa
   candidature

S

sacrifice le sacrifice *n*
salary le salaire
Saturday samedi *m*
say dire
scandal le scandale
scandalize scandaliser
scenario le scénario
scene la scène
scenery le décor
scold gronder
scream crier
script le scénario
search fouiller *v*
secret le secret
see voir
seem sembler, avoir l'air + *adj*
semester le semestre
send envoyer
sentence la sentence
sexy séduisant
share partager
shock scandaliser, étonner *v*
shop la boutique *n*; faire des courses *v*
shopping: to go — faire des courses
short bref, brève; **in —** (en) bref
short story la nouvelle
shot le plan *(film)*
show le spectacle *n*; montrer *v*
sick malade
sinecure la sinécure
sing chanter
singer le chanteur, la chanteuse
skiing le ski; **to go —** faire du ski
slang l'argot *m*
slap gifler *v*

sleep le sommeil *n*; dormir *v*; —
   outdoors dormir à la belle étoile
slim down maigrir
slip: to make a — of the tongue faire un
   lapsus
slowly lentement
slums les taudis *m*
small petit
snake le serpent
snob le, la snob
so si, tellement; **— much** tant,
   tellement
social climber l'arriviste *m, f*
socialism le socialisme
socialist socialiste; le, la socialiste *n*
softly doucement
son le fils
soon bientôt; **as — as** dès que, aussitôt
   que
sorry: to be — regretter; **very
   —** désolé *adj*
sound track la piste sonore
South le Sud
souvenir le souvenir
spanking la fessée
speak parler; **— loudly** parler fort; —
   nonsense dire des bêtises; —
   softly parler bas; **— well, badly of
   someone** dire du bien, du mal de
   quelqu'un
spectator le spectateur
speech le discours; **to give, make a
   —** faire un discours
spend dépenser *(money)*; passer *(time)*
spoiled gâté
spy l'espion *m*; espionner *v*
stage la scène
star la vedette *(movie)*
status quo le statu quo
stay le séjour *n*
stern sévère
stereotype le stéréotype
stimulating stimulant
sting piquer
stop arrêter, cesser (de + *inf*) *v*
store le magasin; **department —** le
   grand magasin
strange étrange, bizarre
strict strict
strike la grève; **to go out on —** faire la
   grève
stroll flâner
student l'étudiant *m*; **bad —** mauvais
   étudiant, le cancre; **off-campus
   —** l'externe *m, f*; **on-campus**

— l'interne *m, f*
style   le style
subjective   subjectif, subjective
subtitle   le sous-titre *n*; sous-titrer *v*
suburbs   la banlieue
subway   le métro
suitcase   la valise; **to pack the —**   faire
la valise
supporter   le partisan
surprised   surpris, étonné
suspect   le suspect *n;* se douter de *v*
suspicious   louche
sweet   doux, douce

T

table   la table
take   prendre; **— a course**   suivre un
cours; **— an exam**   passer un examen
talk   parler; **— nonsense**   dire des bêtises
tape   la bande *n*
taste   le goût *n*; **to have good, bad
—**   avoir bon, mauvais goût
teacher   le professeur; l'instituteur *m,*
l'institutrice *f (elementary school)*
technique   la technique
tell   dire (à + *n* de + *inf*); **— a
story**   raconter une histoire
terrorist   le terroriste
testimony   le témoignage
thank   remercier; **— for**   remercier de
thanks   merci
that   ce, cet, cette, *adj*; cela *pron*
theft   le vol
their   leur, leurs
there   y, là; **— is, are**   il y a
therefore   donc, aussi + *inverted verb* (*p*
125)
think   penser, croire, réfléchir
this   ce, cet, cette, *adj*; ceci *pron*
time   l'heure, le temps, la fois; **at the
same —**   à la fois, en même temps;
from — to —   de temps en temps;
what — is it?   quelle heure est-il?
tired   fatigué
title   le titre
today   aujourd'hui
together   ensemble
tomorrow   demain
tonight   ce soir
too much   trop (de)
totally   totalement, tout à fait
tour   l'excursion *f*; **guided
—**   l'excursion accompagnée

toward   (*p* 209) vers, envers
trade   le métier
traditional   traditionnel, traditionnelle
traffic   la circulation
travel   le voyage *n*; voyager *v*
travel agent   l'agent de voyages *m*
travel bureau   l'agence de voyages *f*
traveler's check   le chèque de voyage
tree   l'arbre *m*
trial   le procès
trip   le voyage; **to take a —**   faire un
voyage
true   vrai, véritable
truly   vraiment
trunk   la malle; **to pack the —**   faire la
malle
trust   se fier à *v*
truth   la vérité
try   essayer (de + *inf*) *v*
tune   la mélodie
twin   le jumeau, la jumelle

U

under   sous
understand   comprendre
unemployed   en chômage; **— person**   le
chômeur
unemployment   le chômage
unfair   injuste
ungrateful   ingrat
unhealthy   malsain
unjustly   injustement
unknown   inconnu *adj*; à l'insu de *prep*
unpleasant   désagréable
upbringing   l'éducation
use   employer, utiliser

V

verdict   le verdict
very   très
visit   visiter *(a place)*; rendre visite à *(a
person)*
vote   voter *v*
vulgar   vulgaire

W

wait   attendre; **— for**   attendre; **— in
line**   faire la queue
walk   la promenade *n*; marcher *v*; **to take
a —**   se promener, faire une promenade

want vouloir
war la guerre
warm chaud; **it is —** il fait chaud
 (weather)
warmly chaleureusement
waste gaspiller *v*
watch regarder *v*
wealthy riche, aisé
week la semaine
weigh peser
welcome accueillir
well bien
well-behaved sage
well-bred bien élevé
well-to-do aisé
what! comment!
when quand, lorsque
whereas tandis que
wherever où que *(+ subj)*
whistle siffler *v*
whoever qui que *(+ subj)*
wholly totalement, tout à fait
why pourquoi

wife la femme
wildly frénétiquement
win gagner
wish vouloir, désirer
with *(p 208)* avec, de, à
witness le témoin
woods le bois
word le mot, la parole *(spoken)*
work *n* le travail, l'ouvrage *m (of fiction,*
 etc.); **in the — of** chez; travailler *v*
worker l'ouvrier *m*, l'ouvrière *f*
world le monde
worst le pire, le plus mauvais
write écrire
writer l'écrivain

Y

year l'an *m,* l'année *f*
yesterday hier
young jeune
youngest le cadet, la cadette *n*

Index